BUILDING DIGITAL ARCHIVES, DESCRIPTIONS, AND DISPLAYS

A How-To-Do-It Manual for Archivists and Librarians

Frederick Stielow

HOW-TO-DO-IT MANUALS
FOR LIBRARIANS

NUMBER 116

NEAL–SCHUMAN PUBLISHERS, INC.
New York, London

Published by Neal-Schuman Publishers, Inc.
100 William Street, Suite 2004
New York, NY 10038

Printed and bound in the United States of America.

Library of Congress Cataloging-in-Publication Data

Stielow, Frederick J., 1946-
    Building digital archives, descriptions, and displays : a how-to-do-it manual for archivists and librarians / by Frederick Stielow.
        p. cm.—(How-to-do-it manuals for libraries; no. 116)
    Includes index.
    Webliography: p.
    ISBN 1-55570-463-8
    1. Archival materials–Data processing–Handbooks, manuals, etc. 2. Archives–Automation–Handbooks, manuals, etc. 3. Web sites–Design–Handbooks, manuals, etc. 4. Digital libraries–Design–Handbooks, manuals, etc. I. Title. II. Series.

CD973.D3S75 2003
025/.00285—dc21
                                                            2003044213

CONTENTS

LIST OF FIGURES

PREFACE

Building Digital Archives, Descriptions, and Displays: A How-to-Do-It Manual for Archivists and Librarians is intended for museums, libraries, and archives seeking to offer digital archives through the World Wide Web. The World Wide Web is a perfect fit for cultural institutions that are rethinking their roles and redefining services for the Information Age. These bodies have the content and reliability that the new medium demands. Moreover, they possess decades of experience with information standards, computerized description, and microcomputer applications—all of which are directly transferable to the Web.

The speed of redefinition and actual change has proved remarkable. By the mid-1990s (only a few years after the Web's birth), users came to expect even the most traditional of repositories to have a "homepage." The Web opened hidden treasures to the world, but problems persist. For example:

- Some professionals hesitate to digitize their holdings, unsure of how to proceed in a rapidly changing environment without permanent answers.
- Costs are uncertain and can scale dramatically.
- Copyright and other legal issues, along with donor relations, loom as potential threats.
- Deference to "experts" or self-trained volunteers can lead to sites that are difficult or impossible for a repository to change or update.
- Adherence to information standards can be expensive and calls for additional resources and staffing.

Building Digital Archives, Descriptions, and Displays is designed to address such questions in a straightforward, step-by-step manner. The intended audiences are professionals in archives, libraries and museums, along with students and those in historical and cultural associations. The book speaks especially to managers trying to gain a handle on their Web prospects and to those with limited resources and without fulltime digital specialists. It should also prove useful anyone struggling to find balance within the day-to-day demands of the information revolution.

What is a digital archive? The definition of "digital archive" continues to evolve. The original concept was the preservation of institutional records that originated in the computer—i.e., were "born digital"—but now the definition also encompasses computerized images of two- and three-dimensional objects, electronic publications, online displays, policies, and a variety of location pointers and professional descriptions.

Definitions must be further refined for their institutional setting. Archives, libraries, and museums bring subtle and not-so-subtle differences from their diverse type of holdings, descriptive practices, and historical perspectives. Yet each also contributes valuable and complementary skills for digital archives on the Web.

Building Digital Archives, Descriptions, and Displays: A How-to-Do-It Manual for Archivists and Librarians recognizes archivists first—they provide the primary descriptive model and have the most experience with digital archives. Archivists are editors who organize, describe, and title groups of materials with unique and enduring value. Archival "collections" feature paper and electronic records, but can include photographs, videos, audiotapes, and artifacts. Second, librarians, by far the largest and most technologically advanced of the fields, catalog and classify published books and periodicals, yet do not supply internal order or titles to their charges. The Web era has stretched library practices beyond purchase to licensing. Third, museums and historical agencies are at the lowest level of automation among the three, but their interpretive skills and Web displays represent the highest level. In addition to making exhibits, curators register, title, and classify unique artifacts of enduring value at the individual or item level.

These three previously disparate fields are being drawn together by a common desire for the digitization of their resources. In the virtual world, this shared commitment may signal a revolutionary change: traditional boundaries based on differences in the types of holdings may disappear; for online patrons there is little doubt digitization blurs the lines among archives, libraries, and museums.

SCOPE AND CONTENT

Building Digital Archives is designed to demystify the new medium and teach readers "how to think web." The text builds on the reader's professional grounding along with ingrained understandings of print and office automation. It provides a series of practical applications and software demonstrations to ensure that digital archives are available to any institution. The bottom line? It will show that anyone who can use a word processor is capable of building digital archives.

ARRANGEMENT

Building Digital Archives begins as a primer for project management and evolves into a general guide for managing such creations.

Chapter 1, "Planning the Digitization Project," provides a planning framework for the project, including setup, systems analysis, and electronic records management. It views the Web as a type of word processing with the special tools of hypertext and metadata. The technological overview explores the Internet, HTML, http, external contributions, and XML (RDF).

Chapter 2, "Understanding Digitized Finding Aids," introduces the archival finding aid as a model descriptive device on the road to digital archives. The chapter is primarily a training exercise in automation project management.

Chapter 3, "Creating Effective Web Finding Aids," expands the training exercise to the Web and introduces HTML and hypertext tool skills as part of a "word-processing" approach to digital archives.

Chapter 4, "Considering SGML/EAD, XML, and Database Options," extends the discussion into more structured and technologically advanced options. The chapter looks at SGML (Standard Generalized Markup Language) and XML (Extensible Markup Language) through an EAD (Encoded Archival Description) finding aid example. Those on-line "publication" directions are juxtaposed against the production-driven alternatives from database management systems (DBMSs).

Chapter 5, "Exploring Leading Automation Systems for Libraries and Museums," looks at the models of legacy automation systems from museums, archives, and especially libraries. The chapter looks at commercial turnkey applications, online bibliographic utilities, established descriptive standards, and the growing Web responses, such as the Dublin Core and Open URL.

Chapter 6, "Establishing Policies and Techniques for Digital Imaging," examines concerns about copyright and other policy issues. The chapter discusses selection criteria for in-house digitization and Web presentation and covers measures for image capture, optical character conversions, and treatments of sound and video.

Chapter 7, "Creating the Web Site and Display Options," presents a top-down view of a model digital archives through four permeable layers: a formal entrance or gateway, displays, descriptive devices, and digital assets. The chapter examines the growing opportunities the Web offers to create an array of displays for new and old audiences—and the accompanying responsibilities.

Chapter 8, "Maintaining and Preserving Digital Archives," offers methods for the maintenance and preservation of digital archives within three types of institutional response.

- **WEB MUSEUMS:** The basic model displays digitized images of an institution's traditional holdings.
- **INSTITUTIONAL RECORDS:** An advanced option is offered for the electronic records management (ERM) of an organization's digital information.
- **DIGITAL LIBRARIES:** An advanced option, this addresses cooperative ventures among major libraries to preserve digital publications and multimedia.

An afterword called "Setting the Historical Context" is a wrap-up for readers interested in tracing the trail that brought us here and where it may lead.

Finally, references are featured in a "webliography" of over 200 useful Internet Sites.

As information professionals, we sit on the threshold of a revolution that is redefining the most traditional services. The World Wide Web is dramatically altering archives, libraries, record centers, and special collections. It is democratizing the past by bringing historical documents and images online for all the people. Change is unavoidable; the opportunities are immense. In addition to new clientele and services, our managerial challenges extend to integrating the Web into the workflow and the very nature of the institutions we serve. *Building Digital Archives, Descriptions, and Displays: A How-to-Do-It Manual for Archivists and Librarians* is designed as the guide for such integration.

1

PLANNING THE DIGITIZATION PROJECT

Project Planning
- Setup
- Systems analysis
- Electronic records management
- KISS and other hints

Web=Word Processing++
- Hypertext
- Metadata

Web Technology Overview
- Internet
- HTML
- http
- External Contributions
- XML (RDF)

Building Digital Archives presupposes that its readers are interested in moving beyond the initial creation of an institutional Web site. The new demand is for guidance on how to enhance the electronic content of extant sites through digital archives.

The move to digital archives may be inevitable because the Web has changed the nature of our patrons' expectations. Not only do scholars want digital access, but a new and emerging public audience assumes that they, too, will encounter digital holdings through the Net. In response to these expectations, the commercial sector is doing its part to guarantee the ascendance of the digital. Just as typewriters have been replaced by computers, analog cameras, copiers, and recorders are rapidly disappearing. The marketplace is making it almost impossible to purchase, let alone maintain, earlier media formats.

Changes in recording media are fated to alter the nature of repository holdings and descriptions. Archival collections increasingly contain computer files and digital media, libraries must deal with online journals and new electronic genres, and museums regularly include digital content in their displays. Moreover, the new media have already impacted professional training and credentials for these fields.

This chapter is designed as a prologue or introduction to set the stage for the automation and digitization applications in the rest of the text. The chapter puts forth planning approaches and a technical framework by offering:

1. project planning techniques rooted in three sets of tool skills;
2. general management guidelines for automation ventures; and
3. an understanding of the nature of the Web that is sufficient to address digital archives.

PROJECT PLANNING

In the "good old days," archival operations were familiar and manual, and stable methods had evolved over the decades in a print environment:

ink on paper was used to control ink on paper and physical objects. The computer and the Web disrupted this comforting scenario. Instead of an archivist or researcher picking up a sheet of paper and reading, a machine had to intercede to transform a data stream into a visible format. Ongoing change and planning for uncertain future capacities became the new managerial norms.

As this text will relate, you do not need to be a computer scientist to master Web basics or build digital archives—you only need a little extra discipline and attention to detail. This chapter offers three sets of initial tool skills for launching its automation projects:

- two components for project setup
- a six-step systems analysis methodology
- three naming principles for electronic records management

SETUP

Two preliminary activities are typically required for any automation project to develop:

- **SELECTING A TEAM:** Since few individuals have all the skills needed for a Web project, one of your first steps is selecting a team. You need an array of complimentary skills for:
  - content determination;
  - description/cataloging;
  - project management;
  - graphic design; and
  - computer and Web applications (they are not necessarily the same thing).

- **SETTING A TIME LINE**: Your next steps are equally vital–establish and then adhere to a time line, e.g.:
  - project preparation, team selection, and definition
  - data gathering period
  - analysis meeting
  - solution discussions
  - pilot stage
  - implementation

SYSTEMS ANALYSIS METHODOLOGY

Systems analysis provides the methodology behind most computer programming and information systems, as well as the direction for this text. The approach is linear; step follows step in a distinct order without "jumping the gun." The book employs a six-tiered approach, which mirrors the preceding timeline:

1. **PROBLEM DEFINITION:** The first stage—gaining consensus on the problem—is arguably the most important and can be difficult for a team. The planner must make certain that everyone is working toward the same end. Archivists, librarians, curators, and technical experts will have their own ideas of how the term "digital archives" should be defined.

DIVIDING THE PROBLEM

A major skill is the ability to subdivide a problem into doable segments or phases—in other words, "Do not bite off more than you can chew." At the minimum, projects can be split between:

1. **PRESENT AND FUTURE CHANGE:** Do not try to do everything at once. Start with building the best possible solution from "X" point in time forward.

2. **RETROSPECTIVE CONVERSION:** When and only when the model is in place and tested, turn to retrospective conversion (recon). Unless the institution has exceptionally rich resources, I normally urge that materials be appraised and prioritized for processing in keeping with informational values and their projected use.

---

2. **DATA GATHERING:** Background research for the projects in this book can be divided into three categories:
   - **INTERNAL** studies of your resources, staffing, and institutional framework
   - **EXTERNAL** comparisons to similar institutions, parallel practices, and standards from the information professions
   - **TECHNOLOGY** factors, standards, and the marketplace for practical implementation and sustainability

3. **ANALYSIS:** The third layer involves sitting down and carefully sifting through the evidence. What are the costs in terms of money and staff time in relation to the expected benefits? Look to what you want to happen, but also the potential for unintended consequences and tradeoffs. Will you need to give up other practices? Don't forget to factor in maintenance and training needs.

4. **SOLUTIONS:** Consider options and draw up plans to satisfy the problem. Generally, you should concentrate on the "biggest bang for the buck" and attack the easiest facets of the problem first.

5. **PILOT:** The fifth step is integral to any R and D (research and development) effort. Too many projects fall victim to the "Fallacy of Perfect Planning." Automation is a trial and error proposition that demands a separate period for testing and debugging. This stage is typically divided between:

    • **ALPHA PHASE:** laying the groundwork for testing

    • **BETA PHASE:** testing and analysis with the potential for returning up the systems analysis tree for debugging or routing to the next stage

6. **IMPLEMENTATION:** Assuming the pilot test results are positive, implementation flows directly from the procedures created during testing. With automation, additional staff training and written instructions are particularly crucial. Yet be aware that solutions are not permanent; ongoing evaluation and adaptability should be factored into your equation.

BRADFORD'S EQUATION AND ZIPF'S LAW

Common sense can be reinforced by heuristics (rules of thumb) from information science. Pareto's Principle or Bradford's equation, the classic 80/20 rule, assists with asset allocation. From it, the manager can predict that 20 percent of the information resources will produce 80 percent of the activity; moreover, closing the gap for that last 20 percent of requests will take at least four times the work. Keep in mind George Zipf's Law of Least Effort in Description, a classic law from the 1950s that argued that one should not expend more energy in description than the value of the information described.

ELECTONIC RECORDS MANAGEMENT

You will be gradually introduced to techniques for managing electronic records. At the start, you will need to be aware of three cardinal "naming" principles:

1. **FILE NAMES:** The first step is insuring a distinct and consistent pattern of names for your files. If possible, avoid codes in preference of mnenomics; choose something that both the human operator and computer can work with, e.g., *tool_kit, note-4/13,* or *mary_pic* rather than *x4568* or *#ga382.*

2. **OPEN SOURCE FORMATS:** Future compatibility and updating depends on saving the files as open formats (program files that are built on shared standards) or those can be easily converted to open formats—e.g., the open ASCII *(.txt),* *.rtf* and *.htm (.html),* but also *.pdf,* and Microsoft Word's *.doc,* et cetera.

3. **DIRECTORY CONTROLS:** Files are stored together within hierarchically arranged directories that also require meaningful names. Figure 1.1 illustrates by dividing a repository's electronic files into two major directories. *"Administration"* holds subdirectories related to general management—e.g., staff files. *"Information_services"* contains the work products—e.g., collections and displays.

KISS AND OTHER HINTS

In addition, project management should be rooted in commonsense and the KISS ("keep it simple, stupid") principle. As summarized in figure 1.2, you will want to concentrate on the front-end of the venture and be sure that you are driven by the institution's needs—not technology's upper limits.

APPROXIMATION-BASED PLANNING TECHNIQUES

You may also wish to consider approximation-based planning, a technique that makes allowances for expected but unpredictable change in hardware and software. Instead of assumed omniscience, managers rely on team expertise and presuppose ongoing reassessment and change. The idea is to be flexible and prepared. Despite following the best rules, standards, and practices—what can go wrong will go wrong.

Fig. 1.1. Sample Directory Layout

```
                    Hard Drive/Local Area Network
                         /Administration/
                            /Building/
                           /Equipment/
                            /Finance/
                             /Staff/
                      /Information_services/
                           /Collections/
                                    holding #
                                    holding #...
                             /Displays/
                                    display x...
                              /Images/
                                    image y...
```

Fig. 1.2. Checklist for Automation Projects

✔ **Plan, test, and retest:** Place your energies at the front-end with detailed planning, but be prepared for extended testing and debugging.

✔ **Be output driven:** The project's goals must be determined by institutional needs—not by what you are told the technology can do.

✔ **Don't reinvent the wheel:** Examine what you are already doing and try to build on it, but also study the successes and failures of others.

✔ **Refer to standards:** Similarly, be especially aware of open systems and the professional guidelines established by your field.

✔ **Look for commercially robust, non-proprietary systems:** Automation is easier with developed product lines and established support mechanisms.

✔ **Integrate solutions into the workflow:** Automation should not be an add-on. The goal is a regular activity that simplifies decision-making to the routine and will produce synergies to ease other services.

✔ **Tackle the easiest problems first:** Technology is evolving too rapidly for perfect solutions. You are entering a process of ongoing change, education, and adaptation. Fortunately, your hard problems may be solved on the way.

✔ **Consider the costs in relation to the benefits:** This includes factoring staff time, equipment, maintenance..., but also what other services may be losing.

WEB=WORD PROCESSING++

The projects in this book call for a modicum of knowledge about the Web. The focus is HTML (Hyper Text Markup Language)—the Web's form of word processing. HTML is an open source or non-proprietary set of codes. It was designed to allow anyone to layout documents for transmission among the different computers on the Internet. The standard comes with two additional features that are of particular interest in the readings: hypertext and metadata.

HYPERTEXT

HTML's major technical flourish is a type of hypertext. Books, articles, and other printed materials are largely designed for linear intake—the reader is expected to follow the path laid out by the author and read through the text to its end. With hypertext, the reader can jump to other places within a document or to totally different locations on the Internet. Hypertext is a stimulating new form of expression or genre—like the Web page itself. The integration and understanding of hypertext will become your greatest challenge.

Chapters 3 and 7 provide insights on hypertext and compositional skills for the Web. For now, please recognize that this remarkable advancement rests on two elementary commands:

> Catalog cards are an exception that foreshadow hypertext.

- **NAME** *<a name="term">* sets anchors or bookmarks within an electronic document.
- **HYPERREFERENCE** *<a href="term">* creates hyperreferences or links to the name within an article or to other locations and bookmarks on external Web sites.

Note: The Web's version of hypertext is "many to one." Each anchor or URL must be unique and have its own distinct name. An infinite number of hyperlinks can go to the anchor or Web site, but a hyperlink cannot go to multiple anchors or sites.

METADATA

Metadata, the buzzword of the Web era, simply means "information about information." For Web sites, the immediate concerns divide into two broad categories:

- **LAYOUT TAGS:** The operational locus is HTML data elements for the layout or syntax of how the document will look onscreen—e.g., bold face, italics, fonts, headings, tables, and background color.

- **ELECTRONIC POINTERS:** HTML also brings ability for computers to locate sites and content— e.g., title, keyword, and descriptive metadata (See also: search engine discussions later in this chapter).

More on Metadata

Information professionals require nuances on metadata beyond basic HTML functions and should be aware of the particular terminology used for professional descriptions and management of the materials. Library parlance, for example, stresses three general categories of Web metadata:

- **STRUCTURAL** metadata reflects both the syntax or layout and semantics or meaning of the material.
- **ADMINISTRATIVE** metadata is data on the technical makeup of the record, including who entered it, when, and for what institution, along with procedural comments on privacy status, preservation, retention, or related actions.
- **DESCRIPTIVE** metadata provides external indicators to the contents and their relations to other material, e.g., keywords and abstracts.

It may be helpful to think of your early grammar classes: is the term a verb, noun, or modifier? On the Web, the advanced focus is on nouns and adding semantics or meaning by categorizing terms (See also: XML discussions at the end of this chapter). One looks to build the collective noun as a point for data entry and then fill in specific entries: e.g., Policemen (collective) can hold Officer Smith, Officer Jones (personal).

> Anne Gilliland Swetland in the Getty Museum's *Introduction to Metadata* presents a solid introduction
>
> (http://www.getty.edu/ research/institute/standards/in trometadata/).
>
> Also see W3C's take (http:// www.w3c.org/Meta).

WEB TECHNOLOGY OVERVIEW

Although you do not need additional background at the beginning, several other aspects of the Web will come to the fore. The Web itself is the union of three elements—the Internet, HTML, and http. Many of the features that we take for granted were actually created by outside developers—such as the common browsers and search engines. And, recently, the original focus on simple word processing has begun to give way to a 2nd-Generation Web, which adds database concerns and computer manipulations through XML metadata.

Reader's Advisory: Portions of the following discussions, especially on the second-generation Web, will be advanced. Those already expert or with milder concerns may wish to return to these pages later. The section is particularly apt in preparation for chapters 4 and 8.

WEB ORIGINS

Tim Berners-Lee of CERN (Centre European de Recherches Nucleaire) in Geneva launched the World Wide Web on August 6, 1991. His revolutionary idea would allow one to control screen design and post work documents for sharing across computer systems. The codes would be openly available and would not require advanced computer knowledge. In his words:

"The Web made the Net useful because people are really interested in information (not to mention knowledge and wisdom) and don't really want to know about computers and cables" (See: (http://www.w3.org/People/Berners-Lee/FAQ.html).

By 1994, the World Wide Web had swept across the globe. Controls passed from CERN to an international World Wide Web Consortium (W3C) at the Massachusetts Institute of Technology. The World Wide Web had become the "killer app" that popularized the Internet. The phrase shortened to Web–a term recognized with unprecedented speed in languages across the globe.

INTERNET

Web creator Tim Berners-Lee had to select an extant communication platform to link disparate types of computers. His choice drew on groundwork laid for the United States military in the 1960s. The government wanted a safe and dependable system to exchange information among its research computers and those of cooperating universities. Rather than a proprietary system or one offered by a single manufacturer, the demand was for open sourcing source coding—one freely available and sharable by all.

The task fell to the U.S. Defense Advanced Research Projects Agency (DARPA), which regulated transmissions by breaking messages into small "packets" with their own addresses and mathematical checks for validation. These packets were routed individually along a compliant wide area network (WAN) before reassembly in the receiving machines.

DARPA's first rule sets were the Transmission Control Protocol with addresses defined through an Internet Protocol (TCP/IP), a concept that helped launch ARPANET. Thanks to the visionary input of Vinton Cerf and Robert Kahn, ARPANET expanded exponentially in the mid-1980s, resulting in the Internet—an international alliance of Domain Name Servers (DNSs) that selflessly route their packets to and from designated IP locations.

Most acknowledge Donald Davies and Paul Baran as inventors of packet switching. Claims have arisen for Leonard Klein-rock

---

IP VERSION 6

The success of the Web helped exhaust the 32-bit IP schema (which allows for 4.3 billion addresses) and other interim methods (e.g., CIDR blocks). IP v6 will address the problem by absorbing locations down to the level of individual household appliances while also promising more security and reliability than available from IPs v1 to v4 (v5 did not come out of development).

HTTP (HYPER TEXT TRANSMISSION PROTOCOL)

> http is normally not capitalized; it is remarkably stable and still in version 1.1

Berners-Lee's second task was to create a transmission protocol to ride on the Internet. His http is only one (number eighty) of the hundred or so TCP/IP protocols. Most are familiar with the @ sign and the IP addressing for the e-mail protocol of Ray Tomlinson, and some have encountered gopher and ftp (file transfer protocol) or even video conferencing. Most are certainly familiar with URLs (Uniform Resource Locators)—http's brand of IP addressing.

Http remains the overlooked workhorse of the Web. On entering *http://,* you engage the TCP/IP "daemon" that declares a Web session is taking place on the Internet. The results are "stateless" transmissions. Http moves information in a walkie-talkie-like session (a "half duplex" mode) from the originating machine to the receiver, and a query transfers a duplicate of the material to the control of the requesting machine. This form of file transfer brings significant policy, planning, and copyright questions, which will be covered in later chapters. It provides two primary methods for communicating:

- **GET:** In simple transactions, the requesting computer posits a short "get" command to retrieve the information listed on the page. Data is then transferred from the host and downloaded as is to the requester.
- **POST:** The other option is to "post" longer and more powerful query strings to the host machine–e.g., addressing through HTML forms, CGI (common gateway interface) scripts, or database queries.

HTML: HYPERTEXT MARKUP LANGUAGE

HTML supplied the display side of the Web equation. Berners-Lee invented HTML 1.0 as a rudimentary word processor with hypertext features, but he soon turned to a related design from the standards world.

THE INITIAL HANDSHAKE

Despite the complexities of IP, Berners-Lee managed to keep things simple and understandable. Initial http contact relies on "get" and involves a two-stage sequence: discovery and transfer. Discovery begins by entering an external URL. Your browser asks a Domain Name Server (DNS) to resolve the URL into an IP address, opens a TCP connection, and starts a three-part handshake. The browser proffers a "get" for the contents of the URL and the receiver sends an introductory outline with a list of the elements to fill the screen. The requesting browser sends packets in "turns" to complete the initial entry—a stage that was significantly enhanced with http 1.1 and persistent TCP communications. Once your browser completes discovery, it starts transferring context through the TCP protocol. The browser in the receiving machine controls the pipeline and resends a request if a packet is lost.

SGML Roots

C.F. Goldfarb authored SGML and its IBM predecessor, Document Composition Facility Generalized Markup Language.

In the mid-1980s, the American National Standards Institute (ANSI) commissioned an open source code to automate its book production by instructing computers to emulate an editor's "mark ups" to typesetters. In 1986, the International Standards Organization adopted the work as the Standard Generalized Markup Language (SGML–ISO 8879).

The standard relies on the ASCII character set and a "kernel" of tags and rules. The latter are native to all SGML endeavors and basic for coding digital archives (See also: chapter 4).

- Individual fields are called *"elements."*
- Coding is within the "lesser than" and "greater than" brackets (< >).
- *Elements* are defined in pairs (*wrappers*) with "start" and "/stop" tags e.g., ****bold tag puts everything in bf until****.
- Tags can be imbedded within tags: *<i>**bold italics**</i>***bold****.
- Tags should be in lower case.
- Elements can have *"attributes."* Modifiers can be strung together and are set in the start tag following the element name with a space and the term="quality." For example, you may want to indicate that a date is the publication date with *<date type="publication">*.
- Most elements are recursive—they can be repeated in numerous places and even within the same element: *<bioghist>…<bioghist>… </bioghist></bioghist>*.

- Results must be well formulated—i.e., in compliance with the preceding rules. To ensure compliance, use a separate validation program before mounting files on the Web (See "XHTML Varieties and Compliance," below).

Instead of making individual layouts for each page and relying on the browser to interpret the tags, XHTML can separate content from layout with separate programs called cascading style sheets (CSS).

Web Pages and XHTML

HTML 2.0 emerged in 1992 as an SGML Document Type Definition (DTD). As illustrated in figure 1.3, HTML produces a three-part document that takes some latitude, but roughly comports to SGML's official syntax. The HTML DTD added new features and evolved through two more generations before approximating true SGML-compliance with XHTML 1.0 (See: http://www.w3.org/TR/xhtml1/), which this book recommends for your endeavors.

Fig. 1.3. Web Page Structure with XHTML/HTML Differences

The Declaration announces the document type or version of HTML (XHTML or XML) e.g., *<!DOCTYPE html PUBLIC "W3C// DTD XHTML 1.0 Transitional//EN">*

<html>
<head> is designed for communicating among the computers and largely is hidden from view. It tells the receiving machines what to expect, can declare stylistic features, and holds title, keyword, and description metadata. </head>

<body> contains the text, formatting, and hypertext codes for the actual display on the computer screen. These follow SGML's grammar and <tag> formatting, but:

- HTML allows for a selection of "empty tags" without a closing entry: *<p>* paragraph, *
* line break. In XHTML (and XML), empty elements must be closed by a stop tag (</p>) or space and "/"—e.g., <br />.
- HTML can use upper case letters. XHTML demands lower case.
- HTML relied on ASCII for coding letters, but XHTML has expanded the choices with Unicode options.
- XHTML and XML favor dividing pages into subsections or divisions <div>, which can be individually managed for style.

</body></html>

XHTML VARIETIES AND COMPLIANCE

XHTML rewrites HTML for XML/SGML compliance, and current software packages are programmed for the change. You can update older pages through Dave Raggett's HTML Tidy (http://tidy.sourceforge.net/), Jonathan Hedley's related HTML Tidy Online (http://infohound.net/tidy), or other validators. XHTML 1.0 comes in three flavors:

- The "Strict" form may not work well with older browsers and stresses separate layout coding with cascading style sheet (CSS) programs.
- "Frameset" allows for deprecated tags, but comes with clear indications of the growing dislike for frames.
- "Transitional" is the option of choice and used in this text. It demands more discipline, but still allows for HTML's familiar features.

EXTERNAL CONTRIBUTIONS

The new medium was eagerly embraced by outside developers. They made contributions that were vital to the popularization of the Web, yet outside the control of W3C. We will focus on three external technologies:

1. **WEB SOFTWARE EDITORS:** A number of entrepreneurs stepped forward with software shells to ease the coding of HTML. Instead of the flat coding with Notepad or other basic text editor, these employed hidden codes with WYSIWYG (what you see is what you get) and GUI (graphical user interfaces) mouse controls. Each product comes with its own learning curve.

2. **BROWSERS:** This software transforms HTML code for presentation on the receiving computer screens. Early Web users relied on Internet Lynx browsers with navigation by tabbing among anchors. In 1993, Marc Andressen added an easy-to-use GUI interface with the Mosaic browser. The next year, he issued its commercial sibling, the phenomenally successful Netscape, which opened the Web to the general public. Browsers stimulated the drive for more HTML features—such as the inclusion of images and media.

3. **SEARCH ENGINES:** Search engines were added to identify resources within a geometrically expanding

universe. Yahoo! led the way in the early 1990s with its human classifiers, followed by software agents with search engine "spiders" that employ complex mathematical models to locate, analyze, and point users to appropriate resources on the Web.

SEARCH ENGINE OVERVIEW

Search engines can be divided into two categories.

- **DIRECTORIES/SUBJECT GUIDES:** Led by Yahoo, these rely on humans to categorize and make listings. You or the search engine editors submit a short description that the software uses for its matches.
- **CRAWLER-BASED:** These utilize three types of software:

1. **Spiders:** These software programs crawl the Web looking at sites, following HTML links to pages within, and reading and gathering data.
2. **Index:** The spider returns the data to its home nest—an index with copies of all the pages crawled that is updated after each visit (Google also employs a "caching" system with the pages stored as an alternative mechanism for users to get the information from a page).
3. **Inference and Searching Software:** These programs respond to queries by sifting through material in the index, finding matches, ranking in order of perceived relevance, and returning results.

Other Contributions

Although beyond the book's scope, other non-W3C developments can be thrown into the mix—in particular, Sun Microsystems' extended HTML with its now standard Java language (See: http://java.sun.com). Java can add programs within a Web page; for example, it can help install complicated chat rooms and interactive forms and can also implant small programs ("applets") to enliven displays.

Finally, we should acknowledge the drive for more bandwidth and speed of delivery. Traditional telecommunications agencies and newer cable and satellite companies have eagerly entered the mix on the delivery side. The government would continue to link to the Internet, but also launched its own delivery system. In 1998, the academic research complex took a parallel path with Internet 2 (The Grid) and a massive increase in bandwidth (http://www.internet2. org).

XML: SECOND-GENERATION WEB

The Web eventually lost a portion of its human-centered innocence and word processing limits. The computational desires of scientists received a major boost in the mid-1990s when W3C opened the medium to e-commerce. According to product developers Jon Bosak and Tim Bray in a *Scientific American* article, the 2nd Generation was driven to respond to business concerns for speedy systems:

> *that take customer orders from customers, transmit medical records, even run factories and take scientific instruments from half a world away.* (http://www.sciam.com/1999/0599issue/0599bosak.html)

Cultural bodies echoed these directions. They sought to go beyond HTML and foster professional information standards for interinstitutional cooperation. The cry came for "well-formulated" documents—those with clearly defined content (words, graphs, images) and an indication of what role such elements played. W3C was similarly intrigued and committed to an open system to enable Web computing. With the added blessings and support from Microsoft, W3C assigned a working group of twelve in 1996.

Rather than a new product, the team offered a radical restatement of SGML (See: chapter 4) and left formatting to HTML. They streamlined the older standard and brought it into conformity with something the http daemon could recognize. The team sought a flexible, hierarchical database system to allow computer operations on the Web. The results were a 1997 proposal for an Extensible Markup Language (XML).

Meta Language

While XML uses SGML syntax, anyone can build a model (XML Schema) with or without reference to SGML or its subsidiary DTDs. XML is, in fact, a metalanguage in its own right. The potential benefits are manifest:

- XML theoretically offers speed advantages. Instead of repeatedly querying a site and having the answers reformulated and transmitted back again and again, XML transfers the database structures and content en masse for work within the receiving computer.
- The approach allows for comparisons among institutional records and even among the records of multiple institutions.

- XML is scalable off the Web to other electronic media. By concentrating on content, it can publish to PDAs, cell phone viewers, or other unforeseen devices.
- XML scales to Braille readers and sound or other media outputs to help insure handicapped access.
- XML offers extra authentication and transaction verification.
- XML also brought along Unicode, a new character conversion standard built on the initial 256 characters of ASCII code, but extended to include coding schemes for all the world's known writing systems.

XML does have limits. It is an admittedly verbose resource-greedy, and rule-driven language that calls for expertise and work well beyond that for the word processing of HTML—for example:

- **XML PARSERS:** Compliance with SGML's syntax (See: chapter 3) demands a formal software review or validation of the tags before it can be mounted on the Web.
- **EXTENSIBLE STYLE SHEETS (XSL):** Onscreen display demands HTML codes, which are rendered through stylesheets *<xsl:stylesheet>*. Such templates insert the font families, margins, header styles, et cetera (See: www.w3.org/TR/xsl for information on such translations; XSL FAQs at www.dpawson.co.uk /xsl/xslfaq.html).

Resources on XML and Web Standards

You can find information about standards and training all over the Web, but anyone can profit from going back to square one. W3C (http://www.w3.org) maintains a trove of information including its own "school zone." You may be interested in the Web Standards Project (http://www.webstandards.org) or sites like C-Net Central (cnet.com) and PlanetIT (http://www.planetit.com). The truly interested can go to the Internet Engineering Task Force (http://www.ietf.cnri.reston .va.us/home.html) and Internic (http://www.Internic.net). For Internet 2, check http://www.internet2.org and look in the applications area.

On XML, start with W3C's XML site (http://www.w3.org/XML/) and the International SGML/XML Users group (http://www.isgmlug .org/). The Organization for the Advancement of Structured

Information Systems (OASIS) is the non-profit outlet for much of XML's commercial development. It hosts Robin Coover's expert commentary (http://www.oasis-open.org) and co-sponsors the *ebXML* e-business format for the UN.

RDF and the Semantic Web

W3C is not finished with XML. The consortium seems uneasy with retrieval from commercial search engines. Its internal goals go beyond commercial applications to a universal machine translator for all communication on the Web. XML's abilities as an exchange format are vital to such directions, but XML's very elasticity gets in the way. The proposed answer is a meta resource for all metalanguages called the Resource Description Framework (RDF). According to W3C's 1999 recommendations:

> *The World Wide Web was originally built for human consumption, and although everything on it is machine-readable, this data is not machine-understandable. It is very hard to automate anything on the Web, and because of the volume of information the Web contains, it is not possible to manage it manually...* *(RDF) is a foundation for processing metadata; it provides interoperability between applications that exchange machine-understandable information on the Web.* (http://www.w3.org/TR/REC-rdf-syntax)

RDF works through a tripartite "sentence." It provides a subject-verb-object for the computer to decode. The approach builds from XML's namespace (xmlns) capacity and allows linkages to trusted formats, like EAD, which are found at a predetermined Uniform Resource Identifier (URI). The implications are no less than a semantic network of all metalanguages.

> RDF was designed by Ora Lassila and others for W3C. It drew from the work of James Hendler at the University of Maryland with the SHOE project: the Web's first knowledge representation language.

> **URLs** can include any addressable spot on the Web: e.g., anchors.

ASSIGNMENT

Your "homework" is to become aware of differences between the Web and print documents. For example, *Building Digital Archives* is constructed with the Web in mind. The book's paragraphs are deliberately short, headings and illustrations frequently used, references made to URLs, and bulleted lists are favored. Yet print cannot reproduce hypertext or scrolling. The view is a horizontal page—not the vertical, half-page view of a computer screen—and so forth.

2 UNDERSTANDING DIGITIZED FINDING AIDS

This chapter will introduce archival techniques and constructs to non-archivists. It also provides a training exercise in automation project management, which establish the underlying techniques for the applications in subsequent chapters.

PRELIMINARIES

As indicated in chapter 1, automation projects typically start by:

1. bringing together a team with complimentary skills in management, design, content, and technology;
2. setting a reasonable time line for the project's stages; and
3. launching systems analysis.

PROBLEM DEFINITION

Our purpose is to create an efficient automated archival Finding Aids, presumably to be mounted on the web. As with most computerized description, the descriptive devices do not stand alone; they require supplemental tools for quality control and access. Consider dividing your efforts for manageability into two segments:

1. **ENTRY MODEL:** techniques for creating new Finding Aids that ensure reliability and future migrations, and facilitate mounting on the Web
2. **RETROSPECTIVE CONVERSION:** a secondary phase to convert preexisting documents into the new model.

FINDING AID BACKGROUND

Finding Aids are a logical choice to begin down a challenging road. A familiar format with established practices and policies, these devices come in manageable sizes for testing, are generally free from copyright and privacy concerns, and, more importantly, they are apt transitional vehicles for digital archives. Finding Aids provide the basis for Encoded Archival Description (EAD)—the American archival community's conceptual model for the electronic delivery of descriptions and access to digital collections.

Reader's Advisory: The chapter invites skimming. Its next section is an introduction for non-archivists. Archivists may want to jump ahead to "Data Gathering."

The Finding Aid is a guide to describe and provide access to archival collections. It is an extremely flexible and powerful tool with a format that can encompass a limitless amount of content and a variety of media. Examples range from less than a page (as illustrated in figure 2.1) to booklets with hundreds of pages.

Fig. 2.1. Sample Finding Aid

E. F. Doree Collection,
1916–1947 (Predominately 1916–1925)
.75 linear feet, 1 1/2 manuscript boxes
1658-IWW

Edward F. Doree worked as a national organizer for the Industrial Workers of the World [I.W.W.] and served as treasurer of its General Defense Committee. The collection focuses on the mass arrest and imprisonment of I.W.W. members in 1917–1918 for alleged violation of wartime anti-sedition acts. Doree was caught in the sweep with his brother-in-law, Walter T. Nef, secretary-treasurer of the Marine Transport Workers Industrial Union No. 100 in Philadelphia. At the time of his arrest, Doree was secretary-treasurer of Textile Workers Industrial Union No. 1000 in Philadelphia. Before receiving a presidential pardon in September 1922, Mr. Doree was released twice from the federal penitentiary at Fort Leavenworth to visit his critically ill son in Philadelphia.

The papers of E. F. Doree were placed in the Reuther Library by Ellen Doree Rosen, the daughter of Mr. Doree, in July of 1996 and opened for research in January of 1997.

Series I: Correspondence 1917–1925, Box 1
Series II: Legal Affairs, 1921–1922, Box 2

Contents

Box 1–Series I

1.	Clippings and E. F. Doree business card, 1922
2–5.	Correspondence; E. F. Doree to Ida S. Doree, Oct 1917, Sep-Dec 1918
6–11.	Correspondence; E. F. Doree to Ida S. Doree, Jan-Jun 1919
12–20	Correspondence; E. F. Doree to Ida S. Doree, Jan-Dec 1921
21–25.	Correspondence; E. F. Doree to Ida S. Doree, Jan-Aug 1922
26.	Correspondence; E. F. Doree to parents, 1916–18, 1925

Box 2–Series II

1.	E. F. Doree depositions on behalf of amnesty for I.W.W. prisoners, Aug 1921
2.	E. F. Doree pardon; corres., etc., Aug-Sep 1922
3.	House Judiciary Committee hearing on amnesty for political prisoners; transcript, Mar 1922
4.	I.W.W. Leavenworth prisoner status lists, 1922
5.	Correspondence; Rebecca Winsor Evans to Ida S. Doree, 1947
6.	E. F. Doree depositions on behalf of amnesty for I.W.W. prisoners, Aug 1921
7.	E. F. Doree pardon; corres., etc., Aug-Sep 1922
8.	House Judiciary Committee hearing on amnesty for political prisoners; transcript, Mar 1922
9.	I.W.W. Leavenworth prisoner status lists, 1922

PARSING

One of the keys to successful automation is parsing or breaking down a document into its constituent parts—i.e., into metadata elements that a machine can understand—like figure 2.2's expansion of figure 2.1:

Fig. 2.2. Parse of Sample Finding Aid

<Title Block>
<Title>**E.F. Doree Collection**
<Dates>**1916–1947 (predominately 1916–1925)**
<Size>**.75 linear feet, 1 1/2 manuscript boxes**
<ID code>**1658-IWW**
<Body>
<Scope and Content> <paragraph>Edward F. Doree worked as a national organizer for the Industrial Workers of the World [I.W.W.] and served as treasurer of its General Defense Committee. The collection focuses on the mass arrest and imprisonment of I.W.W. members in 1917–1918 for alleged violation of wartime anti-sedition acts. Doree was caught in the sweep with his brother-in-law, Walter T. Nef, secretary-treasurer of the Marine Transport Workers Industrial Union No. 100 in Philadelphia. At the time of his arrest, Doree was secretary-treasurer of Textile Workers Industrial Union No. 1000 in Philadelphia. Before receiving a presidential pardon in September 1922, Mr. Doree was released twice from the federal penitentiary at Fort Leavenworth to visit his critically ill son in Philadelphia.

Fig. 2.2. (cont.)

    \<paragraph\>The papers of E. F. Doree were placed in the Reuther Library by Ellen Doree Rosen, the daughter of Mr. Doree, in July of 1996 and opened for research in January of 1997.
\<Organization\>**Series I:** Correspondence 1917–1925, Box 1
    Series II: Legal Affairs, 1921–1922, Box 2
\<Inventory\>
\<container 1\>**Box 1–Series I**
\<folder\>1. Clippings and E. F. Doree business card, 1922
\<folder\>2. Correspondence; E. F. Doree to Ida S. Doree, Oct 1917, Sep-Dec 1918
\<folder\>3. Correspondence; E. F. Doree to Ida S. Doree, Oct 1917, Sep-Dec 1918
\<folder\>4. Correspondence; E. F. Doree to Ida S. Doree, Oct 1917, Sep-Dec 1918
\<folder\>5. Correspondence; E. F. Doree to Ida S. Doree, Oct 1917, Sep-Dec 1918
\<folder\>6. Correspondence; E. F. Doree to Ida S. Doree, Jan-Jun 1919
\<folder\>7. Correspondence; E. F. Doree to Ida S. Doree, Jan-Jun 1919
\<folder\>8. [Repeat title and folder tags to…]
\<folder\>11. Correspondence; E. F. Doree to Ida S. Doree, Jan-Jun 1919
\<folder\>12. Correspondence; E. F. Doree to Ida S. Doree, Jan-Dec 1921 [Repeat title/tags…
\<folder\>to 20.]
\<folder\>21 Correspondence; E. F. Doree to Ida S. Doree, Jan-Aug 1922 [Repeated folder tags…]
\<folder\>to 25.
\<folder\>26. Correspondence; E. F. Doree to parents, 1916–18, 1925
\<container 2\>**Box 2–Series II**
\<folder\>1. E. F. Doree depositions on behalf of amnesty for I.W.W. prisoners, Aug 1921
\<folder\>2. E. F. Doree pardon; corres., etc., Aug-Sep 1922
\<folder\>3. House Judiciary Committee hearing on amnesty for political prisoners; Mar 1922
\<folder\>4. I.W.W. Leavenworth prisoner status lists, 1922
\<folder\>6. E. F. Doree depositions on behalf of amnesty for I.W.W. prisoners, Aug 1921
\<folder\>7. E. F. Doree pardon; corres., etc., Aug-Sep 1922
\<folder\>8. House Judiciary Committee hearing on amnesty for political prisoners; Mar 1922
\<folder\>9. I.W.W. Leavenworth prisoner status lists, 1922

Sample Elements

Finding Aids vary widely by institution, but share certain tendencies. They are hierarchical in nature and, as in our model, typically feature at least:

1. **TITLE:** a block (or complete page) containing basic information:
   a. **Title Proper**—generally the name or "provenance" of the originating person, family, or institution
   b. **Dates**—the period covered in the collection
   c. **Size**—expressed in linear/cubic feet or number of items for smaller holdings

  d. **Identification Numbers**—normally point to an internal accession code

2. **BODY:** a section containing content descriptions and analysis, such as:

   a. **Narrative** with **History** and **Scope and Content Notes** to abstract the holdings at hand;

   b. **Organization** with **Series Note** to explain the arrangement of the materials with a focus on keeping their original order; and

   c. **Inventory** or container lists to specify the contents of the boxes and folders

---

NOTE ON EAD USE

The EAD tag library (http://www.loc.gov/ead) provides the main thesaurus for Finding Aid elements. Its 2002 version lists 146 elements and assorted attributes. The book uses a less restrictive set of terms for visible display, but reverts to EAD for standardized metadata elements and anchor names for computer recognition.

Added prospects

You are well advised to keep things simple at the start and standardize on a limited number of elements in a set order. In addition to the elements above, you may want to consider adding:

In EAD, the Genre indicator is often subsumed as an unlabelled subtitle.

1. **TITLE BLOCK**
   - **Genre or Form Indicator** to qualify the generic term "Collection" by adding terms to distinguish among personal papers, institutional records, photographic or oral history holdings, et cetera
   - **Author/Editor Citation** for the creator of the Finding Aid
   - **Date of Publication** or completion of the Finding Aid
   - **Repository or Publisher** information that may include the address
   - **Copyright Symbol** to demonstrate intellectual ownership

2. **BODY**

- **Table of Contents** may be present for longer Finding Aids
- **Biography or History Notes** about the subject of the collection
- **Chronology** as a subset of Biography/History or Scope and Contents
- **Subject List** of key topics, places, and events under Scope and Contents
- **Correspondent List** of those with letters under Scope and Contents
- **Related Collections** or list of other resources under Scope and Contents
- **Note on Materials Removed** for destruction or housed separately
- **Administrative Notes** on the origins, state of processing, restrictions, and preservation—each of which could be a separate note
- **Index** or alphabetic rearrangement of the box/folder listings

Subject and Correspondent Lists are best tied to authority files for consistency and cross-collection research.

FINDING AID STUDIES

Gregory Hunter's *Developing and Mounting Practical Archives* in this series provides a solid introduction to the archival field. Frederic Miller's *Arranging and Describing Archives and Manuscripts* (Chicago: Society of American Archivists, 1990) is a good resource on descriptive apparatus. Although more critical analysis on the descriptive devices is in order, user studies and publications about EAD implementation are rapidly emerging.

DATA GATHERING

Data gathering balances internal factors with external practices, standards, and current technologies. Documentation is important, so open a folder and begin to record your findings.

INTERNAL RESEARCH

Your research begins at home. The team will want to examine a representative sample of in-house print and computer versions. Check, too, on extant written or verbal polices, current practices, and staff opinions to determine:

- **ADMINISTRATIVE BACKGROUND**
  - Are there financial implications (e.g., significant revenue coming from the reproduction of Finding Aids)?
  - What contracts or other institutional expertise and possible funding sources are available?
  - What is the nature of the staff and their expertise in regard to Finding Aids and automation?
  - What are your current policies—e.g., copyright, privacy, copying?

- **USE FACTORS**
  - How many collections are processed or unprocessed?
  - How does staff use the Finding Aids?
  - What type of researchers use the archives and how do they approach the Finding Aid?
  - What collections are most important and most used?
  - Are there privacy or copyright questions (e.g., exhibiting a Finding Aid on a collection that will be closed for a number of years)?

- **PRODUCTION STATUS**
  - How many Finding Aids are produced in a typical year?
  - How many are currently available?
    - How many are word-processed or in other program formats?
    - How many are available only in a typed hard copy?
  - What is the range and norm in terms of the number of pages?
  - Which are the most used or detail the most valuable collections?

- **PARSING THE LAYOUT**
  - Can you list the data elements and the order in which they are encountered?
    - What is in the Title Header?
    - What do you find in the Body?
  - What terms are being used?

- Are there differences in layout or terminology in your sample?
  - If so, is there any historical pattern to the changes?
  - Are there notable differences among current staff members?

EXTERNAL RESEARCH

A portion of your time is spent looking at Finding Aids in other archives; encourage team members to discuss practices and other skills or tools with the archivists at such institutions. Look, too, for personal assistance from colleagues in archival organizations and by attending conferences/workshops.

Standards

See: Victoria Walch's *Standards for Archival Description* (http:// www .archivists.org/catalog /stds99/index.html)

As part of their drive for automation, American archivists began to collaborate on descriptive standards in the 1980s, producing an interim consensus on library cataloging and Finding Aids which consisted of a special MARC-AMC format and Steven Henson's rules for content entry— the *APPM Manual (Archives, Personal Papers, Manuscripts*; see chapter 5). In the 1990s, the Web pushed efforts toward a global stage and calls for further standards, including:

- Canadian RAD (Rules for Archival Description); see http://lib74123.usask.ca/scaa/rad
- European ISAD(g) (General International Standard of Archival Description); see http://www.ica.org/ biblio/cds/isad_g_2e.pdf
- CUSTARD (Canadian United States Task Force on Archival Description), which is currently under development and scheduled to resolve international differences; see http://www.archivists.org/news/ custardproject.asp
- SAA's EAD (Encoded Archival Description), which, as previously indicated, provides the data-entry framework and controlled terminology; see http://www.loc.gov/ead

AUTOMATION FACTORS

Hardware questions have largely vanished from the table because most institutions can afford powerful desktop models with almost unlimited storage capacity. Instead, software commands the team's technical attention.

Software TYPES

There are a variety of options for encoding Finding Aids:

- **WORD PROCESSORS** are by far the most commonly used software. The "Killer Application" of the 1980s, word processors turned the microcomputer into a consumer fad. They began as simple text editors to replace typewriters, but quickly expanded with style controls, spelling, thesaurus, grammar checking, et cetera, to rival the output of a printing shop. With time, they evolved into office suites with ready exchange to companion DBMS, spreadsheets, presentation software, and even direct export to the Web.

  Staff are expected to be familiar with the ubiquitous word processor and similar technology–ergo reducing the need for extra training. Equally important, most programs allow for open formats.

TEXT FORMATS

The American standard common integer set—*ASCII (.txt)*—has long provided a way to exchange text among programs. In the mid-1990s, Microsoft added *rich text format (.rtf*—the industry-wide standard to capture both text and graphics. The latest arrival is Unicode, which expands the ASCII set to handle all types of languages and scripts.

In 1970, IBM's E.F. Codd reported the mathematical principles for interlacing relational tables to replace the linear tags of early mainframes.

- **Developed in the 1980s, DBMSs are** a more powerful solution than "flat" word-processed files because, unlike word processing programs, they can unite across records to facilitate comparisons and convert lists to tables through relational mathematics IBM's underlying SQL (Sequel–now SQL:1999), the open system standard, sets the rules for creating and manipulating databases. DBMS product lines are well developed with good support and a solid commercial base and have also been converted by object-oriented programming for hierarchical retrieval and, as discussed in chapter 4, Web applications.

- **DEDICATED COLLECTION MANAGEMENT SOFTWARE**: Turnkey archival and records management software, mentioned at the close of chapter 5 as part of the larger discussion of integrated library systems (ILSs), offer a separate set of DBMS-related possibilities for the production of Finding Aids.

- **SGML SOFTWARE EDITORS,** developed to parse books for automated printing in keeping with Standard Generalized Markup Language, are also adaptable to the production of Finding Aids (See: chapter 4 for analysis).

ANALYSIS

Although it is almost impossible to avoid some analysis during data-gathering, now is the time for you and your team to stop, look at your data, and weigh all the variables, including the possibility of unintended consequences.

GENERAL ASSESSMENT

The strengths of automation are self-evident. Most institutions have already proceeded with the automation of Finding Aids. Word processing provides the compositional strengths of the printing press with the ease of updating and correction. And, as demonstrated, automation should bring additional layers of quality and authority controls that can standardize layout, facilitate spelling and syntax checking, and ensures consistency in terminology and naming.

Since results vary from institution to institution, this section can only provide general pointers on layout and software selections. You are striving for a product that is useable, easy to put together, and will not take a great deal of staff time to implement.

Audience Concerns

In theory, audience is *the* prime component for effective communication instruments. While Finding Aids may be tuned to the work and language of archivists and manuscript curators, the intended audiences are seasoned researchers.

Production, however, must still remain comfortable and doable for your personnel. Effective information systems require realistic means of data entry, so reconsidering any established format can be a daunting proposition. Project designers should rely on simplicity and play close attention to established methods of description.

Content Factors

Analyze the inclusion, order, and terminology of elements for your new Finding Aids. Based on your observations:

- Are there elements that you want to add?
- What terminology is most appropriate for your layout and your users?
- Are all the elements within your final product worth the time and effort?
- Which of the remaining are mandatory; which are prefixed with permanent information; and which are an option, especially for larger and more important holdings?
- Do you want to include authority controls for names and places?

AUTOMATION FACTORS

In addition to bottom-line or cost/benefit factors, a commonsense evaluation will consider the following questions:

- Does your current software (or newer versions of the line) meet present or projected needs for Finding Aids?
- Do you have an administrative mandate or other reasons to adopt a different product line?
- What is the level of staff competence and projected training demands for product introduction?

- Does the selection meet the open standards (e.g., *.rtf, SQL*) to translate among other products and ensure future migration?
- Does it have a solid commercial base and offer good customer support?
- Do you have access to other internal or external support for the product—e.g., IT department, users in the institution, or ties to a group project?

Software Selection

Unless there are overriding imperatives to change (e.g., a grant, participation in a group project)—stay with what you know. The simplest alternative and lowest learning curve involves using extant products or upgrading to a newer version of the line. For most readers, the choice is between word processing with ASCII, *.rtf,* and MS Word formatting or an SQL-compliant DBMS. The ease of use of the word processor must be measured against the higher power and greater complexity of the DBMS—and there are tradeoffs. At the introductory level and for our initial demonstrations, the word processor emerges as a logical choice.

Output Considerations

Computerized Finding Aids can be conditioned as "read-only" and mounted on a stand-alone computer or LAN for user access, allowing word-processed forms to be individually retrieved and searchable through the computer's string or keyword options. DBMS versions can extend searching across collections.

Yet the computer has a limited viewing area. Access is largely serial, like a microfilm, allowing the user to scroll up and down through the text. Moreover, the investment of funds and space for computers may prove too much for some institutions.

Print, on the other hand, has the advantages of comfort for in-depth research, and it offers random access and the strengths of skimming. Researchers can have several individual copies on the table at the same time, right beside their other materials. Automated Finding Aids will thus likely remain supplementary to the printed copy in most repositories for some time. Finding Aid automation will likely be focused primarily on printing, and, as covered in the next chapter, external publication through the Web.

Supplemental Supports

As you gathered data, you may have noticed that museums, libraries, and archives have developed sophisticated methods for human retrieval—e.g., catalogs, directories, and finding aids. Computer access demands even more structure. As discussed in the pilot section, you will want to consider:

- project control guides for managing the operations;
- authority records to control names, places, and subject entries; and
- supplemental navigation lists to give users a variety of methods to locate the Finding Aids.

RECON CHOICES

Your approaches do not have to be all or nothing. The team may consider a second phase of retrospective conversion or "recon"—a selective conversion of the more important holdings. Treatment selection varies by the storage media:

1. **PRINTED VERSIONS:** These require scanning with OCR (Optical Character Recognition) conversion before use (See: chapter 5).
2. **PREVIOUS WORD PROCESSING:** These files may be useful as is, and it may not be worth the effort to convert fully to your new model. You do need to consider updating obsolescent or non-standard formats and reformatting items for the Web in *.rtf.*
3. **DBMS FILES:** If you are already parsing into a database, turn to chapter 3 to pull your data naming into conformity with EAD.

SOLUTIONS

You and your team have reached another plateau and stopping place.Now is the appropriate time for the team to model and debate the most appropriate solution from the tentative solutions discussed during the analysis stage.

Some use this moment to purchase equipment or software and provide background training in preparation for piloting. The stage can also address missing protocols for the management of electronic records.

AUTOMATION APPROACHES

Word processors provide an affordable initial software solution for most environments and are part of a robust commercial marketplace (See also: chapter 3 for MS Word examples). For our model, the needs are modest, and the package need only have such features as:

- **PRINT COMMANDS:** The print command is typically found on the *Formatting Tool Bar* to designate type font, size, bold face, italics, and justification.

- **TABLE:** This tool, among the most useful for creating and controlling layout, is also significant for sorting and mathematical operations. It allows for the conversion of word-processed formats into data elements for more powerful spreadsheets or SQL-compliant database management systems, and it converts directly to the Web.

- **TAB:** This assists with any layout, but also offers *Tab delimited* output. Delimiters work in conjunction with the *<return>* or *<enter>* key, which marks the end of a line. Consistent use of tabs lines up textual content for ready conversion to a table (See: figure 1.2).

- **STYLE MENU:** This is of particular interest for later conversion to the Web. As discussed in the next chapter, this menu can automatically set the size and type font for normal text and various levels of headings.

- **SAVE AS:** This command is found on the *FILE* or first pull-down menu on the top of the screen. Look for:
  - *READ ONLY* option is needed for mounting patron copies.
    - *RICH TEXT FORMAT* (*.rtf*) is the industry standard for sharing word-processed text and graphic files, but MS Word also serves as a current de facto standard.
    - *SAVE AS WEB PAGE/HTML* includes options for title and keyword entry, plus

These are preferred over *Frames* for Web design. Avoid **Columns** as they are awkward and a non-Web command.

Comma, dash, colon may also be used as delimiters.

Web Styles: Interpretation was originally defaulted to the browser, but is now possible with cascading style sheets (CSS).

background administrative metadata for author, date of entry, etc.
- *TEMPLATES* are also of interest, but call for practice and may not work for later con version to a Web page.

- **LISTS (numbered and bulleted):** Lists are quite useful and translate to the Web.

With luck, your present software will suffice or may demand a mere upgrade. The research for this book found 1997+ versions of Microsoft Word and WordPerfect adequate.

FILE Naming Conventions

The title proper (provenance) of the collection may be best for humans and normal in-house use—e.g. "The Paula Rosenfeld Papers." However, this approach presents problems for the computer, because personal names are often duplicated and may be very long or confused by the use of aliases. Successful sorting demands the extra step of putting the last name first.

The preferred alternative is to assign an identification or accession number of the collection. Codes should be distinct, easily manipulated, and typically reflect the order received. They can take on several forms:

- Many are a running accession number in a four or five digit sequence.
- Some employ a two-position museum practice with year code + accession # (98–013).
- Suffixes and/or prefixes are often used to coordinate multi-unit projects and records management environments—e.g. 246-uaw-vp or uaw-246-vp would signal "United Automobile Workers Union, Vice-President's Office, collection number 246."

New operating systems make the file naming job easier by allowing up to 256 spaces. The examples in this book will initially be more constrained, because they try to comport with the older DOS and Unix base. Terms form within the traditional 8(dot)3 or *xxxxxxxx.yyy* pattern—the initial eight for a name and the three-digit extension for the type of format–e.g., *.rtf, .htm, .gif.*

MODELING

Based on your analysis, draw mock layouts, discuss with the team, and select the most appropriate layout for the pilot stage. As figure 2.3 demonstrates, the model can be surprisingly spare. Graphics and layout can be kept simple, uncluttered, and close to the printed version.

Fig. 2.3. Sample Finding Aid Layout *(fa_form.rtf)*

TITLE + Genre
Dates
Size
ID #
©Publisher (Repository Name)

SCOPE AND CONTENTS NOTE

Correspondents

Related Collections

CONTENTS

Series

CONTAINERS

Findingaid:02:perm

Embellishments

Elements not used in the completion of an individual Finding Aid are easily erased after data entry. Field names within the Title Block are so recognizable in print that you could ignore them—resist the temptation. You should feel free to play and explore the layout options—for instance, your word processor can easily add:

Lists

Correspondents and Related Collections entries work well as bulleted lists:

CORRESPONDENTS

- Harry Anslinger
- J. Edgar Hoover
- Elliot Ness
- John Dillinger

Tables

Figure 2.4 illustrates a simple technique to expand the form above with the table function. In addition to looks, this enhancement offers advantages for the Web and sorting that are not possible in print (Note: lines can be made invisible or converted back to text).

Fig. 2.4. Automated Finding Aid with Inventory Table	
TITLE + Genre Dates Size ID # **©Publisher (Repository Name)**	
SCOPE AND CONTENTS NOTE Correspondents Related Collections **CONTENTS** Series CONTAINERS	
Box:Folder	Container Contents
1	
1:1	
1:2	
2	
2:1	

SUPPLEMENTAL MATERIALS

The Finding Aid cannot stand alone. Management and access to both manual and electronic records rely a web of mechanisms, for example:

Authority Records

"Controlled Vocabularies …on the Web" is a convenient source (http://www .lub.lu.se/metadata/subject-help.html).

Authority records are important to the Finding Aid, but can become complicated, requiring high-level expertise and checking against national lists. The Library of Congress has taken the most difficult lead with the multi-volume Library of Congress Subject Headings. On the museum side, the Getty Museum has stepped to the fore with the *Provenance Index* (http://www.getty.edu/research/tools/provenance/) and the *Thesaurus of Geographic Names* (TGN; see http://www .getty.edu/research/tools/vocabulary/tgn/index.html).

Systematic reliance on national and international authorities is the way to go. But archivists have had difficulties in implementing cooperative authority projects and sharing findings. A collection may have dozens of unique names and nicknames in addition to the main "author" entry. The International Council of Archives is moving to change this picture through an International Standard Archival Authority Records (ISAAR; see http://www.ica.org/biblio/cds/isaar_eng.pdf).

Figure 2.5 offers a homegrown approach for those without access to such venues or only currently interested in word-processing ventures.

Fig. 2.5. Manual Name-Authority File

NAMES *Last name, first, middle (alias, maiden name)	DATES birth-death	CITATIONS (ID # or HEFA Link) *name:02.perm*

*The "last name, first" convention is vital for subsequent sorting routines.

FORM NUMBERS

Form numbers—the codes you see popping up in the headings of forms—are an expected records management device and basic to the control of information systems. The book's version, e.g., *findingaid:02-c:perm*, reflects a three-part code:

- *Form Title Code:* (duplicates as file name)
- *Version_year* + *-update* code for significant model changes in the year*:*
- *retention_period.*

Note: The last element can be used to automatically schedule electronic records for destruction or archiving.

List of Automated Finding Aids

Instead of retrieving printed guides from a shelf, computer and Web access relies on intermediate lists in automated and print versions. The devices also can help coordinate staff efforts, avoid duplications, and act as a "pick list" for cut-and-pasting resources into other lists. As demonstrated in figure 2.6, the outputs should include an update area to highlight the most recent additions.

Fig. 2.6. Finding Aid List *<holdings/fa_list.rtf>*

Repository Name
Automated Finding Aids

fa_list:03:updated

Last Updated: _____

Latest Additions-Test Area:

Sally Bowles Papers, 1920–1936	568
Committee Against Premature Aging, 1978–2000	569

A — **ID Number**

George Abbott Papers, 1926–83	113
Henry Aquanaut Papers, 1943–1992	056
Association of Angry Archivists Records, 1989–	365

B

Thomas Batten Papers, 1898–1917	113
Sally Bowles Papers, 1920–1936	568
Joseph Johnson Oral History Project, 1926–30	487-oral

Return to top

Project Log

The Finding Aid is a subset of the overall arrangement and description of a collection. Most institutions have established methods in place for assigning and supervising larger endeavors. Although exceptions can be made for a handful of items, typical procedures call for a project log (e.g., figure 2.7), which may be on paper or in the computer.

RETROSPECTIVE TACTICS

Based on resources and an appraisal of the extant holdings, you have several responses for converting older versions to the new model.

- At one extreme, you can do nothing, or perhaps defer a decision for Web conversion.

- At the other, you can update everything.
- In the middle, you may choose to update a prioritized selection of the most important or used items.

Fig. 2.7. Finding Aid Log				
Collection/ID #	Staff Initials	Date Assigned–Finished		Notes *Proj-log.02.1yr*

Assuming the charge is to act, you face three sets of conditions based on your software situation:

1. **PRESENT SOFTWARE LINE** works—open files and *Save as...ID number* in *.rtf* (or word processor format)

2. **NEW VERSION OF LINE** needed—once installed, again, simply open files and *Save as...ID number* in *.rtf* (or word processor format)

3. **NEW SOFTWARE:**
   - Can previous files be opened as one of the options within the new word processor and then named and saved as above?
   - If not, and you have the older software available, does the package offer *.rtf*?
   - If not, can you save as ASCII file (.txt), reopen with the new package, and save as *.rtf*?
   - Should you consider the option of commercial conversion packages that are available to assist with large projects?

PILOT

While there is always more information that can be gleaned, proper planning must give way to practical problem solving. However, do not push forward without taking the time to correct the inevitable mistakes and avoid potential embarrassment. This pilot stage divides into an alpha phase for physical preparations and a beta stage for testing and debugging.

ALPHA PREPARATIONS

The project demands a workable model for data entry along with solid attention to detail. Alpha preparations build on established conventions, such as the naming principles for electronic records management in the Prologue. We are about to create the foundations for an electronic records management environment.

Engineering the Models

Open the word processor and begin construction of the model Finding Aid and its supplemental supports.

1. Based on your drafts, enter the selected terms in order.
2. Use the various formatting options to create a pleasing and functional outline.
3. Save the file with the appropriate name and format and in the correct directory. Save a duplicate or back-up copy.
4. Review the output and be ready to fine tune.

Instructions

It is crucial that the instructional guides and hands-on training are tailored to the policies and technical approaches at your institution. They should be reviewed with staff for clarity, nomenclature, and quality control. As illustrated in the next chapter, instructions should be standardized with at least a title, date of issue, plus any revisions.

Directory Conventions

Your computer or LAN should be prepared as a test-bed to receive the project. Directory controls may range from the creation of a single *holdings/*directory to a large number of finding aids resembling figure 2.8.

Fig. 2.8. Project Directory Configuration

*...***/holdings/*** directory with subdirectories

- ***holdings/done*** (for processed and supplemental files on the Web site)
- ***holdings/old*** (for previously word-processed files)
- ***holdings/tool_box*** (a list of files and/or "sub-subdirectories" for forms and guides)
    - fa_guide.rtf
    - name.rtf
    - proj-log.rtf
- ***holdings/working*** (if needed, as a temporary work area)

BETA TESTING

Very few automation projects emerge without unforeseen problems and the need for "workarounds." It is time to test and debug.

New Model

If possible, encourage experienced processors to lend their expertise to the production of the new Finding Aid. You will also want to:

- Set a reasonable time frame for testing.
- Begin with the smallest and least complicated collections.
- Provide training and written instructions.
- Have the processors keep notes on their progress and problems.
- Review results periodically and be willing to redesign.

Recon Pilot

The recommendation, to convert extant word-processed Finding Aids into *.rtf* or a format that will work for conversion into HTML for the Web, is essentially a queuing and production matter.

1. Pick a reasonable subset of your extant collections—e.g., ten to twenty.
2. Ensure the collections are in *holdings/old.*

3. Prepare a project log.
4. Provide staff with training and a companion set of instructions.
5. Convert samples to a standard format—e.g., *.rtf.*
6. Review and revise procedures and instructions

MONITOR/EVALUATE

The team must observe and make pragmatic adjustments during the course of the pilot:

- What works—what does not?
- How much time does it takes to complete a version?
- Can you extrapolate from that for full implementation? Remember that you will learn along the way and speeds will improve with practice.

At the end of the trial period, review the results. Be willing to redesign the format and retest as necessary—or even abandon the initiative.

BACKUPS

Any sensible automation endeavor presupposes regular backup procedures such as streaming to a tape system or saving to zip drives, CDs, DVDs—even simple floppy copies. If possible, you should arrange to have the backups stored off-site for added protection (See also: chapter 8 on preservation).

IMPLEMENTATION

Depending on the evaluation during the pilot, the time comes to implement and the test-bed becomes the working bed. Most of your procedural bugs should have been removed, but fine-tuning may be necessary. Assuming there is a backlog, prioritize to ensure that the most important items are captured. Again, begin with smaller and less complicated collections so you will develop skills that will come in handy with more elaborate versions. Make sure that staff receives formal training and access to the project findings along with the rationale for the effort.

Prepared instructions, training materials, and production guides will pay dividends over time—especially for the education of new staff.

The pilot added several permanent components to your information system, including *holdings* and directories for *forms* and *guides.* These structures will resurface periodically along with other records management controls.

Finally, do not become complacent. We have only begun down the R and D road to automation in the Web era, so Expect that the Web will affect future description and that the layout of the Finding Aid will evolve and perhaps be replaced by newer formats. The goal is a set of integrated structures that weave together the management of the institution.

NOTE ON SYNERGIES

Look for synergies in the automation techniques for the Finding Aid that are not only part-and parcel of general procedures, but also enhance and ease the work for other endeavors. In later treatments, for example, the data in the NAMES column of an authority record is available for cut-and-pasting into correspondent lists, speeding implementation, adding conformity, and reducing typing errors. Similarly, you can copy the hyperlink citations from Web Finding Aids List (See: chapter 3) into CITATIONS. The Name-Authority File then takes on power as a retrieval device and mechanism—one that can expand beyond the limits of the Web's many-to-one form of hypertext.

3 CREATING EFFECTIVE WEB FINDING AIDS

This chapter continues the training exercise from chapter 2, adding HTML, hypertext, and Web design to your technological tool set for building digital archives. The instructions include a brief tutorial on the construction of Web Finding Aids through Microsoft Word software.

PRELIMINARIES

Project planning requires expanding the previous team to include Web expertise. As before, you need to establish a time line:

1. How long for data gathering (e.g., one to three months)?
2. How long for the analysis and solutions (e.g., one month)?
3. How long for a pilot stage (e.g., three to six months)?

EXERCISE

This exercise is an extension of the Finding Aids treatment from the last chapter. Your next task is to develop a production plan to place those instruments and their supporting mechanisms on the Web. This process transforms an in-house research tool into a Finding Aid that is an instantaneous, international publication—one that can act as a new interactive genre and gateway to digital documents.

MORE DATA GATHERING

You can use your information and analysis in the previous exercise in the creation of a Web Finding Aid. This time, you will adjust your research to the specific opportunities and demands of the Information Highway.

INSTITUTIONAL RE-RESEARCH

Data gathering looks in particular at how others deal with Finding Aids on the Web. You should be especially conscious of layout, terminology, and hypertext. Several sites can help you locate external resources for your survey:

- Terry Abraham's *Primary Resources* (http://www. uidaho.edu/special-collections/Other .Repositories.html)
- Lee Miller's *Ready 'Net Go!* (http://specialcollections .tulane.edu)
- UNESCO *Archives Portal* on the international side (http://www.unesco.org/webworld/portal_archives/)

SOFTWARE FACTORS

With the Web, software concerns take on broader scope than in-house computerization. In addition to the internal selection of software to encode pages, the team needs to be aware of the audience and a Web environment that includes browsers, telecommunication, and search engines factors.

Software Choices

Converting a Finding Aid into HTML for Web mounting is technologically straightforward. Any of the type of products below will fill the bill, but be sure to allow time for training and practice to build skills in your choice.

- **TEXT EDITORS:** One approach is to program HTML code directly through a non-WYSIWYG text editor—e.g., Windows NotePad or Macintosh SimpleText.
- **WORD PROCESSORS:** You can use a word processor as a text editor for entering HTML codes if you save the document as "text only or .txt" with the raw ASCII code, but none of the program's hidden formatting. Alternatively, you can insert hypertext into MS Word, WordPerfect, and other modern products and convert it to HTML. The results are more than adequate, but direct encoding produces smaller file sizes.

- **WEB EDITORS:** Most sites are programmed using HTML editors. At the time of this writing, Dreamweaver (http://www.macromedia.com/software/dreamweaver) and GoLive (http://www.adobe.com/prodindex/golive/main.html) headed the list of full service programs. Microsoft's FrontPage (http://www.microsoft.com/frontpage) is an easy-to-use program within its office suite. Even simpler and less expensive are BBEdit for Macintosh (http://www.barebones.com) and HomeSite for Windows (http://www.macromedia.com/software/homesite/).
- **BROWSER EDITORS:** Netscape, Microsoft's MSN Network, and other portals have long provided the tools for users to create pages for mounting on their sites. Recently, true browser-based WYSIWYG Web editors have made their appearance. Site Point's Editize (http://www.sitepoint.com) is reasonably priced, and you can get the same functionality for free with htmlArea (http://www.interactivetools.com/products/htmlarea/), which also offers an interface to its companion content management system.

PDF OPTION

PDF provides an interesting alternative to HTML. A quasi-proprietary product from Adobe, PDF has become a de facto standard for document capture from word processors and has been enhanced for hypertext insertion and limited search engine discovery. PDF output requires the purchase of Adobe's Acrobat product (http://www.adobe.com) or is available through WordPerfect with its "Publish to *.pdf*" option. (See: chapter 6 for further discussion)

Browsers

See **Browser Watch** (http:// www.ski.mskcc.org/browserwatch/) for developments.

Effective Web design takes into account how your design will look on different *browsers*—the software used to view Web pages and interpret HTML formatting. Simplicity remains the ideal—try to ensure that the vast majority of viewers can see your materials without having to download an extra "viewing patch" (The examples in this book meet such a test).

Although browsers achieved rough conformity following the appearance of HTML 3.2, one must still compare outputs between the dominant Microsoft Explorer and Netscape Navigator products. Each produces subtly different images, color representations (they share only

A Mac dash (-) is OK for Navigator, but Explorer defaults to (?).

216 colors of the RGB palate of 256), and occasional anomalies. Be aware, too, of differences between displays on a Macintosh and Windows-based PC.

Telecommucations

Your main external concern is download times for users. Finding Aids can become larger than the typical Web document, which means they can overwhelm browsers and require inordinate loading times. Based on today's 56 K modems, the rule of thumb favors initial pages of 50K (i.e., ten seconds or less for complete download) with an outside limit of 100K.

Search Engines

See **Search Engine Watch** (http://www.searchenginewatch.com) for comparisons and developments.

Search engines define your virtual visibility. While regular researchers and patrons may know to come to your site and look for its digital archives, most users arrive by way of a search engine. The text takes part of the burden if you inject search engine capacities such as metadata into your designs (See also: chapters 1 and 7).

THE GOOGLE FACTOR

Take note of the direction set by Google, the leading search engine of the early twenty-first century. In particular, Google:

- focuses on the HTML title;
- does not rely on your metadata efforts;
- makes its own "description" tag;
- bases evaluation on the number of links to a site; and
- limits indexing to the first 100K or so of a page.

HTML ELEMENTS

Fortunately, you do not need to know a great deal about HTML to make studied decisions for Web Finding Aids. This book relies on the most basic of codes within HTML 4.01 and its replacement XHTML standard (See: chapter 1). We need add only three concepts beyond normal word processing—headings, hypertext, and metadata.

Reader's Advisory: The next sections are intended for newcomers. Experienced Web hands may want to push ahead to the analysis section. A number of books and Web sites are available to help in going further with the HTML language—e.g., NCSA Beginner's guide to HTML (http://www.ncsa.uiuc.edu/General/Internet/WWW/HTMLPrimer.html) or HTML Help (http://www.htmlhelp.com).

A. Headings

> Search engines can target and weigh heading levels for retrieval purposes.

Rather than bold facing and using a large font size to mark divisions in a text, HTML has a system of tags to declare headings that range in size from the largest *h1* to the smallest *h6*. For headers, browsers typically default to boldface Times-Roman type at 24, 18, 14, 12, 10, and 8 points (Designers often limit to no lower than level *h4* to ensure visibility). Equally important, headings can reflect hierarchies and relationships—e.g., an *h1* has precedence and owns any *h2s* that follows it.

B. Hypertext

This revolutionary approach supplies the greatest difference and greatest potential for enhancing the Finding Aid beyond print. As described in chapter 1 and illustrated at the close of this chapter, the Web's form of hypertext rests on two sets of instruction:

- *<a name="bookmark">* places anchors (to go to places) in HTML documents.
- *<a href="reference">* comes in three types:
    - **INTERNAL**—*"anchor name"*—to link to a place within the same page
    - **RELATIVE**—*"file name.htm"*—to connect to records in the same directory or *".../directory/file name.htm"* to those on other directories in the site
    - **ABSOLUTE**—*<"http://www.location.edu/external_record.htm">* uses the *http* protocol to tie to locations on the site or anywhere on the Web.

C. Metadata

The final considerations are largely hidden from view and reside in the Head at the top of the HTML record. That section holds data for computer use, including three types of metadata of potential interest to search engines:

- **TITLE:** *<title>***PAGE NAME***</title>* This is the most important—and the only visible—form of

HTML metadata. The entry produces the title in the center top border of the Web page, which is vital for search engine identification and helps Web users orient themselves. Although the title can display sixty characters, search engines may only focus on the first few words.

- **KEYWORD:** *<meta name="keyword" name="xxx, xxx, xxx">* The most hyped and abused tag, keywords are limited to 1,000 characters, but with an emphasis on the first 200 spaces. Search engines are starting to ignore this feature.

- **DESCRIPTION:** *<meta name="description" contents="summary sentence">* This short sentence summary of up to twenty-five words (roughly 180 characters) is used to categorize the site. The element may be supplied by the site or generated by search engines.

WEB PAGE DESIGN

With the above concepts in place, we can examine the trappings of a typical Web page. Your canvas is a computer screen that is roughly half the size of a sheet of paper. The opening image has two main purposes:

1. to identify the location and purpose
2. to provide navigation to its contents

Reader's Advisory: These treatments are cursory. This text does not pretend to hold definitive guidance or aesthetic leadership. The goal is to provide an introduction and to keep things simple (See also: chapter 7 on overall site requirements).

Identification is straightforward, but Web navigation calls for hypertext insertions. The goal is to change the opening image from a flat, postcard image into an interactive magazine cover—one with an automated table of contents. The computer screen offers a limited number of areas for such a feature:

The *Tables* command is prefered to *Frames* in HTML for columns; XHTML also allows one to duplicate the effect by blocking areas.

LEFT- OR RIGHT-HAND COLUMNS: The right-hand variety is ergonomically superior (most people are right-handed and have the mouse on the right), yet the dominant convention is to use a left-hand column to hold the main navigation buttons.

TOP BUTTON BAR: This approach seems to be gaining favor. It is effectively limited to seven or eight buttons, but these can be packed through pull-down menus and sup-plemented by navigation columns.

BOTTOM BUTTON BAR: Unless the top image is kept to a narrow slice, the bottom of the page can easily disappear from immediate view, making it an impractical place for a navigation bar. **Note:** The bottom is, however, often reserved for a rough site map.

A Star or Burst pattern with links radiating from the center is another alternative.

COMBINATIONS: The four locations can be arrayed in combinations. Many Web portals have adapted a "newspaper style." This approach features a masthead with a top button bar or a button bar below the title. The head is followed by a body of three or four headlined columns, which may include additional navigation blocks. This design leads readers to scroll down the screen.

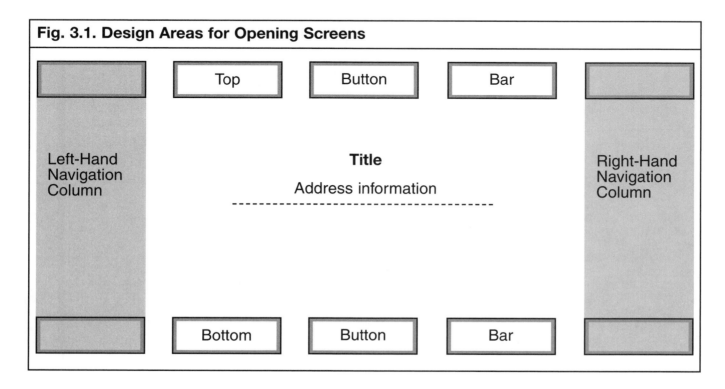

Fig. 3.1. Design Areas for Opening Screens

WEB DESIGN RESOURCES

The number of Web design experts, books, and sites is legion. As someone perhaps better equipped to recognize a good design than create one, I hesitate to give directions. Yet some web design sites do stand out. Yale's Style Manual has stood the test of time (http://info.med.yale.edu/caim/manual/contents.html). HTML Help (http://www.htmlhelp.com), Dmitry's Design Lab (http://www.webreference.com), and Open Source Web Design (http://www.oswd.org) are often helpful. My favorite remains Web Pages That Suck (http://www.webpagesthatsuck.com/).

Other Navigation Links

This book covers two additional types of hypertext links that typically are used for navigation on a Web page:

- **CONTENT TIES:** These are used to tie a citation within the narrative to external or internal referents— e.g., from a series description to the related area in the box inventory, from "related collections" to the collection's Finding Aid, from a box or index heading to the box listing, or directly to the digitized content.
- **DIRECTIONAL POINTERS:** These are the standard links that users expect to encounter on a Web page:
  - Navigation within the site—e.g., *Return to Homepage, To Collections List*
  - Return functions at the ends or within long runs of text—e.g., *Return to top, Previous page, Next Page*
  - Ties to disparate, but commonly used files— e.g., *Return to Main File, To Inventory*

HYPERTEXT CODING METHODS

Project planners must take account of different types of data entry for hypertext:

- **PRECODED:** The easiest options for general staff applications are those programmed in place or set for simple cut-and-pasting within a template or model.

- **REAL TIME ENCODED:** Some elements, like those between main and subfiles, must be coded in real time during the creation of the Finding Aid. The use of this approach may not be suitable for general implementation by current staffs and may require the selection of an editor.

ANALYSIS

In most cases, user desires and the popularity of the medium make your underlying decision a *fait accompli*—repositories should have Web Finding Aids. Still, do not take the step lightly. Each institution is unique and will need to factor in its own particular nature.

- What do your patrons want or say they need? It may be that less is more.
- Are there intervening institutional, grant, or political forces at play?
- What will be the effects on the workload and other services?
- Does the staff already possess skills with HTML and related software programs?
- What about the in-house Web site? Note its stylistic conventions and methods of navigation to keep things consistent.
- Think about the possible location of the Finding Aids on the site and within an integrated network of description. Where would they fit best?
- Do you need to add distinguishing features to the Finding Aids?
- How does the layout function with hypertext in mind?
- Are there features that you find desirable and may want to duplicate in an automated version?
- How much metadata do you want to enter?

WEB MOUNTING

As we have already concluded, print still has its place. Web Finding Aids will not become the sole resource for in-house access to traditional documentary collections—especially for experienced researchers. The Web Finding Aid, however, will become the gateway for external users such as the offsite researcher, who may use it to make travel or photocopying decisions. It provides a key method for direct access to digital images and broadcasts the materials' presence to the search engines.

SOFTWARE CHOICE

The choice of software will likely come down to staff expertise and any current method of encoding for the Finding Aids. For our exercise, we find:

- **NOTE PAD ENCODING** is too difficult and awkward to recommend for the large-scale production of individual Finding Aids.
- **WEB EDITORS AND BROWSER EDITORS** are not well suited for production lines and fast delivery of dozens of Finding Aids. The sites offered through portals are also often ignored by search engines.
- **PDF** represents an interesting alternative, but it is proprietary and calls for additional software purchases.
- **WORD PROCESSING** continues to offer the simplest route.

OUTPUT OPTIONS

Several types of output are available for Web Finding Aids. Advanced XML/EAD applications are discussed the next chapter. This treatment concentrates on two simpler HTML options:

- **DIRECT CONVERSION:** The easiest method is to convert the word-processor's printing format (e.g., ASCII, *.doc, .rtf*) into http-addressable HTML (XHTML) or PDF files.
- **HTML-ENCODED FINDING AIDS (HEFAs):** The middle route involves adding hypertext navigation flourishes to turn the print form into a true Web document. This tactic applies to both new entries and cut-and-pasting for recon.

Your decision between those two should take into account several factors:

- What are the costs of direct conversion versus those for making HEFAs?
- What are the HEFA's added benefits for your institution, users, and as a transitional mechanism for involving staff with the Web?

- Would you consider a mixed solution? Direct conversion could be employed for the bulk of the recon, but HEFAs could be used for all new—and, perhaps, a selection of the most valuable—extant Finding Aids.

SOLUTIONS

Either choice results in a straightforward application but a significant addition to the workflow. You may want to consider adjusting the project plan by:

- altering the time line.;
- naming an editor for quality control, metadata, and external hyperlinks; or
- adding a training component that could extend to hiring a consultant.

1. DIRECT CONVERSION

Conversion is simply a matter of deciding which materials have a higher priority and should be converted sooner. You can prepare a word-processed Finding Aid for the Web by merely engaging "*Save as Web Page,*" but I strongly advise that you go at least one step further and insert a key piece of metadata:

TITLE TAG helps human users and search engines identify the contents. While the ID Number is needed for internal file management, you will want to use the collection's normal title for your Web title (e.g., Edward Jury Papers). You may want to add the repository's name if space allows. This is an important point of identification for those "deep linking" (linking directly to certain items) within your site.

- Begin with the Finding Aid's title and dates—"Mary Elington Smith Papers, 1918–1964."
- Place the repository's name after the title.

2. HEFAs

You can code HEFAs individually, but it's best to use front-end planning and create precoded templates to be filled in. This book presents two prospects in figure 3.2 and 3.3 that reflect the model in figure 2.6. The design adds EAD standards and Web interactivity and structures.

Fig. 3.2. Sample HEFA 10-Box Layout *<hefaform-10.rtf>*

HEFA/EAD

Help
Scope and Content
- *Correspondents*
- *Related Collections*
Contents
- *Containers*

To Web Finding Aids

Title:
Genre:
Dates:
Size:
ID #:

©Repository Name

HEFA.03.perm

Scope and Contents

- *Instructions (to be erased)—paste all contents here.*

Correspondents

Related Collections

Return to Top-End Scope

Contents

Series I:

To Series I

Series II:

To Series II

Series III:

To Series III

SeriesI SeriesII SeriesIII [*Instructions (to be erased)—cut and paste* **"Series#"** *as anchors*]

Container

Return to Top

[Box1] [Box2] [Box3] [Box4] [Box5] [Box6] [Box7] [Box8] [Box9] [Box10]

1-Box 2-Box 3-Box 4-Box 5-Box 6-Box 7-Box 8-Box 9-Box 10-Box
[*Instructions (to be erased)—cut and paste* "**X**-Box" *as anchors*]

To Container
Return to top-End Finding Aid

Fig. 3.3. Sample HEFA Template with HTML tags

HEFA/EAD <a name="hefa_header"> <table>

Help

Scope and Content <a href="scopecontent">
• *Correspondents* <a href="namegrp">
• *Related Material* <a href="relatedmaterial>
Contents <a href="dsc">
• *Containers* <a href="containers">

To Web Finding Aids <a href="http://www. repository.edu/holdings/fa_list.htm">

Title: *<h1> <a name="unittitle">*
Genre: *<subheading>*
Dates: *<subheading>*
Size: *<subheading>*
ID #: *<subheading>*

©Repository Name *<h2> <a href="http://home">*

HEFA.03.perm <a name="archdesc">

Scope and Contents *<h2> <a name="scopecontent">*

• **Recon Instructions** *(to be erased)—paste all contents here.*
<normal text>

Correspondents *<h3> <a name="namegrp">*
<ul (list)> <normal text>
Related Material *<h3> <a name="relatedmaterial">*
<normal text>
Return to Top-End Scope <a href="title">

Contents *<h2> <a name="dsc">*

<normal text>
Series I: *<h3>*

To Series I <a href="arrangement_1">

Series II: *<h3>*

To Series II <a href="arrangement_2">

Series III: *<h3>*

To Series III <a href="arrangement_3">

SeriesI *<a name="arrangement_1">* **SeriesII** *<a name="arrangement_2">*
SeriesIII *<a name="arrangement_3"> [**Instructions** (to be erased)—cut and paste anchors]*
<table>

Container *<h3> <a name="container">*

Return to Top <a href="title">

[Box1] [Box2] [Box3] [Box4] [Box5] [Box6] [Box7] [Box8] [Box9] [Box10]
<a href="container_#">...

1-Box 2-Box 3-Box 4-Box 5-Box... *<h4> <a name="container_#">...*
<normal text>
To Container <a href="container">
Return to top-End Finding Aid <a href="title">

Hypertext Navigation

The heart of the model is the one-time preparation of hypertext navigational elements for the various parts of the Finding Aid.

- **INTERACTIVE TABLE OF CONTENTS:** The navigation box is set as a left-hand column that links to headings in the body of the text, but also includes a link to *Help* resource and a link back *To Web Finding Aids* list.

Fig. 3.4. HEFA Title Box with Right-Hand Navigation Box

Help *Scope and Content* • *Correspondents* • *Related Collections* *Contents* *Inventory* *To Web Finding Aids*	**Title:**

- **RETURN FEATURES:** *Return to the Top* entries link to the *<title>* anchor.
- **DIRECTIONAL POINTERS:** As illustrated in figure 3.5, you can build on normal alphabetic and numeric classifications to create very simple, yet powerful navigation aids.

Fig. 3.5. Index Navigation Table and Alphabetic Anchor

Index *Return to Main File*
Scroll down or click on a letter below
A B C D E F G H I J K L M N O P Q R S T U V W X Y Z
• *Instructions (to be erased)—The letters below are anchors to be cut-and-pasted before contents)*
A, B, C, D, E, F, G, H, I, J, K, L, M, N, O, P, Q, R, S, T, U, V, W, X, Y, Z

BOXES AND NUMBER SORTING

There is a similar use of hypertext for linking to box inventories. Note: The "1-Box" convention facilitates sorting routines under the *Table*. Be aware, too, that you need to "zero-fill"—add 0s in the tens, hundreds, etc. positions (008, 080, 800)—to guarantee a proper sort.

Added Encoding

Several standard elements require coding during the creation of individual Finding Aids.

- **TITLE AND KEYWORD METADATA**
- **RELATED MATERIAL:** This is an extremely powerful addition that offers researchers the ability to transit directly to related collections, as well as to subject path finders and even to external resources.
- **FILE TO SUBFILE CONNECTORS:** To move from the main file of collection number 328 to a subfile of its contents (328-contents), block the ***Contents*** terms in the main file and hyperlink: e.g., the relative *"328-contents.htm"* or absolute *"www.repository.edu/ holdings/328-contents.htm."* The subfile requires *Return to Main File* links: *"328.htm"* or *"www.repository.edu/holdings/328.htm."*
- **CONTENT CONNECTORS:** You can consider adding cross-file navigation from the main file to features within subfiles—such as to anchors for series. References for series in the main file are routed to the resource location: *"328-contents.htm #arrangement_2"* or *"www.repository.edu/holdings/ 328-contents.htm #arrangement _2."*

SUPPLEMENTAL RESOURCES

The Web Finding Aid does not stand alone, but is part of a collection of resources within the digital archives. For example, our model includes links to two supplemental files that must be prepared and uploaded to the Web site: the extremely important list of *Web Finding Aids* (See: figure 3.7) and the expected "Help Page" illustrated below.

Fig. 3.6. Finding Aid Help

<u>**Repository**</u>

Finding Aids are devices created by professional archivists to describe collections and help you locate information.

- **Title Box:** You first see the collection's name and the time frame represented within it. Size is in linear feet or by the number of items for smaller holdings. The ID number is our internal device to help retrieve the boxes. Be sure to write down the collection's name and number to help subsequently retrieve materials.
- **Body:** The archivist has analyzed the holdings and provided essays to help you understand the subject and the particular contents of this collection. We may include lists of significant correspondents and related collections.
- **Organization:** You should look for "series" descriptions, which will tell you how the materials are organized.
- **Inventory:** The last section includes specific information about the boxes and names of folders inside them. Note the box/folder locations to help us in retrieving the material.

For questions or further information-E-mail: *staff@repository*.

<u>Return to Web Finding Aids</u>

OTHER HELP RESOURCES

A number of archives and manuscript repositories provide general "Help" data that may be useful as links for your Web visitors:
- Bentley Historical Library of the University of Michigan (http://www.umich.edu/~bhl/bhl/refhome/refhome.html)
- National Archives and Records Administration (http://www.archives.gov/research_room/alic/research_tools.html)
- National Archives of Canada (http://www.archives.ca/04/0416_e.html)
- Reuther Library on HEFAs through the *Help* button on each booklet or http://www.reuther.wayne.edu/services/hefa_resources.htm.
- Social Welfare History Archives of the University of Minnesota (http://special.lib.umn.edu/swha/manuscripts.html)
- Yale University's Archives and Manuscripts Division (http://www.libraryyale.edu/mssa/tutorial/tutorial.htm)

PILOT

Many of the preparations from the last chapter are part of the pilot stage. We again divide between an Alpha phase for physical preparations and Beta for testing.

ALPHA STAGE

Now is the time to build and test your various descriptive apparatus and HEFA model (See: Microsoft Word Training section for examples).

List of Web Finding Aids

The *Finding Aids List* (figure 2.6) is updated and integrated into a production model for the Web (figure 3.7). When new Web Finding Aids become available for downloading to the site during the Beta phase, the editor updates the list in a parallel posting. The "Latest Additions" label can be expanded to indicate that this area is a "test-bed" and part of a work in process. The list itself comes with synergies beyond its primary purposes. It can act as a "pick list" for cut-and-pasting resources into the "related collections" field and to enhance authority records with interactive links to the collections. The basic features are listed below:

- The internal title anchors are coded as *<title>*.
- The repository name is linked to the homepage—a navigational convention to be used throughout the site.
- "Last Updated" and "Latest Additions" areas are present.
- Internal navigation links are preprepared—in this case, a hyperlinked alphabetic list.
- *"Return to top"* links to the title anchor are available.
- There is a descriptive title/metadata: e.g., "Web Finding Aids at Repository."

Training and Instructions

Both the HEFA and direct conversions will require training sessions and written instructions.

Fig. 3.7. Web Finding Aid List-<holdings/fa_list.rtf>

Web Finding Aids
©*Repository*

fa_list.03.update

Last Updated: _____

Scroll or click on a letter below to search
A B C D E F G H I J K L M N O P Q R S T U V W X Y Z

Latest Additions-Test Area:

A	ID Number
George Abbott Papers, 1926–83	113
Mary Alberghetti Photographic Archives, 1990–2000	246-photo
Association of Angry Archivists Records, 1982+	365

B

Return to top

Fig. 3.8. Direct Conversion Guidelines for Web Finding Aids

December 13, 2002

1. Check the Project Log for your assigned area (or the Web Finding Aid List).

2. Go to *holdings/done* and open the chosen document.

3. Click on the *FILE* button in the top tool bar.

4. Use the direction arrows or the mouse to click on: ***Save as Web Page...***

5. The *ID Number* file name is automatically filled in with an *.htm* (or *.html*) suffix.

6. Click the ***Web Options...***button and go to the **General** tab

7. Fill in the Collection Title with date range in the box after *Web page title*.

8. Click the OK button on Web Options form

9. On the Save As Web Page form, save in *holdings/webmount* directory.

10. Save by clicking OK button

11. Enter completed collections in the Project Log.

Fig. 3.9. HEFA Quick Entry Guide (MS Word)

November 15, 2002

1. **Select Finding Aid/Duplication Check:** look under *holdings/done*; pick collection—check for duplication in *holdings/tool_box/list_rtf*

2. **Prep Text:** open, select all, copy, exit, don't save

3. **Select Form:** open *holdings/tool_box/fa_form.rtf*

4. **Paste Finding Aid into Form** [Note: Verdana type face is preferred, 11 point for body]

5. **Paste Title Box Entry:** cut-and-paste title information from collection to HEFA

6. **Save:** Under *File/Save As...* click for *Rich Text Format* in *Name:* enter *ID #*

7. **Paste Body Entry:** complete cut-and-paste; put Series descriptions after CONTENTS

8. **Add Navigation Tools:** cut-and-place alphabetic and box anchors in Contents area (note header level); copy and add *return to index* and *return to contents* links as you see fit

9. **Add Web Title and Metatags:** (Advanced option) *Click File/Properties... /Summary:*
   * enter narrative title in Title box (default is "HTML-Encoded Finding Aid")
   * enter your name in Author box (default is "Staff")_
   * enter names from Correspondent List or major subjects in Keyword box

10. **Create and Link Supplemental Files:** (Option—May revert to HEFA editor)
    * save Header and Narrative Information, including Contents with series descriptions as the main file
    * add *To Inventory* or *To Series* external navigation links in Contents area and perhaps Navigation box__
    * create new files from the Inventory sections
    * name files as extension of main file-e.g., *id#-s1.rtf* for the text version of Series I, *id#-i* for single inventory
    * include the Web title for each supplemental file
    * insert *Return to main file* hyperlinks in title header and at end of file

11. **Delete Navigation/Anchor:** check body and navigation box; delete unused elements

12. **Test/Save Document:** TEST ALL LINKS, SAVE

13. **Save as Web Page/Web Title (Option):** *Save as Web Page...* to *holdings/webmount*; check Title under *Web options...* Close and click to reopen as Web page

14. **Retest:** check links again, make corrections in *holdings/web's .rtf* file; resave

15. **Delete** any Web folder with the collection number when images are not included

Directory Preparation

The in-house test-bed must expand to receive the new tools. Web Finding Aids require the insertion of new forms and guides in the *tool_box* section on the LAN. In addition, you can create a new subdirectory as a transfer station for the Web—e.g., *holdings/webmount*.

The *holdings/done* file remains as a back-up and the area for staff to make corrections and additions to the *.rtf* masters.

Web Directory

You need to add a mirror directory for the Web site. The */holdings/* directory receives the HTML files to be uploaded. It can also store the various list and help files, or these can go in a separate directory. The *Holdings Directory* emerges as the address to access your materials—e.g., *<http://www.respository.edu/holdings/id#.htm>*.

Fig. 3.10. Directory Set-ups

LAN/Computer	Web Directory
.../holdings/	**.../holdings/**
holdings/done	116.htm
116.rtf	458.htm
458.rtf	458-s1.htm
458-s1.rtf	458-s2.htm
458-s2.rtf	fa_list.htm*
fa_list.rtf	hefahelp.htm*
hefahelp.rtf	
holdings/old	
holdings/tool_box	
fa_guide.rtf	
hefaform.rtf	
hefatool.rtf	
names.rtf	
webguide.rtf	
holdings/webmount	
028.htm	
694.htm	
holdings/working	

* Could be placed in a separate directory

BETA TESTING

Make sure that you have prepared a Project Log, training materials, and written instructions.

> **Note:** If you are using a hybrid solution with HTML-saves and HEFAs, employ a file name convention to separate the formats—e.g., hefa-id#, web-id#; or id#-hefa, id#-web.

- **CODERS:** Assuming the initial data entry went well, staff will want to view their efforts through a browser and retest all links. They may note changes that call for additional fine-tuning. Avoid attempting to make changes in the *.htm* file. Go to the *.rtf* versions in *holdings/web*, correct, and then resave the Web page in *holdings/webmount*. Test again until satisfied.
- **HEFA EDITOR:** The editor plays a pivotal role as coordinator of the pilot and ongoing implementations (See: figure 3.11—HEFA Editor Guidelines). The individual will need to:
  - add any requisite external links;
  - ensure a fast loading first page and dividing the rest into manageable file sizes (for large finding aids only);
  - periodically check the templates to ensure that the links are still functioning (Note: You are free to blame losses to the computer gremlins.);
  - control entries in the Web Finding Aids List;
  - coordinate uploading of the List and Finding Aids on the Web site; and
  - test the new additions for their appearance on the Web (they may change in unanticipated ways—see gremlin note) along with double-checking the links.

Fig. 3.11. HEFA Editor Guidelines

(1/26/2003)

1. **Transfer** recon and new files to *holdings/working*

2. **Open Listhefa:** This is the working file to make initial hypertext citations, which can then be cut-and-pasted into the other appropriate lists. **Check to avoid duplication.** Open any other supplemental lists.

3. **Examine and test HEFA:** (In MS Word 2002, View as *Web Layout*
    a. **Does the** file name conforms to the convention (e.g., hefa_287)?
    b. Do the links work? Are the fonts and letter size correct?
    c. Are there "Title" tags or other metatagging? Check under File/Properties.
        i.   If not, add at least Title (Name of Collection, dates).
        ii. Consider adding a few keywords—e.g., names of major figures, subjects, locations.

4. **Make corrections** in .rtf version.
    a. Save as .rtf
    b. Resave as Web Page
    c. Recheck .htm file

5. **Check .htm file size:**
    a. File levels: The first or lead file is the most crucial for size control—hold to no more than 100K. Secondary files can range to 1000K. Any secondary file larger than 1000K must also be divided.
    b. Main File can typically hold all the header information, Scope note, and Contents/series.
    c. Secondary Files may be needed for the container inventories and indexes (EAD's <dsc>).

6. **Dividing large files:** (Note the need to add navigation hyperlinks to model; MS Word—Insert/Hyperlink…).
    a. Making Secondary Files: There are two basic approaches.
        i.   Copy to new File: Block the information, cut-and-paste into a new document. (Note: leave "Finding Aid End" tag in lead file).
        ii. Delete materials from the original and rename the altered file.
    b. Adding navigation to secondary file: Include ***"Return to Main File"*** links in the opening and at the end of the file: e.g., *www.repository.edu/ holdings/###.htm*.
    c. Name new file(s): File name (e.g., hefa_###) add (-) and suffix "s" for series—893-s1, hefa_893-s2…
    d. Save as *.rtf*
    e. Save as HTML. Remember to add the collection title as a metatag.

7. **Reformating Lead File**
    a. Correct hyperlinks in Navigation Box (Instead of linking to the anchor below, you may reprogram to go directly to secondary file).
    b. And/or add **"To Contents"** or other links from set headers to Secondary Files to allow users to navigate there. (e.g., *www.repository.edu/holdings/###-s1.htm*)

Fig. 3.11. (cont.)

---

    c. Test internal links
    d. Save as *.rtf* in *holdings/done* directory
    e. Save As Web Page in *holdings/webmount*. (MS Word 2000—Save as type/Web page, filtered).

8. List Entries:
    a. listhefa: Enter Collection title—<tab>###. Block Collection Title and insert hyperlink to lead file: e.g. Institution for Checking 1456
    b. Copy entire line and paste under new additions, then where appropriate in other lists.
    c. Save as *.rtf* when all HEFAs are entered.
    d. Save as Web Page…and place in *holdings/webmount*

9. Notify Web Master

10. Recheck Web: Once the new files are mounted, go to the New Additions area and check to see that the items are in order. Double check links between main and secondary files.

Evaluation and Going Public

Testing takes on great importance with a Web site. Once mounted, your wares are available for the entire world to see. Take a moment to sit down with the team and perhaps the users to evaluate the results of the pilot—as well as plan your next steps:

- Were the products of suitable quality?
- Were there unexpected problems—e.g., strong staff or user objections?
- Were the methods workable and not too costly or labor intensive?
- What types of improvement should or could be made?
- Are these significant enough to jump back in the planning loop and rethink solutions and repilot?

Hint: You may want to consider keeping the initial placement quiet. You do not need to advertise or provide pointers to the exercise until things are debugged. Consider labeling the initiative as a "Pilot Project" or "Testing Area" when you do go public.

IMPLEMENTATION

Assuming positive pilot results and only minor modifications, the test-bed again converts into the working bed. But you have several matters to consider.

- **UPDATE SCHEDULE:** Do you want to establish a regular schedule for uploading completed Web Finding Aids?
- **AUTOMATED FINDING AIDS:** During the pilot stage, you maintained separate operations for finished word-processed print production and Web Finding Aids. Those opting for a direct *.pdf* or direct HTML conversion will need to keep both. Those going the HEFA route may consider eliminating the word-processed view.
- **PUBLICITY:** With everything in good shape, you should consider publicity. The movement to Web Finding Aids is a significant step for any repository. At the least, you should inform regular clients and higher administration of the advance.

MS WORD TRAINING

Ease of use and familiarity with a software product are keys to successful implementation. Commercial software manuals and Web sites may help, but expertise takes time. The following are minimalist and compromise approaches drawn from the trial and error of working with Microsoft Word 2001 for Macintosh and more recent exposure to Word 2002 for Windows.

MS WORD ALERTS

Word processors have become too smart. MS Word employs Bayesian math to infer what the user is doing from the structure of the document. One result is the well intentioned, yet occasionally annoying "paper clip" on-screen helper. While you can turn off such features, they still seem to reappear mysteriously. A related problem with Word 2001 is its tendency to insert headings without user commands. Such tagging goes unnoticed in a word processed or printed version, but comes alive online, resulting in extra space and bolding.

Word's normal Web save is subject to "bloatware."—the program adds a long array of print fonts and other extra stylistic flourishes. Word 2002 offers a more straightforward HTML 4.01 option.

The good news is that Word is extremely easy to use. Anyone can make powerful Web Finding Aids with only a handful of commands. The art form is how you apply them.

A. **VIEW AS WEB PAGE:** I recommend setting the screen image under the *View* menu to <u>*Web Layout*</u> for a better idea of the end product.

B. **HEADINGS AND STYLES:** Next, set the HTML heading levels. Headings command the entire line and can be declared anywhere on the line. The easiest method then involves pulling down the *Style* menu on the *Formatting* toolbar and clicking on your selection.

Fig. 3.12. Style Selection

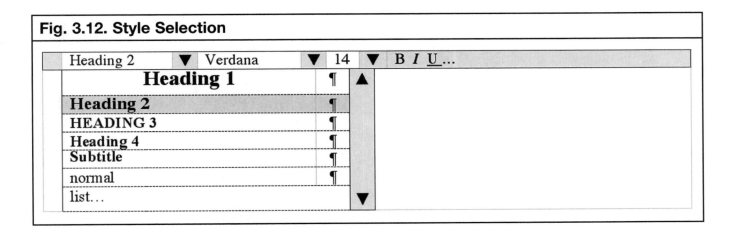

Headings can also be engaged under the *Format* button on the main menu bar by clicking the *Styles and Formatting* selection. You have the option of programming your own style for a CSS, but you may be best advised to leave matters to the browser's defaults.

C. **HYPERTEXT:** The next stage involves precoding anchors and adding hyperlinks within the model.

MS Word refers to its hypertext features as *Bookmark* and *Hyperlink*. Their encoding sequences are located at the bottom of the *Insert* menu on the top menu bar—or by the keyboard shortcuts of *control+k* and *control+i*. In addition, you can reach *Hyperlink* on a separate menu by right-clicking on the mouse, which activates a small screen menu.

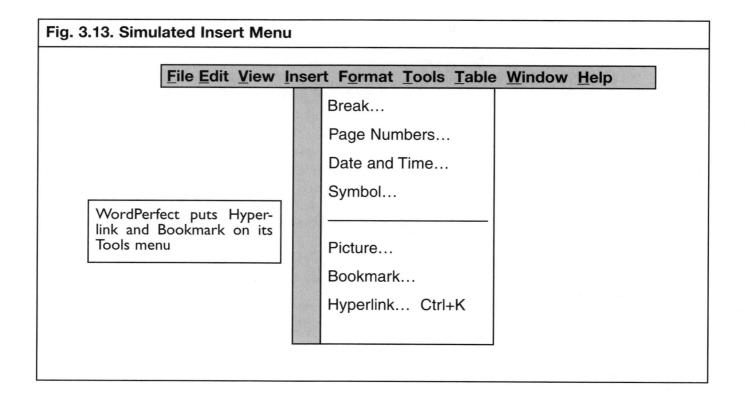

Fig. 3.13. Simulated Insert Menu

1. BOOKMARK: Set the anchors in place before creating hyperlinks.

   a. To set an anchor, go to a desired location—e.g., a HEFA label.

   b. Block the term or position your cursor at the end of the phrase. (Avoid placing the cursor inside. The imbedded anchors will produce awkward spacing on the Web screen.)

   c. Open *Insert* and click on *Bookmark*...a form (figure 3.15) will appear.

   d. Type the designated term in the entry box near the top.

   e. Click the *Hidden bookmarks* box or a line will appear under the anchor.

   f. Press the Add button. The entry is made.

Fig. 3.14. Word Bookmark Form

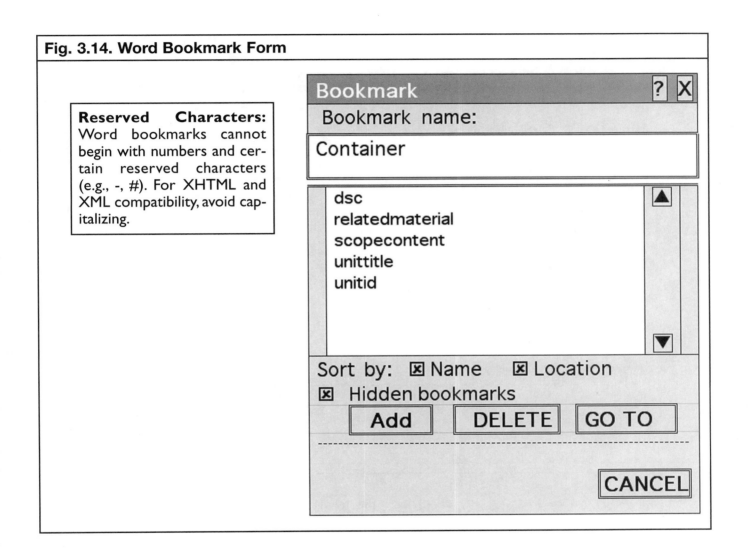

2. **HYPERLINK:** Word provides several points for hyper references. For new entries, e.g., the URL for related materials, you can simply type *"http://"* or *"www."* The program will automatically create a link. The display of a term with its Web address takes up valuable space and may not be aesthetically appealing—Word can bury the actual address within the entry. Instead of "To National Archives http://www.archives.gov," you enter "To National Archives" with the URL invisible.

Fig. 3.15. Word Insert Internal Hyperlink

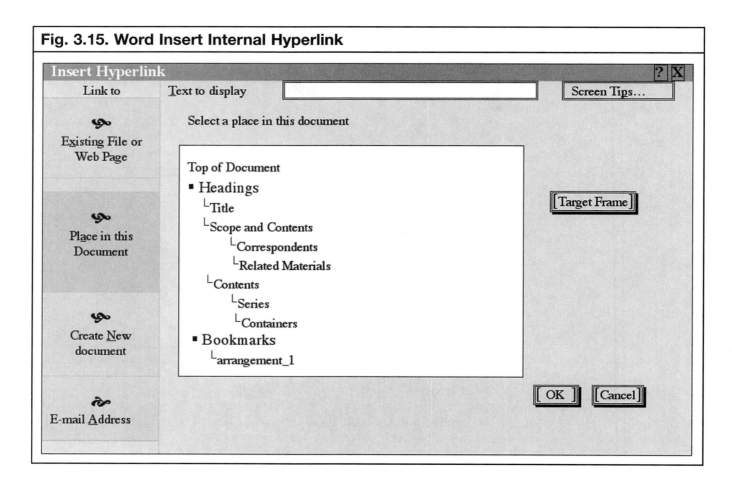

1. Block the term to display—e.g., ***Contents*** in the navigation box.
2. Open *Insert* and click on *Hyperlink...*
3. The *Insert Hyperlink* form appears with four choices on the left:
   a. **Existing File or Web Page:** This is the default screen and includes a range of assistance to help you locate the appropriate resources. For entering URLs behind the display term:
      - Locate the Address entry box in the bottom center of the form.
      - Type in *"http://..."* or start an address with *"www."* and the program will automatically fill in the former.

- For documents on the same server, instead you may want to use a relative link (*"...//directory/file.htm*) instead.
- Click the OK button to enter.

b. **Place in this Document:** This is the menu displayed below. It will:

- show the term that you highlighted to link from;
- provide a pick list of available headings and bookmarks; and
- allow you to click on your choice and OK to engage.

c. **Create New Document:** This is used for entering a placeholder for files that you will create in the future.

d. **E-mail Address:** A menu will open to enter an e-mail address (mail to: name) and optional subject line.

WordPerfect 10 uses *File/ Publish to HTML.*

D. SAVING AS HTML: The final stage is to convert the document into HTML. In Word, the transformation for the Web comes with a single command under—*Save as Web Page...* in the *File* menu of the main tool bar. Once clicked, a form appears with a Save and Cancel button. A simple Save is all that is needed to complete the conversion.

Finally, don't rush. As shown in figure 3.16, you have the opportunity to recast the title. **Note:** Word 2002's automatic save approximates XHTML files with heavy overhead. The *Web page, filtered* option converts it into a much smaller HTML file, but you will lose most metadata entries.

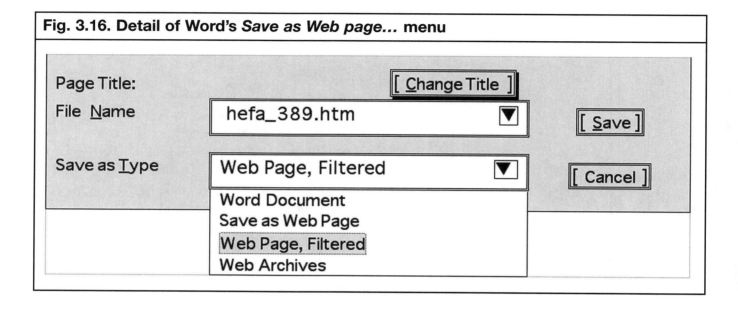

Fig. 3.16. Detail of Word's *Save as Web page...* menu

Fig. 3.17. HEFA/EAD Crosswalk

Term	HEFA Anchor(s)	HTML	Parallel EAD Term
HTML-Encoded Finding Aid (hidden codes)	hefa_ead hefa_header	normal text	<ead> <eadheader>
Title	*unittitle	title (head) and h1	<unittitle>
Type	*genreform	subtitle	<genreform>
Dates	*unitdate	subtitle	<unitdate>
Size	*physdesc	subtitle	<physdesc>
ID #	*unitid	subtitle	<unitid>
Repository (Publisher)	*repository (publisher)	subtitle	<repository > (<publisher>)
hefa.02. perm	end_header archdesc	normal	</eadheader> <archdesc level = "collection">
Scope and Content	*scopecontent	h2	<scopecontent>
Subjects	Subject	h3	<subject>
Correspondents	Namegrp	h3	<namegrp>
Transfers	separatedmaterial	h3	<separatedmaterial>
Related Collections	*relatedmaterial	h3	<relatedmaterial>
End Scope	end_scopecontents	normal	</scopecontents>
Contents	dsc (description of subordinate units)	h2	<dsc type="combined">
Series Description	*arrangement	h3	<arrangement type= "series">…,
Container	Container	h3	<container>
Series in Inventory	arrangement_#	h2	<cO1 type= "series"> Series…
#-Box (#=number)	*Box_#	h4	<c02>box #…, or <container type= "box">box #…
End Containers	end_container	normal	</cO1>
Index	Index	h3	<index>
A, B, C, D…	label_# (letter)	h4	<label>#</label>
End Index	end_index	normal	</index>
Finding Aid end	end_dsc end_archdesc end_hefa	normal	</dsc> </archdesc> </ead>

*Core HEFA elements

4 CONSIDERING SGML, EAD, XML, AND DATABASE OPTIONS

SGML Introduction
- Data entry

Document Type Definitions
- Tag libraries
- Easing into the EAD DTD
- Problems

XML Phase
- Getting started
- XMetal examples

DBMS Options
- DBMS overview
- Web convergence

The addition of the Web's database capacities and computational power offers significant advantages, but demands added institutional commitment, discipline, and investment.

EAD (Encoded Archival Description) is used in the examples in this chapter. The treatment addresses potential confusion between SGML and the Web approaches of its XML derivative and discusses parallel DBMS options for dynamic HTML applications.

The book's tactics change from this point forward. The text will concentrate on expanding the range of background information, analysis, and tool skills for building digital archives, and formal project management planning will be left in your hands.

> **Reader's Advisory:** This chapter is somewhat advanced. Many repositories will be more than satisfied with the quasi-fax machine and hypertext features of the original Web for digital archives. Such readers may wish to skip to the next chapter.

SGML INTRODUCTION

SGML (Standard Generalized Markup Language ISO 8879–1986) emerged from ANSI and the standards community in the mid-1980s. SGML was developed as a set of rules and computer-recognizable tags to mimic the mark ups from editors to typesetters and automate the production of technical manuals (See: chapter 1 for basic syntax and grammar).

Within a computer environment aimed at number crunching, the standard filled a void for human-computer communications. SGML became the metalanguage for subsequent metalanguages and advanced knowledge management.

DATA ENTRY

SGML, designed for large-scale projects and production runs on the mainframe computers of the mid-1980s, produces a hierarchical database with complex tree-like structures. Such power demands rigor and attention to detail. Software programming options, however, are limited and include:

- **SGML EDITORS:** Specialized software editors are available, but have the reputation of being expensive and hard to implement.
- **NOTE PAD–TEXT EDITORS:** Many people enter raw code through text editors like Note Pad.
- **WORD PROCESSOR SGML EXPORT:** Word Perfect and Microsoft Word offered SGML markup editors and parsers as secondary add-ons.
- **DBMS:** As illustrated at the archives of the University of California, San Diego, a DBMS for EAD can be programmed with SGML tags. The program can then report or export the appropriate SGML files.

DOCUMENT TYPE DEFINITIONS

As indicated in chapter 1, SGML lends itself to specialized subsets or Document Type Definitions (DTDs).

DTDs address particular production demands and are available in a vast and growing range of options. They can offer computerized production for the cuneiform of Ancient Sumerian and complete lists of every aircraft part with their suppliers. The Text Encoded Initiative (TEI) DTD provides a descriptive language for the control of all historical printing formats.

TEI

The Text Encoded Initiative (TEI) grew out of a conference at Vassar College in 1987 and set the stage for the use of DTDs in the arts and humanities. What followed was an international research project and then a consortium (http://www.tei-c.org) sponsored by the Association for Computing in the Humanities (ACH), the Association for Literary and Linguistic Computing (ALLC), and the Association for Computational Linguistics (ACL) whose goal was a product-neutral markup language for computer production of every form of text in the humanities.

The project issued the first version of TEI in the pre-Web era of 1990, demonstrating the degree of complexity available from strict adherence to the parent SGML. Given the breadth of possible publications, TEI's 400 elements were further subdivided into prose, verse, drama, spoken, dictionary, terminology, general, and mixed base tag sets.

Fortunately, one does not have to read the full 1,300 pages of TEI's P-3 manual for implementation. The University of Virginia offers a reduced set of some forty tags for TEI's "Lite" version (http://etext.lib.virginia.edu/standard.html).

TAG LIBRARIES

A DTD calls for a maintenance agency and "tag library" of its rules and acceptable terms. The typical tag library usually is presented in both print and online versions. Each element is articulated within ordered, but specialized treatments with its own specialized vocabulary.

EAD Tag Library

As illustrated in figure 4.1, EAD's tag library features seven components:

1. **TAG:** a short, often mnemonic code within "greater than" and "less than" angle brackets (< >)—e.g. *<tagname>*
2. **ELEMENT NAME:** the phrase that humans use to identify the tag
3. **DESCRIPTION:** a narrative definition of the element and its relationships with other elements. The first paragraph frequently looks to supporting standards and authorities, and other paragraphs illustrate the element's use, related terms, and possible areas of confusion.
4. **MAY CONTAIN:** a list of other elements that may be wrapped or included within this element
5. **MAY OCCUR WITHIN:** a list of all the possible parent elements
6. **ATTRIBUTES:** a list of descriptive terms that can be added
7. **EXAMPLES:** a sample of the coding using indentations to indicate hierarchical relations; helps readers put the element's use into perspective

EASING INTO THE EAD DTD

Our EAD example contains a number of potential enhancements to the HEFA word-processing model. By parsing into distinct data elements, the database tactics promise a higher order, stability, and abilities to share information across institutional boundaries. EAD codes can produce greater depth of description for retrieving digital holdings. The approach can:

- provide metadata with meaningful semantics by setting off elements—like *<title>*, *<scopecontent>*, and *<bioghist>* as searchable fields;

Fig. 4.1. Encoded Archival Description Tag Library–sample page

<filedesc> File Description

Description:
A required subelement of the <eadheader> that bundles much of the bibliographic information about the finding aid, including its author, title, subtitle, and sponsor (all in the <titlestmt>), as well as the edition, publisher, publishing series, and related notes (encoded separately).

This element has been modeled on a Text Encoding Initiative (TEI) DTD element and includes the following subelements, in this order: a required <titlestmt>, an optional <editionstmt>, an optional <publicationstmt>, an optional <seriesstmt>, and an optional <notestmt>. The <filedesc> provides information that is helpful for citing a finding aid in a bibliography or footnote. Institutions that catalog finding aids separately from the archival materials being described might use the <filedesc> elements to build a basic bibliographic record for the finding aid.

Do not confuse this with the <profiledesc> element, which describes the encoding of the finding aid. Do not confuse it with <archdesc> elements, which refer to the materials being described rather than the finding aid itself.

May contain:
editionstmt, notesstmt, publicationstmt, seriesstmt, titlestmt

May occur within:
1eadheader

Attributes:

altrender	#IMPLIED, CDATA
audience	#IMPLED, external, internal
encodinganalog	#IMPLIED, CDATA
id	#IMPLIED, ID

Examples:
```
1. <eadheader>
      <eadid> [ . . . ] </eadid>
        <filedesc>
           <titlestmt>
              <titleproper>Guide to the Bank of Willows Records,
                 <date>1880–1905</date>
              </titleproper>
           </titlestmt>
           <publicationstmt>
              &hdr-cst-spcoll;
              <date>&copy; 1999</date>
              <p>The Board of Trustees of Stanford University. All rights reserved. </p>
           </publicationstmt>
        </filedesc>
        <profiledesc> [ . . . ] </profiledesc>
      </eadheader>
2. [ . . . ]
```

- bring coherence to previously undefined lists: e.g., *<subject>*, correspondent *<namegrp>*, chronology *<chronlist>*, and other groups;
- parse into hierarchical databases for enhanced computer manipulations; and
- enhance searching through an individual collection or foster cross-collection and even cross-institutional research.

Deconstructing EAD

The SAA EAD Working Group's *Encoded Archival Description Application Guidelines* provides the best introduction to SGML/EAD procedures. The following presents a more tailored "KISS" approach that looks from several different angles to help you understand \an admittedly complex set of techniques.

With 146 elements, EAD is of middling to small size for an SGML DTD. The vocabulary and *<element codes>* are generally straightforward and understandable: *<scopecontent>* means scope and content note; *<subject>* means subject. While the bulk of terms define Finding Aid categories, EAD has a few special types of tags.

- Twelve levels of components—from *<c01>* to *<c12>*—are available to create hierarchical relations within the inventory or *<dsc>* wrapper.
- Digital archival object *<dao>* provides EAD with a way to approximate Web hypertext links.
- EAD includes a few formatting constructs: notably, *<head>*Header, *<p>*paragraph, and *<tbody>* for making tables.
- If nothing else fits, EAD offers an *<odd>* (Other Descriptive Data) element.

View 1—EAD Structure

The outer layer "wraps" all the content of a Finding Aid within *<ead>* and *</ead>* tags like an envelope. As originally conceived, the area between those tags is set for three major subwrappers: Header, Front Matter, and Archival Description.

EAD BACKGROUND

Work on the standard was decidedly "cutting-edge." Daniel Pitti fathered the initiative in 1990 as part of a cooperative Berkeley Finding Aid Project for California run through the university's famed Sun site (http://sunsite.berkeley.edu/FindingAids). In this pre-Web era, Pitti began by seeking a substitute to the Internet's text-based Gopher daemon for the transmission of Finding Aids.

By the mid-1990s, the Web had taken hold, and the archival field awoke to new opportunities. Archivists had never been fully comfortable with the 1980s extension of MARC cataloging (See: chapter 4). MARC was not intended to replace Finding Aids, because it did not allow for the inclusion of large narratives and excluded the all-important inventory sections.

A number of major archives—the Bentley Library of the University of Michigan, University of Virginia, University of California—Irvine, and the Library of Congress—saw the wisdom of joining Pitti and made significant contributions. With funding from the Council on Library and Information Resources (CLIR), the Society of American Archivists (SAA) played a pivotal role by pushing forward the work of the Bentley Fellowships Finding Aid Team. Things came together in 1998 when SAA published the *Encoded Archival Description Tag Library* and proselytized the product through influential training sessions. In 1999, SAA adopted EAD as its official encoding standard for Finding Aids.

EAD applications arose from multi-institutional and grant-funded projects, and a number of granting agencies would begin to demand EAD compliance as a prelude to funding. The standard has taken hold and is making inroads internationally and also beyond archives as possible information exchange format for museums and other bodies.

Fig. 4.2. EAD Simple Structural Model

```
<ead>

<eadheader>
        Web publication statement
</eadheader>

<frontmatter>
        Electronic title page
</frontmatter>

<archdesc>Archival Description
        <did> Descriptive Identification
                Complete Title Elements
                Other Narrative and Descriptive Elements </did>
        <dsc type> Description of Subordinate Units
                Components with Series and Container Lists </dsc>
</archdesc>

</ead>
```

View 2—Element Order for EAD Finding Aid

Figure 4.3 provides a rough hierarchical schema based on our previous HEFA and printed Finding Aid models.

Fig. 4.3. EAD Basic Structural Layout

```
<!DOCTYPE ead PUBLIC"-//Society of American Archivists'
Encoded Archival Description (EAD) 1.0 (DTD)//EN">

<ead>
    <eadheader>
        <eadid> ... </eadid>
        <filedesc>
            <titlestmt><titleproper> ... </titleproper></titlestmt>
            <publicationstmt>name of repository and date of publication/copyright
            </publicationstmt>
        </filedesc>
    </eadheader>
    <archdesc level="collection">
        <did>
            <unittitle> ... </unittitle>:
            <date> ... </date>
            <physdesc> ... </physdesc>
            <unitid> ... </unitid>
        </did>
        <scopecontent>... </scopecontent>
        <relatedmaterial> ... </related material>
        <dsc type="combined">
            <arrangement> ... </arrangement>
            <c01>[repeated with <c02>for boxes and <p> within]</c01>
        </dsc>
    </archdesc>
</ead>
```

View 3—Sample Elements

As demonstrated below, EAD selections can be kept to a manageable number of perhaps twenty-odd terms to describe the Finding Aid. Be aware that EAD is a tool that offers a myriad of possibilities and acceptable solutions and the example offers only one limited set of suggestions.

Fig. 4.4. Sample EAD Elements

DECLARATION: Like all SGML DTDs, EAD documents begin with a statement to identify the DTD and its authorizing body:

<!DOCTYPE ead PUBLIC"-//Society of American Archivists' Encoded Archival Description (EAD) 1.0 (DTD)//EN">
<ead> **Start EAD** tag.
<eadheader> **EAD Header** is a required section.
    <eadid> **EAD Identifier** is a mandatory element and unique code to identify the resource–often its URL or URN location on the Web.

> ### ATTRIBUTES FOR *<eadid>*
>
> The EAD Identifier offers a range of attributes that link to external standards–*<eadid attribute="code">*. With the exception of foreign language centers, American respositories do not have to worry about these codes. EAD automatically defaults to:
>
> - *audience="external"* (internal will hide from view)
> - *encodinganalog="MARC"*
> - *langencoding="iso 639–2"*
> - *countryencoding="iso3166–1"*
> - *dateencoding="iso8601"*
> - *repositoryencoding="iso15511"*
> - *scriptencoding="iso15924"*

<filedesc> **File Description** is another mandatory element. It need only hold a title statement, but I recommend inserting the name of the repository as the publisher, copyright symbol (©) and publication date.
<filestmt>
    <titlestmt><titleproper> Name of Collection *</titleproper> </titlestmt>*
    *<publicationstmt>*name of repository and date of publication/ copyright *</publicationstmt>*

> ### OTHER <filedesc> ELEMENTS
>
> In addition to my selections, you may want to consider <author> for the creator of the Finding Aid and <date type="publication"> to better define the publication date. <profiledesc> is available to add information about the creation of the electronic document and <revisiondesc> can hold data about subsequent changes to the record.

    </filedesc>
</eadheader>

<frontmatter> <u>Not required.</u> Frontmatter offers a type of electronic title page, but reproduces the same information as in the high-level description of the body. Some use it to hold standard information on the repository that will be reproduced in each Finding Aid. With the notable exception of RLG, however, most avoid it as a print atavism.</frontmatter>

<archdesc level="collection"> **Archival description** is a required wrapper and holds the body of the record. The start tag demands a level attribute to distinguish the highest level of description within the document: typically *level ="collection"* (the recommended default) or *="record group."* The tag may also include attributes for legal status, type of finding aid, or language, for example: *<archdesc level="collection" type="register">*.

> *<did>* **Descriptive Identification** normally focuses on the initial or "high level" entry, which is required to hold the "title" information about the collection.
>> *<unittitle>*collection title*</unittitle>* This may be a restatement of the information in the Header. The examples here add more detail and subtitle information as distinct elements in the *<did>*.
>> *<date>*dates covered in the collection*</date>*
>> *<physdesc>*physical description or size*</physdesc>* is normally stated in linear feet or number for items for smaller holdings.
>> *<unitid>*internal control number*</unitid>*
>> *<repository>*repository name*</repository></did>*

<scopecontent> **Scope and Content** is an optional but expected element intended for narrative treatments that describe the nature of collection at hand. Entries are tagged as paragraphs *<p> </p>*. This wrapper may be used to hold elements like *<subject>* or *<namegrp>* for correspondents.

<bioghist> **Biography or History** provides a similar narrative option for the biography of the individual or history of the institution. In addition to the text, you can add or sustitute a chronology *<chronlist>*.

<relatedmaterial> **Related Material** is an option to point to related resources outside the collection that is being described—much like links on the Web. It should become more important and overlap with *<subject>* tags to controlled vocabularies. Do not confuse this with *<separatedmaterial>*, which is reserved for items that were pulled from the collection.

<admininfo> **Administrative Information** offers the optional of information about the nature of the acquisition and processing status. Data is set in paragraphs *<p> </p>* and the element may be divided by function for added detail: e.g., *<acqinfo>* acquisition information *</acqinfo>*, *<accruals>*, *<accessrestrict>*, *<appraisal>*, *<custodhist>*, *<prefercite>*, *<processinfo>*.

<dsc type="combined"> **Description of Subordinate Components** is a highly recommended wrapper that envelops the contents and their hierarchical relationships.

It demands a type attribute (analyticover, combined, in-depth, othertype), but you can easily default to: <dsc type= "combined">.

> *<arrangement>* **Arrangement** provides one method to indicate the organizational pattern—e.g., *<arrangement type="series">*.
>
> *<c or c01-c12>* **Component** is used to establish the hierarchical relationships of the materials and EAD's most powerful contribution.
>
> *<container>* **Container** is used by those who like to code the inventory of their holdings by box—*<container type=box>*Box #*</container>*.

</ead> End EAD Document:

EAD-LITE

Note that few archives use the hierarchies beyond one or two levels and most settle on a standard order for their appearance. The following are additional hints for a "lite" approach to EAD.

BODY <ARCHDESC>:

- Produce only a single high-level description for the title and narrative treatments— resist additional *<did>*s.
- Keep to straightforward narratives and try to avoid the extra coding for recursive elements.
- Avoid administrative elements *<admin>*. Such additions are of questionable value for external researchers, may raise security or privacy issues, and are better handled in an offline environment.

FORMATTING OPTIONS:

Instead of hierarchical levels, especially below *<C01> <CO2>*, consider substituting formatting commands to reduce the amount of coding.

- Distinct elements for folders or lists can be replaced with start/end paragraphing tags *<p> </p>*.
- Headers *<head> </head>* can play a supporting visual role.

PROBLEMS

The Berkeley Finding Aid Project's work on EAD was a landmark that united the resources of a variety of archives in a joint and ongoing effort. Users had ready access to materials long hidden from view and were eager for more. EAD captured the interests of the archival profession, but there were glitches that we can learn from.

Displays

A number of the initial examples have layout problems. Designers relied on frames, which were the rage at the time, but now have become suspect.

A good portion of the screen in figure 4.5 is given to maintaining navigation links, which, in turn, severely reduce the screen space for viewers interested only in the content. Users tend to print the wrong material because their cursor may be in a different frame. More importantly, search engine spiders generally scamper away from frames. Unless one knows the institutional location, materials are not easily to find.

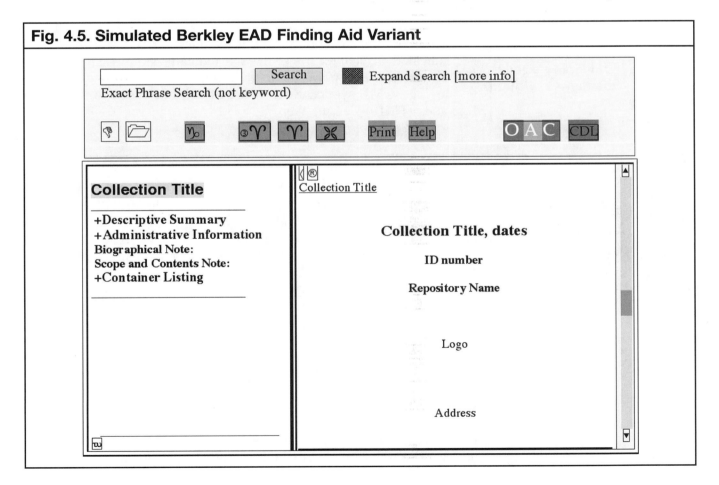

Fig. 4.5. Simulated Berkley EAD Finding Aid Variant

> SGML can be read on the Web—but only with SGML viewers like Panorama;—or interpreted on the fly by a server like Enigma's DynaWeb.

Web Disjunctures

SGML/EAD products create a much bigger dilemma. SGML is designed for complex documents, large-scale production, and long-term storage, and does not equate to the short, flexible, computer-screen presentations that dominate the Web. Although HTML 2+ is an SGML DTD, the Web itself is a separate creation resulting from the marriage of HTML with http. HTML's adopted SGML parent lacks direct access to the new household with its Internet in-laws. Hence, most common Web browsers do not recognize SGML documents and SGML/EAD Finding Aids remain invisible to most Web users.

For those looking to post to the Web, SGML EAD documents had to be converted into HTML. With this conversion, SGML's advantage of data-defining tags with their semantic content was lost—replaced instead by HTML word-processing structures.

XML PHASE

> XML extends ASCII by using Unicode and can signify "empty" elements within one <tag/>.

If placing Finding Aids on the Web is the question, XML is an answer. As indicated in chapter 1, XML is a radically simplified subset of SGML—a new and powerful metalanguage in its own right. While employing SGML syntax, XML is specifically designed to work with http and HTML—i.e., the Web.

EAD COOKBOOK

With XML, most of EAD's coding could be directly transferred to the Web. In July of 2000, Michael Fox of the Minnesota Historical Society led the way from "classic SGML" to XML with the *EAD Cookbook* for XML applications. Fox's text included XML coding techniques for Word Perfect and a new product—the XML software editor with SoftQuad's XMetal. By the next year, SAA's workshops were reconfigured to reflect the new order.

GETTING STARTED

Those committing to XML EAD can find a variety of support mechanisms. The EAD help site at the University of Virginia (http://jefferson.village.virginia.edu/ead) has a number of valuable resources, including Fox's *EAD Cookbook* and software downloads that are vital for XML data entry. The other starting spot is EAD's official maintenance site at the Library of Congress (http://www.loc.gov/ead), which also includes links to participating repositories and two resources of immediate interest:

- *EAD Application Guidelines*
- *EAD Tag Library*

I highly recommend establishing joint operations under the leadership of a repository experienced with EAD or, at the least, borrowing templates from established programs. Above all, anyone choosing EAD should take a course through an archival education program or enroll in the workshops offered by the Society of American Archivists. Indeed, this chapter draws heavily on an excellent SAA workshop by Kris Kiesling and Fox in August of 2002.

EAD 2002

EAD is still a work in progress. SAA's EAD Working Group constantly seeks input, and international practitioners, especially those interested in ISAD(g), have certainly not been shy. Their input led to a revised *Encoded Archival Description Tag Library–Version 2002*. You should expect further revisions.

XMETAL EXAMPLES

At the time of this writing, Microsoft has announced integrating XML editors in its new office suites.

At the moment, the main software option for EAD/XML is the XMetal XML editor, a highly rated Windows product from Softquad (http://www.softquad.com), a Canadian company that was purchased in 2002 by Corel Software (http://www.corel.com). Corel also owns the other major XML/EAD word processing option with WordPerfect.

XMetal has a thesaurus, spell checker and ability to make macros along with standardized templates for data entry. You can either type in your own rules schema or download the ASCII or binary files of a DTD—e.g., for EAD, pick "ead.rlx" from http://jefferson.village.virginia.edu/ead. You can then script the product with entry and quality control features, make elements mandatory or voluntary, and limit the selection of elements to those on a control list.

Once the rules are in place, the program guides the production of a well-formulated document. As illustrated in figure 4.6:

- Entries are set within ⌐crayon⌐> tags < ⌐/crayon⌐ . XMetal uses these "crayons" to clearly mark the tags (see figure 4.6).
- Engage the start tag and type or cut-and-paste the entry.

- Attributes and rules for the element are displayed in a set of boxes below the upper right hand corner of the screen.

- Subelements can be imbedded within the envelope for display and are retrievable from the lower menu block on the right-hand side.

- When complete, a simple button will parse the document and tell you if it passes muster for mounting on the Web.

Fig. 4.6. Simulated XMetal Entry Screen

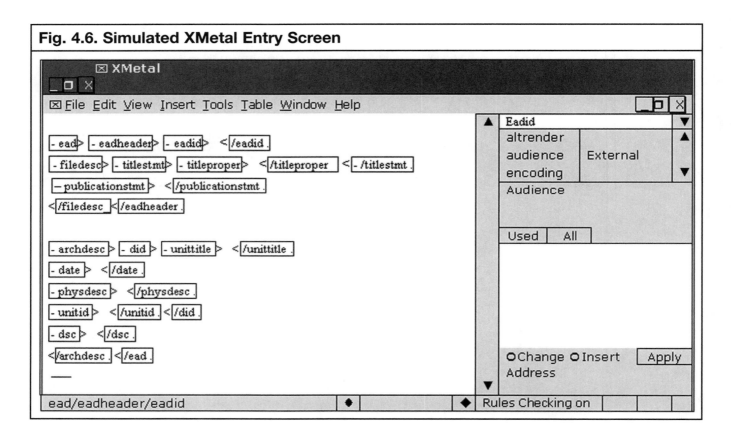

View 4—Sample XML/EAD-Encoded Finding Aid

The following is a lightly coded example of a Finding Aid produced and parsed through Xmetal by a naïve user (me) in roughly thirty minutes.

Fig. 4.7. Sample XML/EAD Finding Aid

```
<?xml version="1.0"?>
<!DOCTYPE ead SYSTEM "C:\Program Files\SoftQuad\XMetaL 2\Rules\ead.dtd">
<ead>
     <eadheader>
          <eadid>www.reuther.edu/collections/ead_1968</eadid>
          <filedesc><titlestmt><titleproper>E. F. Doree Collection</titleproper>
              <subtitle>1916–1947</subtitle></titlestmt>
              <publicationstmt><publisher>Walter P. Reuther Library, ©2002
              </publisher></publicationstmt>
          </filedesc>
     </eadheader>
     <archdesc level="collection">
          <did><unittitle>E. F. Doree Collection</unittitle>
              <unitdate>1916–1947 (Predominantly, 1918–1922)</unitdate>
              <unitid>1958-IWW</unitid><physdesc>.75 linear ft. (1 1/2
              manuscript boxes)</physdesc></did>
              <scopecontent><p> Edward F. Doree worked as a national organizer for
              the Industrial Workers of the World [I.W.W.] and served as treasurer of its
              General Defense Committee. The collection focuses on the mass arrest
              and imprisonment of I.W.W. members in 1917–1918 for alleged violation
              of wartime anti-sedition acts. Doree was caught in the sweep with his
              brother-in-law, Walter T. Nef, secretary-treasurer of the Marine Transport
              Workers Industrial Union No. 100 in Philadelphia. At the time of his arrest,
              Doree was secretary-treasurer of Textile Workers Industrial Union No.
              1000 in Philadelphia. Before receiving a presidential pardon in
              September 1922, Mr. Doree was released twice from the federal peni-
              tentiary at Fort Leavenworth to visit his critically ill son in
              Philadelphia.</p></scopecontent>
              <custodhist><p>The papers of E. F. Doree were placed in the Archives of
              Labor and Urban Affairs by Ellen Doree Rosen, the daughter of Mr.
              Doree, in July of 1996 and January of 1997. </p></custodhist>
              <separatedmaterial><head>Transfers</head><p>Several photographs
              received with the collection have been placed in the Archives Audiovisual
              Collection</p>
              </separatedmaterial>
              <arrangement><head>Series Overview</head>
                   <p> Series I: Correspondence 1917–1925, </p>
                   <p> Series II: Legal Affairs, 1921–1922 </p></arrangement>
          <dsc type=combined><head>Containers</head>
              <thead><row><entry>Box/Folder</entry><entry>Contents</entry>
              </row></thead>
              <c01><did><container>Box 1</container></did>
                   <c02><did><container>1.1</container><unittitle>Clippings and
                   E. F. Doree business card, 1922</unittitle></did></c02>
                   <c02><did><container>1.2</container><unittitle>
```

```
                              Correspondence; E. F. Doree to Ida S. Doree, Oct 1917, Sep1918
                              </unittitle></did></c02>
                              <c02><did><container>1.3–5</container>
                              <unittitle>Correspondence; E. F. Doree to Ida S. Doree, Oct 1917,
                              Sep 1918</unittitle></did></c02>
                              <c02><did><container>1.6–11</container><unittitle>
                              Correspondence; E. F. Doree to Ida S. Doree, Jan-Jun 1919
                              </unittitle></did></c02>
                              <c02><did><container>1.13–20</container><unittitle>
                              Correspondence; E. F. Doree to Ida S. Doree, May-Dec
                              1921</unittitle></did></c02>
                              <c02><did><container>21–24</container><unittitle>
                              Correspondence; E. F. Doree to Ida S. Doree, Jan-Apr 1922
                              </unittitle></did></c02></c01>
                    <c01><did><container>Box 2</container></did>
                              <c02><did><container>2.1–4</container><unittitle>
                              Correspondence; E. F. Doree to Ida S. Doree, May-Aug
                              1922</unittitle></did></c02>
                              <c02><did><container>2.5</container><unittitle>
                              Correspondence; E. F. Doree to parents, 1916–18, 1925
                              </unittitle></did></c02>
                              <c02><did><container>2.6</container><unittitle>
                              Correspondence; Rebecca Winsor Evans to Ida S. Doree,
                              1947</unittitle></did></c02>
                              <c02><did><container>2.7</container><unittitle>E. F. Doree
                              depositions on behalf of amnesty for I.W.W. prisoners, Aug
                              1921</unittitle></did></c02>
                              <c02><did><container>2.8</container><unittitle>E. F. Doree
                              pardon; corres., etc., Aug-Sep 1922</unittitle></did></c02>
                              <c02><did><container>2.9</container><unittitle>House Judiciary
                              Committee hearing on amnesty for political prisoners; transcript,
                              Mar 1922</unittitle></did></c02>
                              <c02><did><container>2.10</container><unittitle>
                              I.W.W. Leavenworth prisoner status lists, 1922
                              </unittitle></did></c02>
                              <c02><did><container>2.11</container><unittitle>
                              Feige (Fanny) Nef; corres., etc., 1920–23
                              </unittitle></did></c02></c01>
          </dsc></archdesc></ead>
```

RDF AND EAD

You should also consider adding RDF references by inserting a pointer at the start of the record to the XML namespace at RDF, which then links to the EAD tag library for automatic look-up:

<RDF xmlns = "http://w3.org/TR/1999/PR-rdf-syntax-19990105#"
xmlns:EAD = "http://www.loc.gov/EAD/taglibrary#">

CONSIDERING XMETAL STYLESHEETS

While largely intuitive, XMetal is not suitable for a Finding Aid production line. Even with a well-designed template and predetermined elements, XMetal will demand staff with knowledge about both the product and EAD, and each Finding Aid will require a stream of decisions.

Alas, too, your work is not done. While the XML export can be placed on the Web, the visual results will be far less than pleasing or readable. XML Web layout relies on HTML. Similar to XHTML's cascading style sheets, XML demands its own XSLs (extensible style sheets), which are programmed with the XSLT language.

Since content is separated, XSL stylesheets do offer a number of significant advantages. You can produce a limitless variety of layouts for the same document and scale to PDAs or other delivery vehicles. Instead of individually encoding the format in each document, the XSL program acts as a rough template that is preprepared with the desired HTML codes and stored for retrieval in the site's directories. As illustrated in figure 4.8, the programming can be modularized for each division within the Finding Aid. Luckily, such coding may only need to be done once, and Fox has prepared a new workshop on XSL for SAA.

> SAA has a new series of workshops to teach XSL techniques.

Fig. 4.8. XSL High-Level DID and Output

```
<xsl:template match="archdesc/did">
    <h2><center>
        <xsl: apply-templates select="unittitle"/>
        <xsl: apply-templates select="unitdate"/>
    </center></h2>
    <h3><center>
        <xsl: apply-templates select="physdescr"/>
    </center></h2>
    <h3><right>
        <xsl: apply-templates select="unitid"/>
    </right></h3>
</xsl:template>
```

Jane Smith Collection, 1916–1947

18 Cubic Feet

ID Number 568

XML BROWSER EDITORS

Online WYSIWYG editors for XML are entering the marketplace. Authentic 5 Browser Edition from Altova (http://www.altova.com) lets you edit XML forms on the Web, and XSLT stylesheets are put in place first. As one edits an XML form, the program incrementally parses and validates each division on the fly.

DBMS ALTERNATIVE

DBMSs, including specialized turnkey products for records center and knowledge or content management, can be queried across the Internet, but such applications call for a solid level of staff expertise or outsourcing.

SOFTWARE OVERVIEW

Following the logic of familiarity, the DBMS is most appropriate for institutions that are already using such a product. Current packages will likely be more robust and with better-established track records than their XML editor counterparts. Most DBMS products act as open systems by adhering to the SQL standard and have informal and formal channels for assistance—e.g., user list serves and product help lines—with years of answers based on long-term development and quality controls.

Products include high-end and expensive products like Oracle (the first SQL DBMS), Informix, Lotus Notes, and Sybase, but most readers will deal with less-expensive microcomputer products like Access, FileMaker Pro, and FoxPro, which store their information in tables, have great flexibility, are generally easy to use, and are appearing more often on the Web.

Basic Techniques

Begin by creating definitions and establishing rules for the terminology to be used. The controls for XML and DBMS are at the subitem level. Each record requires details for its individual data elements, resulting in a powerful array of metadata, including:

- **FIELD NAME:** These terms are unique identifiers and can be drawn from DTD elements.
- **REPEATABLE:** The ability to reiterate the same type of field—e.g., repeating folder lists—is a powerful option in some DBMSs.
- **LENGTH:** In the past, one often needed to declare the maximum length of the DBMS fields.
- **FIELD TYPE:** For example:
    - **Alpha-Numeric:** This contains the normal narrative and terms to be identified through the equals function. It includes numbers that are not subject to math—you cannot have multiple street addresses or phone numbers.

- **Numeric:** This includes the material that is open to mathematical operations. This tag may have subsections to declare decimal or monetary values.
- **Dates:** This is a class of data that is also open to range manipulation by greater than (>) and less than (<) functions
- **Hypertext:** This field links to other reference resources or imports images and media.
- **Logical Operators:** This is a convenient off/on or yes/no switch that ties data entry into a single switch or button or a controlled list of terms—Agree: [] Yes; [] No; [] Maybe.
- **Memo/Notes:** This acts a catchall for narrative discussions and is often set out in 64K blocks for data entry
- **Key (or linking) Field:** Each record will have a major identification field (like the collection ID number), which may be used to tie together and coordinate among different files.

Once you have set the definitions, the staff expert or consultant can create an appropriate template for data entry. Implementation will require training and, as always, written instructions.

WEB CONVERGENCE

DBMSs have made immense strides toward integrating their programs with the Web. In the earliest informal methods, content could be exported as static reports, which were then reframed with HTML tags or through CGI scripting, which enabled one to post queries through interactive forms. But DBMSs have pushed forward with their own services:

Web Forms

DBMSs provide the option of creating and using the database through interactive forms or CGI scripts for posting to the site. If you do not run your own servers, operations can be outsourced to an Internet Service Provider (ISP) or an Application Service Provider (ASP).

Dynamic HTML

In an HTML environment, you make changes in a document, save it, and then upload the file to replace the previous Web page. In dHTML, you update on the fly and reissue the file in HTML code, allowing changes made in the database to be instantly available for the site. While the Web site can literally be generated by queries to the database, most dHTML sites are a hybrid. HTML coding sets the basic screen framework and its fixed information. Database links are available to handle complex transactions beyond the scope of a word processor and tie to frequently updated material (like a current news section).

Many DBMS programs have been adapted for dHTML operations on the Web. You can discern such an approach by the presence of "post" commands, which use questions marks (?) in the query strings on the browser. dHTML greatly enhances the power of the site and helps circumvent updating bottlenecks, but calls for substantial skills to setup.

THE INVISIBLE WEB

An unfortunate side effect of DBMS applications is that they are likely to become part of the "Invisible Web"—a region removed from normal search engine searches. Estimates are that the Invisible ("Deep" or "Hidden") Web may hold anywhere from five to five-hundred times the amount of material found on the Open Web. The dark side is made up of sites that:

*   demand passwords or other steps to enter (—e.g., [] I declare that I am 21 years of age and may legally enter this site);
*   require separate queries to extract information (e.g., DBMSs);
*   are generated on the fly (look for the (?) in their URLs);
*   have inadvertently blocked access through the use of frames or "splash pages"—the high tech animations that sometimes lead into the homepage;
*   elect not to be found (e.g., they may issue a "no robot" command to ward off search engine spiders); or
*   may be only intermittently available or determined of little interest by the search engines companies.

XML Export

The biggest initial problem on the XML scene has been compatibility with DBMS databases. Too many institutions were committed to DBMSs, and that software was too powerful to consider a direct XML takeover. XML toolmakers tried their own solutions, but the greatest advances are coming from the DBMS scene.

By 2002, companies like Oracle and FileMakerPro offered DBMS XML modules, allowing us to have our cake and eat it too. An XML schema like EAD can be downloaded to provide a controlled vocabulary and data entry rules. The DBMS solution for the Invisible Web is to allow XML files to be downloaded as a report or updated on the fly as part of the normal flow of business—making them available to search engines. More enhancements will be available as XML definition and export become regular features of office automation suites.

Final Thoughts

Like our other approaches, the DBMS is an imperfect but still an attractive option. Technical problems mirror those for XML options. Complex applications may require additional resources to reach a level of expertise. Large enterprises may encounter problems with server load. Complex queries can take an inordinate amount of time to fill, the depth of questioning may be limited, and sites can be inundated with too many requests. The solutions are similar to those for pure XML sites—a larger server, mirroring, and load leveling through auxiliary sites or accelerator programs.

Most repositories should be firmly on the database path, but it is not required. Small organizations and those considering a DBMS will want to consider:

- What are the costs/benefits in relation to word processing and HTML solutions?
- Do you have the staff and skills to address a DBMS?
- What are the costs and benefits versus a simple HTML operation?
- What are similar comparisons to using an XML editor?
- What other options do you have—e.g., a turnkey system or outsourcing?

5 EXPLORING LEADING LIBRARY AND MUSEUM AUTOMATION SYSTEMS

Libraries and Cataloging
- MARC
- NUCMC option

Commercial Partners
- ILS Partners
- Database Aggregators

Online Bibliographic Utilities
- RLG
- OCLC

Web Ferment
- Persistent URLS
- Open URL
- XML and MARC DTD

Museum Context
- PastPerfect software
- CIMI and MIDIIS DTD

Although this book concentrates on homegrown methods for building digital archives, many readers will need to consider expanding from their extant automation systems. This chapter touches on the leading automation packages for museums. The focus, however, is on libraries' descriptive techniques, automated systems marketplace, and cutting-edge responses to the Web. As will be discussed here and in chapter 8, the field contributes much of the leadership for the technological and metadata applications in digital archives.

LIBRARIES AND CATALOGING

Library cataloging provides the most recognized forms of automated description for the public and a significant option for electronically listing digital archives. Rather than the extended narratives and inventory of a Finding Aid, cataloging uses short phrase structures that harken to its origins in printed 3 × 5 inch card sets. The modern apparatus include economies of scale and relies on international standards. It has fostered automation and Web research with three complimentary sets of players:

- the Library of Congress (LC), along with leading libraries and consortia;
- commercial software vendors and licensing agents; and
- OCLC and the Research Libraries Group (RLG) Online Bibliographic Utilities.

Reader's Advisory: The opening sections give a cursory background on library methods and the marketplace for non-librarians, along with an easy method for submitting catalog entries. Librarians and the informed may wish to skip ahead to the Online Bibliographic Utilities section and subsequent treatments of Web advances.

MARC

The Library of Congress pioneered MARC (Machine-Readable Cataloging) in 1968. The approach was developed in tandem with pre-existing entry guidelines under the *Anglo-American Cataloguing Rules (AACR)*.

MARC provided a groundbreaking adaptation of the computer for bibliographic and cultural purposes. The approach drew on the linear file structures and arrays of mainframe computers from the 1960s, with numerically sequenced tags working as "buckets" to hold structured data. Unfortunately, commercial software lagged behind for a decade and only arrived in proprietary form—not in the open source programming envisioned by the field.

> MARC became ANSI's Z39.2 in 1972 and led the way for 1979's landmark OSI (Open Systems Interconnect).

MARC 21

By the mid-1980s, LC was looking to update and ensure a more technologically enforceable standard. The resulting MARC 21 family of the 1990s included communication parameters along with separate bibliographic, holdings, authority, classification, and community information formats (http://lcweb.loc.gov/marc/). Instead of the previous pattern of separate formats for different genres, the revision put forth a single, unified bibliographic record.

FINDING AIDS AND MARC

Archival approaches contributed to the development of the unified record. In the early 1980s, SAA's National Information Systems Task Force (NISTF) recommended adapting MARC for archival automation. Steven Henson produced a preparatory content standard with the *APPM Manual (Archives, Personal Papers and Manuscripts),* and SAA worked with LC on a new format—MARC-AMC (archives and manuscript collections)—which could embrace any variety of media from documents to photographs or even artifacts.

In theory, the MARC record describes the completed Finding Aid—not the collection. In practice, MARC records may be treated as an interim descriptive device to announce the presence of a collection. MARC records require a number of compromises for translating to the archival domain. In particular, the narrative elements are limited and reduced in size to catalog-card like entries, constraints are often placed on the number of added entries, and the inventory is absent.

Bibliographic Record

The MARC bibliographic record has a leader and directory to assist with technical interpretation and a body that includes a set of fixed field descriptors and variable-length entries. The latter comes in a preordered sequence and can offer something on the order of 800 variables—many of which can be repeated. While cataloging is not for the faint of heart, matters can be simplified—as with the following list of MARC elements for our sample Finding Aids:

035 = Collection ID Number

100 (110) = Provenance Name for Main Entry

245 = Genre (e.g., Papers, Records) and Date Range

300 = Size, physical description

520 = Scope and Content Note (typically a shortened form)

545 = Biography or History Note (typically shortened)

600 = Correspondents (repeatable field)

650 = Subjects (repeatable field)

851 = Repository Name and Address

856 = Links to the Repository Web site, HEFA, and potentially other digital archives content

NUCMC OPTION

Those not directly in the bibliographic loop can still use MARC—some have been able to secure cataloging entries from cooperating libraries. RLG has opened several options, and a traditional recourse also exists for placing museum and archival listings online for Web access.

Before MARC, LC began offering cataloging services for manuscript holdings through the NUCMC (National Union Catalog of Manuscript Collections) in the late 1950s. Twenty-five years and twenty-nine volumes later, NUCMC's printed reports total 72,300 manuscript, archival, and oral history collections, which are in over 1400 repositories and command more than a million index terms.

While MARC technically describes the Finding Aid, NUCMC describes the collection. Since 1996, NUCMC catalogers have converted records from over 250 institutions into MARC for mounting in the RLG database, and these listings are available as a free service for archives and manuscript repositories in the United States on two conditions—the repository must:

- be open on a regular basis to researchers
- be unable to contribute to national cataloging (through OCLC or RLG).

Eligible repositories mail or enter information in the NUCMC Web site (http://lcweb.loc.gov/coll/nucmc/). As simulated in figure 5.1, the data sheet asks thirteen questions—most of which may sound familiar.

Fig. 5.1. NUCMC Data Sheet

National Union Catalog of Manuscript Collections (NUCMC)
DATA SHEET

Date:

1. Name of repository (include city and state):

2. Does this repository catalog manuscripts on a computer database?   O NO   O YES
   If yes please specify
   [Required eligibility statement]
   (NB: Repositories that catalog on a national database, such as OCLC or RLIN, are ineligible for participation in NUCMC.)

3. Name and title of person to be contacted for information about the repository's collections:

Mailing address and telephone number of contact person (also provide fax number and Internet address, if applicable)

4. Principal name around which the collection is formed (MARC 1xx); i.e., person (full name, birth and death dates), family, business, society, governmental agency, or some other corporate body:

   a) Commonly known form of name:

   b) Give relationship of the above to the collection; i.e.,   O Creator   O collector   O other (if other please specify)

5. Name of collection, inclusive dates of material, and bulk dates (MARC 245)

6. Number of shelf feet
   or number of items
   O linear   O cubic
   O known   O estimated

7. If this is, or was, part of another collection, state name and relationship (MARC 500):

[Generally ignore] ▲▼

8. If the collection contains _copies_ of manuscripts, describe the form(s) of reproduction (e.g.: transcripts, photocopies, positive or negative microfilm) and give the approximate number of each kind. Give location of originals, and dates when the copies were made (MARC 500):

[Generally ignore] ▲▼

9. Occupation or type of activity of the principal person, family, or corporate body; significant events and dates in the career or activity; corporate history and name changes; and place of residence or location of activity (MARC 545)

▲▼

10. Description of scope and content of collection (MARC 520) This description should cover: types of papers (e.g., correspondence, letters, diaries, documents, etc.); dates, subjects, and types of groups of materials that bulk largest; relationship of the material to specific phases of the career or activity of the principal named in item 4; full names, dates, and biographical identification of other persons and names of corporate bodies significant (by quality and/or quantity of material) to the collection, showing dates, types, and subject matter; geographical areas covered; specific events, topics, and historical periods with which the materials deal; and particular items of extraordinary interest. This description may be continued on an additional sheet, if necessary.

▲▼

11. Nature of acquisition (gift, permanent deposit, etc.). Date(s) and source(s) of acquisition and former owner(s) (MARC 561):

[I suggest leave blank] ▲▼

12. Research   ○ unrestricted   ○ restricted
If restricted state nature of restriction and when it will be terminated (MARC 506)

[I suggest leave blank] ▲▼

13. Is there any published or unpublished description, guide, index, calendar, etc., available in the

repository for this collection?   ○ yes   ○ no
     If published, give full citation (MARC 555)

[Use to include Web locations too] ▲▼

EMAIL ADDRESS OF SENDER

Submit   Reset

ArchivesUSA

Chadwyck-Healey, a subsidiary of ProQuest, has a long involvement with archives, museums, and special collections. Its ArchivesUSA product began with microfilmed versions of Finding Aids, but has evolved into a subscription-based Web information resource that features:

- **NUCMC:** Pre-1997 volumes of NUCMC are available online along with indexes, which can be employed for authority purposes.

  - NUCMC's Personal Names, 1959–1984
  - NUCMC's Subject and Corporate Names, 1959–1984

- **NIDS:** ProQuest's National Inventory of Documentary Sources in the United States is a microfiche directory that has been broken down into name and subject indexing for over 52,000 collections.
- **COLLECTION DIRECTORY:** This is a resource of some 125,000 collections of primary materials from almost 5,500 repositories across the United States, with perhaps 5,000 links to online Finding Aids in other sites.

Making Contributions

Repositories can add their own entries to ArchivesUSA through its web site (http://archives.chadwyck.com) via a simple e-mail link and a two-part form:

A. **Repository Information**
   - repository name
   - address
   - telephone
   - fax
   - e-mail
   - Web address (URL) of the repository home page
   - days and hours of service
   - materials solicited
   - description (overview of all holdings)
   - inclusive dates
   - total volume

B. **Collection Information** (Note the overlap with other systems)

- collection name
- collection dates
- type (papers, records, etc.)
- extent (feet, boxes, etc.)
- main topics (main people, places, events in collection)
- description (if there is a finding aid for this collection, indicate where it is available on the Web)
- URL (indicate if the format is HTML or SGML)
- any primary source materials from this collection (with their URLs)

Z39.50 INTERNET PROTOCOL

Libraries also made significant contributions to Z39.50, the Internet's standard for cross-platform database connections. Once in operation, the results are powerful. Participating libraries set their systems to conform to Z39.50's Bath Profile (http://www.nlc-bnc.ca/bath/bp-current .htm), allowing their patrons to engage in one-stop, cross-institutional and cross-platform searches from a single terminal.

Z39.50 BACKGROUND AND WEB APPLICATIONS

Z39.50 emerged in 1988 from a project to link the union catalogs of LC and the online bibliographic utilities. Maintained at the Library of Congress (http://lcweb.loc.gov/z3950/agency/), Z39.50 went through three editions by 1995.

Z39.50 earned a troublesome reputation among developers. The standards community is attempting to simplify and lower the barriers to implementation. Like W3C with RDF, the movement is on to expand the "intellectual/semantic content of Z39.50." Version 1.of the Star-Trek themed "ZING" (Z39.50-International: Next Generation)—was released for comment in October of 2002. (See: http://www.loc.gov/z3950/ agency/zing/).

COMMERICAL PARTNERS

Modern librarianship has remained intimately involved with commercial interests since its birth in the nineteenth century, and such relationships are notably vital in the Web era. Vendors are responsible for much of the practical innovation and library-oriented technologies on the Information Highway.

ILS COMPONENT

MARC's early history demonstrated that a great idea could not work until the commercial sector developed and found it sufficiently attractive to pursue. Library automation is thus normally dated to a decade after MARC and the ventures of the CLSI company in the late 1970s, and the heyday for Integrated Library Systems (ILSs) was delayed into the 1980s. ILSs drew on the comparative ease and power of relational DBMS along with other simplified programming tools. Unfortunately, the resulting products were only partially open, and each interpreted the MARC record in a slightly different and proprietary fashion.

The following is only a gloss. A complete examination of the ILS niche market is well beyond the scope of this text due to the complexity and rapid development of the products. Library schools have a full complement of courses to prepare in the area, but as one who once ran a system can attest, you have to learn the nuances of the program on the job.

Modules

Library automation began with work tools for catalogers, but quickly spread to circulation controls and eventually evolved into a series of interrelated functional modules. Those of potential interest for digital archives include:

- **CATALOGING MODULE** is the heart of library automation. In addition to facilitating copy cataloging, it allows for original cataloging and transmission to the bibliographic utilities.
- **AUTHORITY FILES** have automated and comparative features well beyond the homemade version in chapter 2.
- **PATRON REGISTRATION** is used to identify users and work with the circulation system.
- **CIRCULATION SYSTEM** provides transaction controls for the check in, check out, and use of materials (may have "reserve" functions).
- **OPAC** (Online Public Access Catalog) began with simple line editors, which featured tabbing and carriage returns to navigate on in-house CRT (Cathode Ray Tube) white on black displays. The latter have given way to multicolored screens, GUI interfaces, and Web delivery.

Selection

From the beginning, the purchase and maintenance of an ILS has been a complicated and often expensive affair demanding a trained staff and a significant commitment to an automation and telecommunications infrastructure. Technical support staff would provide the first line of defense for advanced metadata and the mechanics of Web sites in library versions of digital archives.

A trip to the ALA Convention will amply demonstrate the ongoing Web advances of systems like Dynix, Endeavor, Ex Libris, GEAC, Innovative, Sirsi, VTLS, etc.. Fully functional, standards-compliant ILSs are within reach of most pocketbooks, thanks to developments in the education market. For an investment of a few thousand dollars, Follett, Sirs-Mandarin, and other PC-based programs are matching many of the frills of their big brothers.

The companies are converging on the Web and looking for related services to entice clients. One possibility is for the OPAC to do double duty as the repository's homepage or portal to all Web services, and other products are extended to include homegrown electronic pathfinders and educational packets. Those considering such products as part of a digital archives initiative should also look for:

- Z39.50 and full MARC-compatibility;
- integrated authority controls to national and, especially, local resources;
- a strong internal search engine— preferably one that will cover non-MARC resources;
- at least a third-generation ILS, with a flexible Web OPAC module; and
- XML capacities (present in the coming fourth-generation systems).

DATABASE AGGREGATORS

Another set of commercial partners are developing techniques with applicability for a digital archives. Database aggregators negotiate to provide access to the electronic versions of magazines and newspapers and offer the repository licensing to use the publications rather than purchasing paper copies. Such "rented" materials are major digital assets, but their preservation/reuse a significant point of concern (See: chapter 8).

The big three—EBSCO (http://www.epnet.com), Gale (http://www.galegroup.com), and ProQuest (http://www.umi.com)—along with others, are looking to extend operations with digital content and digitization, including Web portals with access to their services, other Web sites, and homegrown resources. In addition, ProQuest touts its digital archives—the Digital Vault Initiative with "500 years of Information." As mentioned in chapter 6, the company also pioneered course-pack software with XanEdu, which allows instructors to build from its resources and other external digital content. EBSCOadmin provides a similar ability to customize services with searching tools and integration with homegrown resources.

ONLINE BIBLIOGRAPHIC UTILITIES

Online bibliographic utilities represent the third element in the library equation. They date to a small group of libraries in Ohio that took the opportunities offered by MARC records to build an electronic cataloging cooperative. The then Ohio Center for Library Cataloging (OCLC) set the stage for new accuracy and economies of scale. Instead of individually detailing each book, libraries could dial in to share "proofed" records and download for simple "copy cataloging." In the mid-1970s, OCLC (http://www.oclc.org) was joined by its university counterpart at the Research Library Group (RLG) (http://www.rlg.org).

OCLC and RLG are major innovators on the Web and are actively seeking new service opportunities. As discussed in chapter 8, the utilities have joined in a national-level initiative for "Trusted Digital Repositories" and are also actively pursuing metadata standards for their customers. Both have announced active outreach and the desire for partnerships with the archival, museum, and publishing communities.

RLG ACTIVITIES

Because of a high concentration of large academic libraries with special collections, RLG took an early interest in digital collections. Its "Archival Services," offered as Web-based, subscription programs (http://www.rlg.org/arr/>), feature access to over a half a million catalog records and thousands of full-text archival finding aids.

At the time of this writing, RLG opted for HTML content over EAD XML or SGML postings.

RLG also embraced EAD for archival Finding Aids. Its *EAD Applications Guidelines* (http://www.rlg.org/rlgead/) appeared in 1998—slightly in advance of SAA's adoption. RLG invites archives to place their EAD Finding Aids in its database, and but also actively solicits HEFAs or other non-EAD Finding Aids for inclusion.

OCLC

OCLC, which focuses on member services with a public library bent, is responsible for key contributions to the Web and toward digital archives.

Dublin Core

The Dublin Core (DC) represents one of the first organizations to respond to the need for systematic metadata standards on the Web. In 1995, OCLC convened a group in its hometown of Dublin, Ohio, to discuss ways to describe resources on the Web. The original idea was a simplified subset of MARC for cataloging Web objects, which spun off from OCLC into the independent Dublin Core Metadata Initiative (http://dublincore.org/). DCMI indicated its dedication to:

> [T]he continual refinement of a "core" foundation of property types and values to provide vertically specific (semantic) information about Web resources much in the same way a library card catalog provide indexes of book properties.

DC (IETF RFC 2413) has emerged as an internationally recognized metadata standard. While looking to expand its descriptive potential with "qualifiers" or attribute extensions, the schema still rests on fifteen basic descriptive elements (See: figure 4.2) that are intended to describe online versions and leave the description of any physical original to traditional methods.

CORC

CORC (Cooperative Online Resource Catalog), one of the first efforts to use DC's as a type of "MARC Lite" for cataloging electronic resources, offers a small suite of tools for selecting Web sites and building electronic subject pathfinders (See: chapter 6). As formally described:

> [CORC] is a metadata creation system for bibliographic records and pathfinders describing electronic resources. You choose which electronic resources to catalog: local and web-based. CORC helps you provide your users with well-guided access to electronic resources. In short, CORC increases the value of the Web for your library and its users, giving you the tools you need to organize, select and describe electronic resources. (http://www.oclc.org/corc/)

Nordic Metadata Template

(http://www.lub.lu.se/cgi-bin/nmdc.pl). The service's user-friendly method for adding metadata to a first-generation Web site demonstrates the international expanse of the Dublin Core. The template allows the user to enter the data and returns verified content to cut-and-paste in the Header of an HTML 4.x file.

The site offers a "short and simple template" with elements 1, 2, 3, 8, 10, and 12. As simulated in Figure 5.2, it also provides for complete entry with all 15 elements and the promise of qualifier selections as they come on line.

Fig. 5.2. NORDIC Dublin Core Entry Form

If you need to repeat a field, just click on the + that accompanies the field

1. TITLE of the resource to be described

Alternative title (Titles other than main title)

2. CREATOR (Name of person or organization primarily responsible for creating the intellectual resource)

Creator name ▼

Creator's (Email) address

3. SUBJECT: Keywords (Your own keywords describing the topic of the resource, **one per box**)

3. SUBJECT: Controlled vocabulary (Keywords from established schemes, **one per box**)

Library of Congress Subject Headings ▼

Library of Congress Subject Headings ▼

3. SUBJECT: Classification (Notations for the resource, **one per box**)

Dewey Decimal Classification ▼

4. DESCRIPTION (Abstract, content description)

Fig. 5.2. (cont.)

5. PUBLISHER (Repository)   Publisher's (Email) address

Publisher's (Email) address

6. CONTRIBUTOR (Name of significant contributors other than the creator)

Contributors name   ▼   ⊟⊞

7. DATE (Date associated with the creation or availability of the resource)

1996-09-23 (ISO 8601)   ⊟⊞

8. TYPE (Category of the resource)

Text.Homepage.Organizational   ▼   ⊟⊞

9. FORMAT (Data representation of the resource, MIME type)

text/html (.htm,.html)   ▼   ⊟⊞

10. IDENTIFIER (Location of the document. Start with 'http://')

11. IDENTIFIER (String or number used to uniquely identify the resource described by this metadata)

URN▼   ⊟⊞

11. SOURCE (Unique string or number for a printed or digital work from which this resource is derived)

Free text ▼   ⊟⊞

12. LANGUAGE of the content of the resource described

English   ▼   ⊟⊞

13. RELATION (Relationship to other resources)

Free text ▼   ⊟⊞

14. COVERAGE (Spatial and/or temporal characteristics of the resource)

Free text ▼   ⊟⊞

15. RIGHTS (Link to a copyright notice etc.)

Free text ▼   ⊟⊞

Digital Preservation Initiatives

OCLC, in an effort to address digital aspects beyond description, offers its members access to a Digital and Preservation Cooperative clearinghouse that includes lists of grant opportunities and cooperative ventures. The utility offers turnkey software to manage special collections on your computer along with parallel options for treatment and storage capacities on its servers. OCLC President Jay Jordan declared his new strategy for "Extending the Library Cooperative":

> *OCLC will extend its cooperative cataloging framework to include new participants, new types of metadata and new automated tools...OCLC will seek the input of metadata from museums, archives, professional associations, publishers and others...*
>
> *Archiving and preservation services, digital conversion services and local content management tools from OCLC will help libraries increase access to their unique collections as well as pass them on to future generations.* (http://www.oclc.org/strategy/)

WEB ADVENTURES

The library community has formed new agencies with the Web in mind—such as the Coalition for Networked Information and Digital Library Federation with its DLIB Magazine (http://www.dlib.org). Special measures are being developed to help bridge the gap between older automated description and the new medium. The following continues our introduction to this vast and occasionally confusing landscape (See also: chapter 8).

PERSISTENT ADDRESSES

One of the most annoying aspects of the Web is Error 404, which indicates that the site that you wanted may no longer exist or has moved without leaving a forwarding address. The Internet Engineering Task Force attempted to address the problem with unique identifiers called URNs (Uniform Resource Names) that allow sites to travel seamlessly among different ISPs and IP addresses (http://www.ietf.org/html.charters/urn-charter.html).

OCLC's PURL (Persistent Uniform Resource Locators) is an enhanced form of URN that creates a system of movable aliases that map the PURL to the URL through tables on a central server. OCLC provides the server software for free (http://www.purl.org/).

LINK CHECKERS

Other methods are available to help ensure persistence. You can rely internally on the supplemental Web lists in chapter 3 (See: figure 3.7). Instead of tying directly to a distinct URL within a Finding Aid or other descriptive device, the link goes to a separate list. and each list is then independently maintained. Modern Web editors, like MS FrontPage, come preequipped with a utility for the initial checks. Link checking software is also available for a fee or through a freeware package—e.g., Funnel Web Analyzer (http://www.quest.com) and Xenu's Link Sleuth (http://www.home.snafu.de/tilman/xenulink.html).

OPEN URL

Open URLs provide a related method to ensure link security, but also to circumvent the limitations of the Web's "many to one" hypertext syntax. A Web *href* link can only go to a single anchor or page, but the new technique extends the potential number of URLs through a stream of actionable metatags that link to independently maintained supplemental resources. In addition, the vendors are provided "hooks" to "reach in" and dynamically expand portions of the descriptive entry. Links are automatically generated to descriptive resources on the Web or elsewhere in the institution.

STANDARDS TRACK

NISO put the Open URL concept on the standard's fast track in 2002. The California Institute of Technology serves as the maintenance, and has even provided an Open URL theme song and video (http://library.caltech.edu/openurl/). By way of comparison, Open URL can offer HTML documents parallel strengths to the "name-space" extensions in XML with RDF for semantic networking.

In current models, a button in the OPAC records provides access to an Open URL information menu with such choices as:

- holdings in OCLC's or RLG's main union catalogs;
- holdings in the catalogs of cooperating or area institutions;
- options for document printing or electronic transfer;
- bibliographic records to download;
- ties to the author's e-mail or Web address; and
- links to related information through a Web search engine.

Archival Collection Example

As projected in figure 4.3, Open URL offers exciting potentials for enhancing the scope of research within digital archives. For instance, the patron uncovering a citation for a collection could engage an Open URL request for:

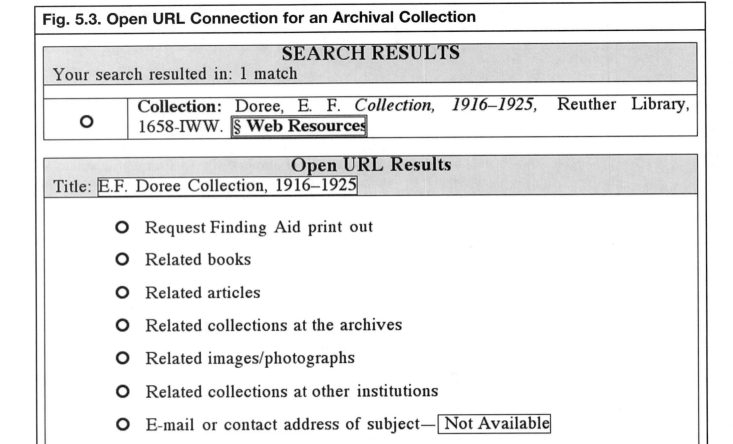

Fig. 5.3. Open URL Connection for an Archival Collection

SEARCH RESULTS
Your search resulted in: 1 match

O   **Collection:** Doree, E. F. *Collection, 1916–1925,* Reuther Library, 1658-IWW. § **Web Resources**

Open URL Results
Title: E.F. Doree Collection, 1916–1925

O   Request Finding Aid print out

O   Related books

O   Related articles

O   Related collections at the archives

O   Related images/photographs

O   Related collections at other institutions

O   E-mail or contact address of subject— Not Available

O   Web Search: Google ▼

EX LIBRIS AND SFX

Figure 5.3 is an extrapolation from Open URL examples from Ex Libris, an ILS vendor that took an initial lead with its SFX Link Server (http://www.sfxit.com). First developed at the University of Ghent in Belgium, SFX connects from a standard bibliographic citation to a separate menu of supplemental resources. At its heart is a link server with SQL programming to create citations on the fly. With SFX, the institution is responsible for programming profiles for the server with:

1. information about the collection/citation;
2. types of services actually available; and
3. rules for the inference engine about those services.

XML AND MARC DTD

With the exception of some Dublin Core entries, library bibliographic resources tend to reside on the Invisible Web. Citations sit within databases that require authentication for access and are effectively hidden from Web search engines (See: chapter 3 discussions). The researcher thus has to be aware of the repository or tied to it through a Z39.50 cooperative search.

XML offers the clearest path to visibility for library descriptions of digital archives. LC began the development of the requisite MARC DTD in 1995, but the complexity of SGML and the MARC record severely complicated plans. A beta prototype only emerged in 1998, but by then, XML had entered the scene to provide a realistic solution for the Web. Several XML freeware conversion packages are now available for MARC (http://www.loc.gov/marc/marcsgml.html); however, instead of that form of retrospective conversion, libraries should be able to experience a rather painless transit through product upgrades into the 4th fourth generation of XML-compliant library automation systems.

DC MARC AND XML RDF CONVERSIONS

The commercial software market is starting to respond to the advances offered by the Dublin Core. The Esprit Soutron Partnership, for example, uses DC to build its XDirectory list management solution (http://www.esprit-is.com/xdir.htm) and DC is also converted into MARC records through a simple freeware program (http://www.bibsys.no/meta/dzm/). Yet none of the major search engines currently employ DC metadata for their retrieval strategies.

DC may be more applicable for an XML environment. Indeed, many of DC's developers took part in W3C's RDF development group. To set an XML/DC namespace:

<?xml version="1.0" ?><rdf:RDFxmlns:rdf="http://www.w3.org/1999/02/
22-rdf-syntax-ns#"xmlns:dc= "http://purl.org/dcelements/1.1/">

Note: There is no doubt about the importance of placing MARC records about unique digital holdings on the open Web. An interesting question does arise, however, when we consider the impact of flooding that venue with listings for multiple copies of the same book in libraries across the world. Will the search engines begin to discount such records and perhaps limit listings of the digital holdings?

MUSEUM CONTEXT

The software and methods used in museum description can provide a model for digital archives. Museums document and authenticate objects along with their use in displays with a Registrar's record, which records the details of artifacts as individual items, including measurements of size, color, and texture.

The museum automation marketplace is smaller and less advanced than the library world (it can be summarized one turnkey system, for example), but museums are certainly progressing and standardization is beginning to take hold—especially through the efforts of the Getty Museum and its affiliates.

PASTPERFECT SOFTWARE

PastPerfect is by far the leading prepackaged software for museums. Distributed by AltaMyra Press (http://www.altamyra.com) and authorized by the American Association for State and Local History (AASLH) (http://www.aaslh.org), the product is built on Microsoft's Visual FoxPro platform, which allows it to work across MS Office Suite and with hypertext links.

PastPerfect is affordable and offers an optional "Virtual Exhibits" module with direct publishing to the Web. As simulated on the next page, the layout features six tabs (I have dropped the accompanying icons for this presentation). Each tab delineates a main function, its subfunctions, and interesting counterpoints.

VIRTUAL TOUR: the program opens to the **ACCESSIONS AND COLLECTIONS** menu. To bring up the Registrar's record, click "Objects."

1. The **OBJECTS** button includes entry space for traditional museum description along with digital flourishes such as an Image Management area, which allows for multiple views of objects along with rulers for size and color test controls.

Fig. 5.4. and Fig. 5.5. Simulated PastPerfect Opening Screens

Main Menu

PastPerfect Museum

Accessions and Collections	Research	Membership	Reports	Utilities	Setup

Objects	Photos	Archives	Library	Lexicon
Temp custody	Accession	Loans In	Loans Out	Exhibits

Objects Catalog   ? X

◀ Prior	▶ Next	🗐 Add	– Browse	✕ Delete	🖎 Edit	8 Spell	K Find	🖨 Print	Œ Exit

records   Help
Sort by   Object ID

Collection				Image _ of _
Object ID		Objname		
Other#		Category		(PICTURE)
Old#		Subcategory		
Accessn#		Other Name		
Source			⇧	
Credit line			Accession	
Home Loc				◀ Image Management ▶

Description	General	Art	Natural History	Legal/ Related	Condition	Location	Subject/classes/ Search Terms/People	Notes	Custom

DESCRIPTION

+
▲

	Early Date	
	Late Date	

Dimensions	**O**in/oz	**O**cm/ar
Oft/lbs		
Height		Width
Length		Depth
Diam.		
Weight		Count

Dimension Notes

▼
▲

2. The **ARCHIVES** button is also of particular interest.

    a. The screen's top half closely parallels the "Objects" registration, but adds a "Container" span note on the Accession line and a ⌷Container List⌷ button to link to a separate form for inventory information:

Fig. 5.6. Simulated PastPresent Container List Form

Container List			Add/Edit List	Print List	Close	Sort by	Entry
Container	Folder	Title	Description				

    b. The bottom half of the main screen provides the museum version of archival description.

Fig. 5.7. Simulated PastPresent Bottom of Archives Screen

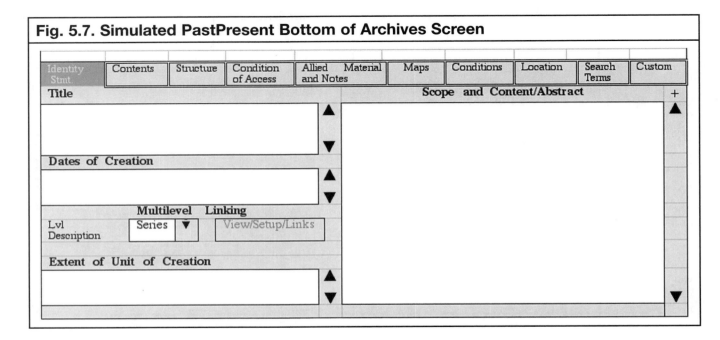

3. The **LIBRARY** button, along with its "Loans In" and "Loans Out" buttons, illustrates interesting museum parallel to ILSs.

4. The **EXHIBITS** button offers valuable controls for online displays and provides a glimpse into museum design planning.

5. The **LEXICON** button provides a particularly fruitful area for comparison and terminology controls. It opens to an authority file, and instead of the library's names, places, or subject controls, we are greeted with a museum classification system. Such a system provides a suitable metadata resource for objects and settings in fully articulated digital archives.

The Lexicon screen includes an interactive definition box to hold descriptions from each of three tiers of controlled vocabulary: major categories, subcategories, and individual object names. There are eleven major categories:

1. structures;
2. building furnishings;
3. personal artifacts;
4. T and E (tools and equipment) for materials;
5. T and E for science and technology;
6. T and E for communications;
7. distribution and transportation artifact;
8. communication artifact;
9. recreation artifact;
10. unclassifiable artifact; and
11. natural history.

CIMI AND MIDIIS DTD

The Consortium for Computer Exchange of Museum Information (CIMI) is committed to standards and the articulation of museum description, and it is actively exploring ways to share, repackage, and reuse such data.

CIMI found problems with both EAD and the Dublin Core. During 2000–2001, the organization began exploring a museum XML DTD with Project MIDIIS: the Museum Initiative for Digital Information

Interchange Standards (See: http://www.cimi.org), an endeavor that examines the types, content, and use of information in museums through structured linguistic analysis. As indicated on the CIMI site and test bed, the MIDIIS is looks at:

- **STRUCTURE:** *What types of rich information resources are currently available in museums and how should they be structured for interchange?*
- **SEMANTICS:** *—How do we understand the semantic similarities and differences in the information resources found in museums?*
- **SYNTAX:** *What format should be used to express complex museum content; can we use eXtensible Markup Language (XML) as the preferred format?*
- **PROCESS:** *What is the overall impact on an organization of information management; what procedures can reduce can reduce the cost of information and increase its value; how can museums reuse existing complex content?*

NON-PROFESSIONAL COLLECTION SOFTWARE

Amateur collectors or those willing to forgo information standards have other inexpensive options for listing their materials. MyStuff (http://www.collectify.com) is one of the newer examples and comes with the ability to import a digital image of objects.

6 ESTABLISHING POLICIES AND TECHNIQUES FOR DIGITAL IMAGING

On the threshold of this digital age, we have one foot in the hard-copy world of physical artifacts and the other searching for solid ground in the digital world. Previous chapters deal with automating descriptions as preludes to, and components of digital archives. Whether through XML editors, word processing, turnkeys, or DBMSs—computerization is a direct process. Data is entered through the keyboard and mouse. The results are "born digital"—the most efficient and logical path to building Web resources.

Yet, patrons expect to encounter "analogs" of documents, photographs, media, and artifacts that were not born digital. Before access, such materials must be digitized into image formats that both in-house computers and Web browsers can handle. Digital imaging raises two distinct, yet related issues:

1. **POLICIES:** legal considerations and the selection framework for digitizing and posting to the Web
2. **PROCEDURES:** physical methods for capturing images and converting to digital files for in-house and Web storage

We will examine each of these issues in turn within this chapter.

POLICY DEVELOPMENT

In the Web era, digitization inevitably will pervade repository activities. The process and potential of this emerging technology is reorienting notions of service, content, and access, and demands studied legal, ethical, and financial consideration. The resulting policies will apply equally to data born digitally and to digital archives as a whole. They will have to resolve copyright questions arising from photocopier reproduction, spell out the parameters for asserting copyright claims, address freedom of access and privacy issues, as well as clarify criteria for appraisal and selection. Fortunately, policy decisions can benefit from a review of past precedents and the practical experiences of others. The following discussions look to the past for grounding, but must acknowledge an ever-changing political and legal landscape.

PHOTOCOPIERS AND COPYRIGHT

Copyright is a crucial consideration—especially when posting materials to the Web. Given its interests on both sides of the copyright fence, the repository must constantly keep abreast of an ever evolving scene. We turn to the 1976 Copyright Act as the foundation of current U.S. copyright law.

1976 Copyright Act.

As holders of copyrights, as well as institutions that provide access to material copyrighted by other parties, repositories have a vested interested in copyright law. Responsibilities escalated in the 1960s, with the reproduction revolution spurred on by new reprographic and audio technology—commercially viable photocopiers and mass-produced cassette recorders. These developments brought repositories, and copyright holders generally, to uncharted legal territory. In the first of a series of responses to this copyright revolution, the United States Congress formulated the 1976 Copyright Act: Title 17 US Code (http://www.loc.gov/copyright/).

The 1976 Copyright Act materially elevated creators' rights and extended the period of protection (see figure 6.1). It guarded the rights to the intellectual and creative work of any person(s) from the moment it was fixed in a reproducible form. Beginning January 1, 1978, "intellectual property" no longer required tradition publication or copyright registration with the Library of Congress to be protected.

One decade later, in 1988, the United States brought U.S. copyright law into rough conformance international standards by becoming a signatory to the Berne Convention of the World Intellectual Property Organization (WIPO). A 1998 revision of the law granted copyright holders twenty more years of protection over the limits established in 1976. It further extended Section 106 regarding rights to reproduce, make derivatives, and use material for performance or display. In related legislation, the Visual Artists Rights Act of 1990 augmented Section 106A to give American artists their first, albeit limited, say over distortions, modifications, or mutilations of their creations.

*1998 Copyright Term Extension Act—a.k.a., the Sonny Bono Act—was declared Constitutional in early 2003.

Fig. 6.1. 1976 Copyright Act Coverage Periods, as amended	
Copyright Category	**Protections**
Materials created after 1/01/1978	Covered for the life of the author plus seventy years (with multiple authors, the oldest living sets the clock); corporate works are the shorter of ninety-five years from the date of publication or 120 years from creation.
Materials created prior to 1/01/1978, but not published	Covered for the life of the author plus seventy years or until 12/31/2002, whichever is greater.
Materials created prior to 1/01/1978 and published prior to 12/31/2002	Covered for life of the author plus seventy years or until 12/31/2047, whichever is greater.
Materials published between 1923 and 1963	Covered under the previous law for twenty-eight years, after which it could be renewed to forty-seven years and could be opened by application for another twenty-year extension.
Materials published from 1964 to 1977	Covered for an initial twenty-eight year term, plus an automatic extension to the sixty-seven year total.
Section 108(h)	Allows some digital and analog copying of published materials during the last twenty years of the extended protection.

Exemptions

Although it imposed limits on the "right of purchase" that dated to the onset of print, the Copyright Act allowed exemptions of considerable importance to repositories:

- **SECTION 107. Fair Use.** This clause established the public's right to access and "reasonable" use of copyrighted material, for personal, research, and other non-commercial uses.
- **SECTION 108. Reproduction by Libraries and Archives.** Archives and libraries, which were open to the public or external researchers and seeking no commercial advantage, could legally make copies (1) for users and (2) to preserve materials. The exemption required record keeping and prominent signage to proclaim compliance with copyright precepts.

PHOTOCOPIERS AND UNPLANNED EFFECTS

In relation to digitization, the photocopying experience offers an object lesson of unintended consequences and new services for archives, libraries, and museums:

- For the first time in history, photocopying enabled individuals to obtain exact copies instantaneously.
- Photocopying introduced the world to a new verb—"Xeroxing"
- Photocopying became an effective preservation tool, reducing wear and tear on originals, and saving the intellectual contents of source materials that could not be repaired.
- Photocopying reduced thefts and mutilations.
- Photocopying made it easier to produce and distribute finding aids.
- Photocopying enabled repositories to produce pathfinders and similar research tools quickly and inexpensively.
- Photocopying produced unexpected revenue streams from copy centers and user-operated machines.
- Photocopying combined with the emergence of facsimile machines allowed consumers to convert printed content into electronic data to be transmitted over telephone lines. This capability related closely to the digital revolution.

DMCA and the Web.

During the 1990s, the seemingly limitless ability to publish and disseminate information on the World Wide Web sparked a fierce debate about copyrights. On the one hand, global access diminished the force of copyright laws, and on the other hand content providers viewed the Web as a vast untapped revenue source for their copyrighted material. The Digital Millennium Copyright Act of 1998 (DMCA) intended to resolve these issues.

- Open Access. Many viewed copyright as a technological anachronism, and approached all Web content as both accessible and free.
- Publishers, information providers, and authors felt differently. Given the nature of *http* transfers, with the material actually delivered to the receiving computer, some challenged the very notion of Fair Use. They sought payment for even accidental encounters with their Web sites.

The 1998 DMCA (http://www.loc.gov/copyright/legislation/dmca.pdf) updated the 1976 legislation, and tried to provide incentives for innovation. The goal was to protect rights holders, while still maintaining a modicum of balance for the public's right to know and access to information. The DMCA brought the United States into further conformance with WIPO, but continued limited special treatment for libraries and archives:

- **SECTION 108:** DMCA's Section 404 tweaked the original exemptions under Section 108.
    - **Subsection (b)** continues to allow the duplication for preservation purposes: "to permit up to three copies, which may be digital, provided that digital copies are not made available to the public outside the library premises." It also grants duplication for computerized resources if the original format becomes obsolete.
    - **Subsection (c)** restricts preservation copying only for damaged, deteriorating, lost, stolen, obsolete conditions where a replacement cannot be purchased at a fair price. In addition, the digital copy may not be outside the premises.
    - Subsection **(i)** makes clear that copying is limited to traditional text and is not meant to apply to a "musical work, a pictorial, graphic or sculptural work, or a motion picture or other audiovisual work other than an audio visual work dealing with the news."
- **SECTION 512(D):** Limitations are granted for the inclusion of information location tools.
- **SECTION 1201(D):** Nonprofit libraries, archives and educational institutions to examine items to make good faith purchase decisions.

Web alert.

e.g., A November 2002 TEACH Amendment added rulings on teaching extension courses

Suffice it to say, repositories are restricted in what content they can post to their Web sites. Whether materials are born digital or converted from hardcopy to digital, one must consider the copyright status of the objects. Do not mount items unless they are in the public domain, owned by the institution, or available under licensing contracts.

KEEPING ABREAST OF COPYRIGHT

Repositories must monitor unfolding copyright legislation and court cases. Valuable online resources abound, starting with the Copyright Office at the Library of Congress (http://www.loc.gov/copyright/). Many traditional law schools maintain sites overflowing with information and links, as do their online counterparts, such as the Cyberspace Law Institute (http://www.cli.org). Law journals and reviews (e.g., the *Journal of Online Law*, http://www.wm.edu/law/publication/jol); and advocacy groups contribute valuable perspectives (the Digital Future Coalition, http://www.dfc.org). Other sources include Kenneth Crews, who provides a useful primer at his Copyright Management Center (http://www.copyright.iupui.edu), and the International Federation of Library Associations (http://www.ifla.org/II/cpyright.htm); A compliance checklist can be found at the Copyright Web Site (http://www.copyrightwebsite.com/info/notice.asp); also and finally, check the European Copyright User Platform (http://www.eblida.org/ecup).

ASSERTING COPYRIGHT

On one hand, cultural institutions generally reflect altruism and sharing. The goal is to put as much as possible on the Web. Unique holdings can be used to establish the organization's "brand" and can lead to expanded virtual traffic on the Web.

On the other hand, the repository should be aware of how a Web presence will impact its foot traffic. More importantly, countervailing economic factors may come into play to suggest that the repository should limit the amount of material it posts on the open Web:

- The repository may garner significant income from reproducing descriptions and materials. Freely available content on the Web site could threaten or eliminate this revenue stream.

- In economic terms, tourism contributes over $3.7 trillion to the U.S. economy alone, and heritage tourism plays an ever-larger role on the world's economic stage. Can your repository's resources be tied into a broader campaign?

- Non-profit organizations conduct financial development campaigns in which cultural treasures, product lines, and "give-aways" play prominent roles.

Methods.

Every repository should thus consider its internal copyright posture when digitizing or granting digital access to its holdings. Those interested in asserting rights for potential profit can work with the

Copyright Clearance Center (http://www.copyright .com). Museums have a licensing cooperative with AMICO (http://www.amico.org). Less entrepreneurial responses include:

- indicating intellectual ownership—e.g., the insertion of the copyright symbol (©) and repository name on the site, in Finding Aids, and perhaps within the digital copy;
- noting that publication or other use require a citation of its origins and may call for written permission;
- for in-house copying, communicating that reproduction does not equate to a transfer of that right; access is granted under Fair Use laws:
    - State this policy on registration and copy request forms.
    - If self-copying is allowed, post the policy notice by the machine and restrict the digital copiers to print output.
    - If publication or other use is granted, state that this is a single, one-time license, —it does not convey copyright, and subsequent uses call for additional permissions.
- for materials on the Web site, declaring that publication or other uses in excess of Fair Use is prohibited without prior written permission;
- instead of complete documents, considering the selective mounting of "teaser" excerpts;
- restricting the quality of the scanned images made available for normal public viewing, or embedding a digital "watermark" copyright restriction on text and images that users can print;
- handling related privacy issues and donor restrictions.

DEEP LINKING

Some institutions object to users bypassing their homepage and directly linking to resources within the site as a copyright infringement. Other institutions may want to encourage deep linking to materials. With respect to policy, I recommend a two-pronged approach:

- The repository's digital assets will be titled to demonstrate ownership.
- The linking party will take the courtesy of notifying and requesting permission from the holding site before linking.

OTHER CONCERNS

The public nature of the Web also casts a different light on privacy and intellectual freedom (IF) issues—one that illuminates ethical differences between libraries and archives.

Intellectual Freedom.

Heretofore, special collections rarely faced censorship. While such institutions are still insulated by prestige and their research mission, Web postings may place them in the open light of other publication and public forums.

With its Office of Intellectual Freedom (OIF) and the Freedom to Read Society, the American Library Association has long marched in the vanguard of the IF movement. The *Library Bill of Rights* proudly proclaims American constitutional rights to the unfettered flow of information. ALA continues its support of that principle, but also recognizes the complexity of the issues in the electronic age—especially for public and school libraries. The library's professional response is the studied creation and addition of "Accessible Use Policies" (AUPs). In addition to checking the OIF site (http://www.ala.org/oif), my book *Creating Virtual Libraries* (New York: Neal Schuman, 1999) in this series provides a good introduction and sample AUPs.

Privacy.

With all repository materials, we must clarify the two-sided issue of privacy. Digital collections in particular can become entangled in two occasionally conflicting sets of privacy rights.

Patron Rights.

Of necessity, library policies aim to guard the patron's privacy, with respect to the materials he or she chooses to check out or read. Such concerns also dovetail with interests in protecting children and patrons from data collecting and solicitations—an almost unavoidable byproduct of accessing the Web. Privacy issues present a unique challenge to archives, in particular. Archives survive based on patron support, which repositories cultivate by developing strong relationships. The service they provide requires archives to know their users' research interests. The computer's ability to profile users and monitor the patron's online selections supplies archives with invaluable information about its users, which can be used to improve customer service.

In managing the digital information gathered about patrons, repositories face three policy and ethical options:

- Do not hold personally identifiable information beyond the bare minimum of time needed for the transactions.
- Retain the information with the user's consent.
- Strip off personally identifiable information, but retain the collective statistics for management purposes.

Donor Rights.

Without donors, most archives would have sparse collections, if they would exist at all. Therefore, archivists have special interests in protecting their donor's rights and ensuring the trust needed to secure future donations. They must faithfully observe all stipulations in a donor contract or deed of gift. Obviously, archives cannot place on the Web items legally restricted from view. Some institutions will even refrain from noting the presence of restricted collections. Such policies dictate that restricted holdings have a lower priority for digitization. Donor relations overlap with other ethical and practical questions, as well. Although legally insulated from slander and libel actions, the repository should consider a modicum of discretion when determining which materials to post on the Web. Opposing considerations can make these decisions hazy at best. If archives cannot establish privacy and trust, donor materials may be lost, at which point the question of intellectual freedom becomes moot. Moreover, maintaining sensitive material in the stacks and providing access to "serious" researchers are accepted practices.

Publishing items on the Web involves conscious choice, which alters privacy traditions and merits thoughtful deliberation before implementation.

PATRIOT ACT

The "War on Terrorism" has added another layer of complexity to the privacy question. The U.S. Patriot Act requires librarians and archivists to respond to formal information requests from Federal agents without informing the patron of any inquiry. When faced with formal requests, repositories find themselves in a dilemma, being legally bound to turn over information their own policies and ethics require them to protect. In addition, digital archives with "sensitive" materials will need to consider security implications and perhaps restricting online displays.

APPRAISAL AND SELECTION

The repository manager needs to weigh a number of practical and professional criteria in making choices for digitizing. The following analysis presupposes limited resources of time, space, staff, and funding, the demands on which should not be underestimated. Few institutions may be able to digitize all their physical assets, whether now or in the future. Repositories fortunate enough to have ample resources to digitize their collections are still advised to implement pilot programs with a representative selection.

This book recommends the archival process of "appraisal." In this flexible technique, every collection may merit an online description—but not every collection is worth the time and effort for digitization. Indeed, not everything in a collection needs to be digitized, and not everything digitized or even "born digital" should be on the Web. The task is rationalizing and prioritizing between the following options:

- **INITIAL SCANNING:** What should you and can you digitize, and when?
- **WEB PUBLICATION:** What portion of those select materials should or can the archives legally published on the Web, and when?

Digitization Criteria.

The appraisal of materials for digitization involves a range of qualitative and quantitative factors:

- **VALUE:** The key variable is quality. Logically, you should pay attention to the most important or valuable materials first.
- **PATRON USE:** A related element is the amount of current and potential patron use. The most-used materials are prime candidates for digitization and publication on the Web (i.e., following the 80/20 principle, concentrate on the 20 percent of the holdings that typically receive 80 percent of the use).
- **PHYSICAL CONDITION: Take into account the impact digitizing will have on** "preservation" of the intellectual content, especially for deteriorating materials that may be beyond repair.

- **OWNERSHIP:** You should verify whether you have permission to digitize materials, especially items on loan or deposit, and those with questionable copyright or licensing.

- **ETHICAL CONCERNS: Relationships with** donors and the community, as well as adherence to the institution's policy, and the profession's code of conduct, should weigh heavily on your decision.

- **PROMOTIONAL VALUE:** Placement in exhibits, which we discuss in the following chapter, may open the door to scanning projects.

- **POLITICS AND GRANTSMANSHIP:** You cannot ignore other practical concerns, like how digitization will affect your ability to secure funding and strengthen the repository in intangible ways.. For example, the "sexiest" items commonly attract the attention of individuals and organizations capable of funding exhibits. Since timing is crucial, instead of addressing the question of digitization of specific items immediately, you could delay conversion until you can implement a strategy to gain external support.

Selection guides.

Several online resources can help with your appraisal and selection:

- Harvard University set the early directions for academic libraries (http://preserve.harvard.edu/resources/digital.html).

- The joint RLG and NPO published its *Guidelines for Selecting Materials for Digitization* online (http//www.rlg.org/preserv/joint/ayris.html).

In her essay in the highly recommended *Handbook for Digital Projects*, published by the North East Documents Conservation Center (http//www.nedcc.org/digital/intro.htm), Diane Vogt-O'Connor adds group nominations and voting by the various stakeholders as a criterion. She prioritizes with an evaluation matrix, which employs a six-point scale to weigh value, risk, and patron use elements. Figure 6.2 expands on her ideas with a ten-point scale.

Fig. 6.2. Digitization Priority Matrix								
Rate each from lowest=1 to highest interest=10 points								
Collection Title	Overall value	Patron use	Physical Risk	Ownership	Ethics	Promotion value	Grants value	Total

Outsourcing.

With selections made and the appropriate financial resources in hand, you may wish to contract a vendor for digitization projects. Large-scale scanning projects especially lend themselves to outsourcing. To determine whether or not to outsource digitization projects, consider the following cost/benefit equation factors:

- **ON-SITE SPACE:** Do you have the room to set aside for a project?
- **OFF-SITE PROSPECTS:** Would it be economical to scan off-site, after you consider the extra dangers to materials and labor for transport?
- **STAFF FACTORS:** Does your staff have the abilities, training, and time to do the work? What work would they have to set aside to do this project?
- **EQUIPMENT CAPITAL:** How much will it cost to purchase and maintain the equipment? Will you have ongoing uses for this equipment after the project ends?
- **ECONOMIES OF SCALE:** Because of their equipment investments, trained staff, and experience, vendors may be able to offer attractive pricing (Some may negotiate lower prices for the publicity value of dealing with cultural materials or prestigious institutions.)
- **DELIVERABLES AND EVALUATION:** Add in your shipping and overhead expenses, as well as costs for a quality review of a representative sample.

Note: Contract issues and requests for proposals/information are discussed in chapter 7. OCLC provides a useful series of questionnaires for prospective clients on newspaper, printed book, manuscript, scrapbook, and photographic scanning projects (http://www.oclc.org/presres/scanning.htm).

PROCEDURES FOR DIGITIZING

Having established the framework for thinking and approaching digital imaging—Policy Development—we turn now to the procedures involved in creating digital images. This section concerns the physical methods for capturing images and converting to digital files for in-house and Web storage.

IMAGING PROJECTS

Imaging projects involve technical issues beyond the initial selection for digitization and in-house storage. You have to consider the prospects of conversions from image to text files; moreover, the Web demands a duplicate or mirror system of its own:

1. **IN-HOUSE:** Which analog originals are suitable for scanning and by what techniques?
    a. **IMAGE CAPTURE**—At what resolution and type of format do you scan; Do you compress or enhance the results?
    b. **OCR CONVERSION**—Do you convert the digital images of textual documents to searchable formats through OCR (optical character recognition) software?
2. **WEB PUBLICATION:** Which of the scanned images do you save and in what depth and formats for mounting on the Web?

SCANNING BASICS

The techniques for making digital facsimiles of documents, pictures, and artifacts begin in a very similar fashion to the photocopying of documents or taking photographs. The underlying capture and storage mechanisms, however, are far different and rapidly evolving. The professional will want to keep abreast of equipment options and aware of some of the subtleties of the processes.

Making digital facsimiles of documents, pictures, and artifacts equates to the measures for taking photographs or photocopying a document. The technological underpinnings and criteria, however, are more complex. The following treatment requires some basic knowledge of the mechanics and variables of digital conversion, which will inform your project management.

> **Reader's Advisory:** If you have minimal interests in technical details, you may want to skip ahead to "PDF Alternatives" or "Equipment Choices" sections that follow this more technical section.

Bitmap.

RASTERS

An alternative approach uses mathematical vectors to outline images.

Electronic scans act like a photograph, but without a physical negative. Instead of exposing silver salts to light, scanners employ light sensors to reproduce a "raster" of dots, recognizable by a computer. Individual dots or pictorial elements are called pixels. As illustrated by the "bitmap" in figure 6.3, the pixel charts the absence or presence of content across a defined grid. Note: Letters can be simulated by this technique, but are only pictures until converted into computer-readable text.

Fig. 6.3. Simple Bitmapped Pixel Display

	0	0	0	0	0	0	0	0	0	0	0	0	0
0	0	0	0	0	0								
	0	I	0	0	I	0	0	0	0	0	0	0	I
I	I	I	0	0	0								
	0	I	0	0	I	0	I	0	0	0	0	I	0
0	0	0	I	0	0								
	0	I	0	0	I	0	0	0	0	0	I	0	0
0	0	0	0	I	0								
	0	I	0	0	I	0	I	0	0	0	I	0	I
0	0	I	0	I	0								
	0	I	I	I	I	0	I	0	0	0	I	0	0

The text follows the tutorial of Anne Kenney, Cornell Library Dept. of Preservation and Conservation, *Digital Imaging Tutorial* (http://www.library.cornell.edu/preservation/tutorial/).

Resolution.

Resolution is the key measure of a digital image. "Optical resolution," based on the number of sensors available on the scanner, determines the depth of detail that can be achieved. The frequency of this sampling is expressed as the number of dots-per-inch (dpi) or pixels-per-inch (ppi). High resolution comes with a trade off: the greater the sensors the better the image; yet high resolution images require extra storage capacity and scanning time.

- **IN-HOUSE ARCHIVING:** You may choose to digitize a high percentage of your collection for documentation purposes and to create a "preservation" master. At one time, 300 dpi was considered reasonable for photographic image capture. The baseline figure went up to 600 dpi (or 360,000 dots in a square inch), which comports to the output of normal desktop printers. As "photographic quality" printers and more powerful digital cameras appear, the number continues to escalate—with figures now reaching to the 5,000 dpi range, especially for in-house documentation or archiving.

- **WEB MOUNTING:** Most images on the Web are set at 72 dpi—the rough limit for the older computer screens. This produces acceptable visual quality and ensures fast downloading. At the same time, 72 dpi images allow only limited protections against secondary use by others. For the Web, consider scanning at the lowest resolution for the quality that you desire. Higher resolution wastes space and slows the process, both for you and the person accessing the Web site. Posting small "thumbnail" images, which can come with the option of expansion, can circumvent this problem.

Pixel Dimensions.

To calculate the number of pixels, simply multiply the number of horizontal units by the number of vertical ones. In figure 6.3, the grid is 20 × 12 and contains 240 squares. Required storage space multiplies dramatically in an automation scenario—an 8 × 10 inch photograph, for example occupies the following number of pixels:

@ 72 dpi = 576 × 720 pixels (total = 414,720)
@ 300 dpi = 2400 × 3000 pixels (total = 7,200,000)
@ 600 dpi = 4800 × 6000 pixels (total = 28,800,000)

Bit Depth.

This measure determines the number of bits that define a pixel and the amount of tonal variation available. Look closely at figure 6.3, and you can see different gradations or tonal levels within the face cartoon. Not unlike the "Pointillism" of painter Georges Seurat, pixels are individual dots, but their grid can convey a deeper range of information—including color schemes. Computer screens and printers deliver images and characters in three forms:

- **BITONAL:** Black or white, 1-bit or simple off/on switches may be all that is needed to differentiate crisply printed letters.

- **GRAYSCALE:** Most documents and especially black and white photographs call for differentiating shades of black into gray tones. The computer world expresses these mathematically as exponents of 2; thus, 4-bit (2^4) produces up to 16 shades, and 8-bit (2^8), the default standard, can represent 256 shades (See: *.gif*).

- **COLOR:** Color employs techniques parallel to grayscale. Indeed, many monitors and images on the Web only display at the 8-bit depth. Effective documentation and representative facsimiles, however, call for higher resolution. For these purposes, you need to scan in "true color" 24-bit RGB (red, green, and blue tints at 2^{24}, or a potential 16,700,000 tones), which begins to approach the quality of a color photograph. Available bit depths of 30, 36, and higher, will produce more realistic images; although, they demand extra storage space and outstrip the capabilities of many current software programs and printers (See: *.jpeg*).

Dynamic Range.

Indirectly related to bit depth, and especially significant for reproducing the continuous flow of photographs, dynamic range reflects the range of light the CCD (Charge-Coupled Device: A type of solid-state sensor used in scanners that captures light reflected or transmitted by original) is able to measure. The scale ranges from 0.0 for perfect white to 4.0 for perfect black; 2.4 to 2.6 are normal for consumer electronics, but the higher the range, the better. For instance, high quality color flatbeds can approach 3.2, and some of the professional drum scanners used by color prepress companies may reach 3.8.

File Size.

Understanding potential storage and delivery requirements is crucial— especially when posting to the Web. Unlike textual records, the image file cannot be subdivided and reconstituted through smaller files. Instead, computers treat image files as whole data units. Hardware and software parameters determine file size: the number of pixels multiplied by the bit depth, divided by the size of the byte used by your computer (e.g., 8-bit, 16-bit, or 32-bit bytes). These numbers are calculated during capture, but compression methods can reduce file size, as well.

- **COMPRESSION.** Codecs (compression/decompression software routines) can greatly reduce the amount of storage required by files. Instead of recording every dot, the program uses mathematical formulas or algorithms to make inferences about data. It might note the start and stop of a string of similar pixels and record the range for fill. Archivists typically shy from such procedures and prefer exact descriptives. But compression programs are a necessary evil when porting to the Web. Without them, uploading and downloading times would become interminable. The next section discusses the main open formats for files.

File Formats.

As introduced in chapter 1, computer users can choose from literally dozens of image file formats. Recall, for example, the value of *.rtf* to manage both pictures and text. Open file format falls into two categories:

- **LOSSLESS:** do not discard information and are recommended for in-house storage/preservation purposes
- **LOSSY:** will use less space by dithering and educated inferences to fill in the dots and tonal qualities; normally employed for images on the Web

For Web applications, many sources limit the discussions to the most current versions of four formats:

- *.gif:* Developed by CompuServe in 1987, the Graphic Information File format is lossless. GIF was the first effective image format for the Web and remains prominent for graphics and black and white images. It uses a bit depth of 8 for 256 possible colors and a LZW (Lempel-Ziv-Welch) compression scheme, which can reduce file size by 5:1.

- *.tiff:* Tagged Image/Interchange File format serves as the standard file-storage format for archival storage. Still images stored as TIFF files can be either compressed or uncompressed. Compressed TIFF files are usually Group IV compressed, a lossless compression that allows all compressed information to be retrieved upon opening the image.

- *.jpeg:* Originally developed by the Joint Photographic Experts Group, ISO "standardized" the format in 1990. JPEGs are the standard for photographs and color representations on the Web. They are lossy with the theoretical capability to reduce by 100:1, but with a practical rate of perhaps 20:1. To compress an image the algorithm divides the picture into tiny pixel blocks, which are halved over and over until the maximum or desired ratio is achieved.

- *.png:* Developed by Microsoft, PNG has the functional strengths of both *.gif* and *.jpeg*. Despite evident strengths, the marketplace has not embraced this format; therefore, we do not include it in the rest of our treatments.

PDF ALTERNATIVES

Chapter 2 introduced PDF as one option for the delivery of text and images. PDF files are either "interpreted" with searchable text or "uninterpreted" photographic images without ASCII/Unicode conversion. Though larger in size when it comes to the storage space they require, uninterpreted PDF files still may be more manageable than *.tiff* or *.jpeg* files. Typical PDF documents are subdivided into compact sequences of page images. The format divides between content and a distinct data record, which contains of metadata to redraw each page and can generate structured tables of contents.

The Adobe company has consistently upgraded the functionality of the PDF format, which now allows hypertext and interactive forms, and has an accessibility patch. It can incorporate Java or other scripting code for dynamic displays and was recently extended for XML and RTF export. Uninterpreted files can be layered with searchable text. PDF also offers notable strengths for security and authenticating documents, including 128-bit encryption, password controls and options to prevent printing.

PDF BACKGROUND

Adobe first issued this "universal document format" in 1993. PDF began as an offshoot of its industry-standard Postscript commands for printing graphics. At the time, this format revolutionized file access and sharing, because it bridged the chasm between operating systems, with its platform-independent, page-description language (http://partners.adobe.com/asn/developer/technotes/acrobatpdf.html). Adobe also opened PDF to third party development—most notably Google, which created Web tools to search PDF text and images. PDF is also available through other platforms, including OCR and digital copier outputs. More importantly, the U.S. government uses it as a standard for distributing official publications, and efforts are under way for a PDF(a) with long-term preservation intent (http://www.aiim.org). Such a development helps to guarantee PDF's viability and future migration Also see PlanetPDF (http://www.planetpdf.com) and PDF Zone (http://www.pdfzone. com>).

Implementation.

You can import almost any kind of electronic document into Adobe Acrobat, or through compatible programs like WordPerfect. The process follows the pattern for the retrospective conversion of Finding Aids in chapter 2. Minor differences in how PDF renders Web page titles—PDF files default to the original file name—may necessitate a change.

Figure 6.4 illustrates the opening "GENERAL" tab for WordPerfect's *File/Publish to PDF...* option. I advise selecting the most recent version of Acrobat, then enter the author's name, consider keyword entries, and choose "PDF for the Web" as the style.

Note: Because each tab has choices that need to be engaged, you will need to click through all the tabs.

- **OBJECTS:** Select compression type JPEG; quality factors run from 2 to 225 (pick the middle of the range).
- **DOCUMENTS:** Click to include hyperlinks and bookmarks.
- **ADVANCED:** Select "Optimize for the Web"; for the color options, choose either "RGB" or grayscale (for the smallest file).
- CLICK OK to make the conversion.

EQUIPMENT CHOICES

Equipment itself is evolving rapidly and becoming easier to use and ever less expensive. Given volatile pricing and rapidly changing technologies, we will avoid product recommendations in deference to a broad overview of current equipment choices:

Fig. 6.4. Simulated Word Perfect PDF Entry screen

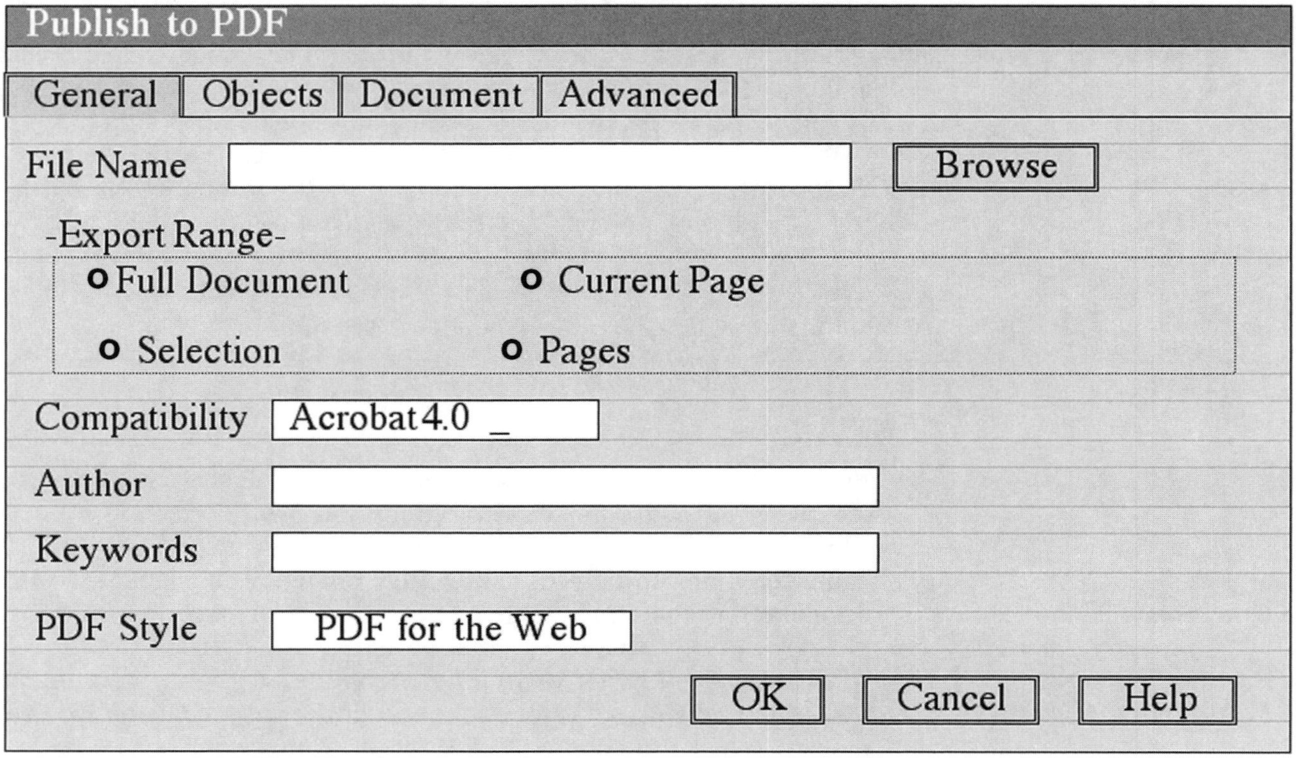

Publish to PDF

| General | Objects | Document | Advanced |

File Name [   ] [Browse]

-Export Range-

  o Full Document   o Current Page

  o Selection   o Pages

Compatibility [Acrobat 4.0 _]

Author   [   ]

Keywords   [   ]

PDF Style   [PDF for the Web   ]

[OK] [Cancel] [Help]

Hardware.

Technology may evolve faster than our ability to purchase, install, and use it. However, certain tendencies in hardware and software are still operable:

- **DESKTOP SCANNERS:** The earliest technology—and a mainstay for digital conversion—is the flatbed scanner. Expensive production models are available, but affordable consumer–grade models perform quite well. An attractive alternative for institutions with limited space and resources is a multipurpose machine, capable of scanning, copying, printing, and faxing, for instance.. The best advice at the moment is twofold:
  - Select a high-level, flatbed color scanner for photographic, pictorial, or graphic images.

- Conversion of the alphabetic and numerical information within such pictures calls for an Optical Character Recognition (OCR) stage. The scanner can be a lower-level machine, but you might consider a sheet-feeder model for mass production.
- **DIGITAL CAMERAS:** A digital camera allows you to capture digital images of artifacts and documents that will not fit on the scanner's screen. Also, digital cameras can capture moving images and sound, but are not appropriate for OCR conversion.
- **DIGITAL COPIERS:** By the early twenty-first century, manufacturers abandoned analog photocopying in favor of digital scanning. Anything photocopied in the past, where the process reproduced the image but captured no data, will hereafter be digitized. The equipment can include hopper feeders for high quantity production, special handling for fragile materials, and adaptation features for microfilm products. These newest options make digitization all but inevitable and demand concomitant policy development.

BEWARE INTERPOLATED RESOLUTION

Some manufacturers advertise the amount of pixels that their machines or software products can mathematically interpolate. They may claim to enhance an original 300×300 dpi scan into a 600×600 dpi. Interpolation allows for "guessing" at the light readings that would have been sampled and inserting new pixels between the old ones. While you may wish to use the technique for display purposes, it has no place in a documentation strategy.

Software.

The digital outputs and software supplied by the scanner or camera will often suffice, but if you do anything outside the default parameters of the equipment, it may be worthwhile to consider image editing software. Production of JPEGs and PDFs may require it, and without it, tinkering with the picture and adding copyright and metadata is virtually impossible.

- Macintosh's built-in iPhoto, Jasc's AfterShot, and Microsoft's Picture It Platinum fill the bill as inexpensive photo editors.

- For full power, consider a complete "freehand painting studio." Adobe's Photoshop (http://www.adobe.com) is the de facto standard, but comes with a higher price tag and significant learning curve.
- Adobe also offers a less expensive and relatively easy to use Photoshop subset called Elements. Unless you are a detailed artist, this product (version 2.0+) should work for most digital archives. It allows for easy:
  - correction of machine-supplied file tiles (e.g., img-0067.jpg) with understandable terms;
  - changing of formats and reducing of image storage size;
  - batch processing to automatically make transformations in all photos in a file;
  - insertion of the repository's name and copy right © symbol to declare ownership, accomplished with Photoshop's layers capacity, which virtually stacks transparent sheets with embedded information on top of the image

PROJECT STRATEGIES

As suggested, the physical process of digitizing is straightforward and is now typically a turnkey operation.

PROJECT-SIZE CAUTIONS

While technological advances in equipment and user familiarity with procedures have simplified digitizing, the size of the undertaking and amount of staff resources involved have not lessened. A testbed to capture and index one hundred images is far from the processing of 100,000 images. Sun Microsystems' (http://www.sun.com) *Digital Library Toolkit* (2000) thus is careful to warn that *"many digital library projects have floundered"*:

Digitizing and converting the images to information are very difficult exercises. The computer hardware and, particularly, software which perform these functions are good and practical, but less than perfect...

All of this means that the process which seems so swift and painless in the salesman's hands with standard texts and simple requirements, may become a painfully expensive reality. This is particularly true if the material is old, in mixed languages, faded, or just voluminous...

Even once digitized, the problems may not be over. Searching and finding digital materials is often still a hit and miss affair for digital material... (p. 17)

ESTABLISHING POLICIES AND TECHNIQUES FOR DIGITAL IMAGING   **141**

Naming Controls.

Digitization projects begin from the same naming conventions that were introduced in the chapter 1. Naming includes the following:

- **FILE NAMES:** Continue to favor natural language and mnemonic devices; however, you will need to use codes for large collections:
    - **COLLECTION ID #:** Start the image file name with the collection identification number. This use retains provenance and builds continuities among your resources.
    - **DESCRIPTIVE TERM:** The name of the person or group in the photograph. The sheer number of photographs may demand coding—e.g., the sequential frame numbers supplied by digital cameras and copiers.
    - **YEAR CODE:** Time is crucial for retrieval, but frequently overlooked.
        EXAMPLE: You can use underlines and dashes to assist with readability: e.g., 694-chicagotrip-1987.jpeg; 249_image#46-1998.jpeg.

- **OPEN STORAGE FORMATS**
    - **TIFF :** for in-house archival storage (600 dpi, 24-color RGB files)
    - **JPEG:** for photographs and color images on the Web (72 dpi)
    - **GIF:** option for drawings and small images on the Web (72 dpi)
    - **PDF:** for preserving text with embedded images and security purposes (Web-enhanced, JPEG output at 50 percent quality)

- **DISTINCT DIRECTORIES:** Directories should reflect the functional hierarchies within the in-house working area and with selected mirrored entries for the Web server. To keep it simple, the normal redress is to name the image directory /image/ or /img/. If using PDFs, you may wish to have those in a separate directory. Figure 6.5 extrapolates a revised layout from the model in chapter 3.

Fig. 6.5. Directory Structures with Image Files

<u>LAN/Computer</u>	<u>Web Directory</u>
../holdings/	*.../holdings/*
holdings/done/	*/holdings/images/*
holdings/images/	*186-family-1987.jpeg*
holdings/old/	*186-johnjones-1956.jpeg*
holdings/pdf/	*423-picnic-1967.jpeg*
holdings/tool_box/	*/holdings/pdf/*
holdings/webmount/	*045-image#1.pdf*
holdings/working/	*045-image#2.pdf*

The Pilot.

As a reminder, any initiative calls for a pilot phase. In keeping with the methods described in earlier chapters, you need to select a reasonable subset for digitizing, write out clear instructions, evaluate the quality of the images and plan of work, and redesign if necessary.

- *Queuing.* Finding Aids, books, scrapbooks, and microfilm come with an inherent order and often a unity of image size. The production queue is thus rather straightforward. Manuscripts, artifacts, and loose photographs demand more organization and thought:

  - Preserve the provenance through naming and document the "original order" of the items. The arrangement and placement or order of images conveys information that can easily disappear.

  - Photographs may come with sleeves or enclosures that have information inscribed and writing on the back (verso). Negatives can have selvage entries around their sides. You will need to consider whether to scan and/or enter this data as text.

  - Artifacts require multiple images to capture their entirety and suggest the inclusion of a ruler and perhaps a color chart for documentation purposes.

  - Production rules of thumb and preservation guidelines suggest you should:

- keep like medium together (e.g., prints separate from negatives);
- treat like sizes together;
- record sizes and types of image storage—negative, albumen print, glass plate, 35 mm slide, etc.

- *Project Controls.* Oversight requires documentation, which should, in turn, inform description. You can employ a DBMS for tracking or project management software. The Scanning Project Log in figure 6.6 is a simpler alternative. It can act as a running inventory to show relationships (If configured in a landscape mode, the document could be expanded to include genre and size information.).

Fig. 6.6. Scanning Project Log

			Outputs			Scan-log.03.1yr
Coll ID #	Image title	File Name	.tiff	.jpeg	.pdf	Date/Staff

- *Web Mounting.* HTML manages pictures as addendums through a process called "imbedding." In a manner similar to making hypertext links to external sites, the program imbeds a reference to resources outside the HTML document. For instance, *<img src="images/doree.jpg">* tells the browser to retrieve and insert a photograph of Mr. Doree—e.g., to add an image to the Finding Aid in figure 2.2. Let us break down coding by way of explanation:
  - *img* (image) tag signals an image

- *src* (source) attribute opens to the location of the picture file to be displayed
- ="**address**" is the path and can be either absolute or relative

    ABSOLUTE: An absolute path relies on the *http* protocol and IP addressing with the complete Web address of the image file—*<img src="http://repository/images/doree .jpg">*. Because this approach takes extra time for loading, normally you avoid this approach, unless you are linking to an external source for the images—e.g., a photo sharing site.

    RELATIVE: A relative path specifies an internal path within the site— *<img src="images/doree.jpg">* where the computer would go to a subdirectory within the document's file. Most image groupings, however, are in parallel directories. The address will need to refer up to its level—*<img src="../images/doree.jpg">*.

    Note: If the routing is off, Netscape issues a "broken image" icon and Explorer a little square with an X in it.

- *Evaluation.* Although technical measures are available, your eyes produce the best quality checks. Begin the project with close inspection, and once the set-up is functioning, you are advised to continue sampling the output.

    Managers must consider the actual costs of image conversion, which may be shockingly high. In a 1999 article in RLG *DigiNews,* Steve Puglia uncovered a range of from $1.85 to $42.25 per image with an average cost of $17.65. His figures broke the costs roughly into thirds among physical conversion, cataloging/metadata, and administration/quality controls.

METADATA CONCERNS

A picture is worth a thousand words—and therein lies the rub. How can we successfully index and retrieve images? The answers are not fully in place, but will come from a combination of sources. Metadata standards are emerging—e.g., NISO's Z39.87–2002 *Technical Metadata for Digital Still Images* is under review until the end of 2003 (http://www.niso.org/committees/committee_au.html). As discussed in chapter 7, you will have to decide the degree to which you will apply these standards. Fortunately, digital hardware and software products make it possible to insert many of the key tags automatically. Computer science is contributing promising work on shape analysis that may eventually become practical—e.g., Carnegie-Mellon's Informedia Terabyte project (http://www. informedia.cs.cmu.edu).

OCR OPTIONS.

Optical Character Recognition (OCR) systems extract the images of letters and numbers from digitally scanned pictures and convert them into computer-recognizable codes—e.g., ASCII or Unicode. With OCR, what started as image management moves into document or even knowledge management.

High-end OCR packages are available for large-scale production. These are beyond the scope of an introductory text. Most institutions can rely on serviceable consumer options. Such software often comes bundled with the scanner—or can be inexpensively purchased on the side. The products make OCR projects easier to implement. You either import scanned *.tiff* files, or the program can take control of the scanner for input. The software guides you through a series of steps (or, increasingly, one step) to produce a text file. The converted material is then proofed and installed in the regular text production line—no different than its born-digital compatriots.

OCR BACKGROUND

OCR programs began with GIZMO in 1951. By 1954, a prototype machine was capable of reading one character per minute of upper case letters. IBM speeded development with the first commercially viable product in 1959. This "task-specific reader" could interpret one font in one size and was used to process mortgage loan applications. It set the stage for other "template matchers," which compare only to specially selected fonts and set sizes. By 1966, additional accuracy was ensured with the codification OCR-A (American, ANSI X3.17–81) and OCR-B (European, ANSI X3.49–75) fonts.

Kuzweil Computer Products produced the conceptual breakdown for flexible "general-purpose readers" in 1978. It used a learning system with "rule-based" approaches to break characters into lines and curves, which could be expanded or contracted to deal with different font sizes and shapes. Eight years later, Calera Recognition Systems turned to neural networks with self-learning algorithms drawn from thousands of samples. By the 1990s, Calera, Caere, and others were adding contextual intelligence, language analysis, artificial neural networks, and the inference projections of Bayesian mathematics into the mix. Modern programs poll and weigh the interpretations from a number of expert engines before issuing their most likely selections.

Fig. 6.7. OCR Hints

The following recommendations are based on trial-and-error experiences with Caere's OmniPagePro, which is touted as the best of the consumer-level OCR programs.

- OCR works best with very clear copies—avoid fuzzy or smudged documents.
- It is most accurate with mono- or typewriter-spaced fonts like Courier and the standard Times-Roman.
- The recognition of non-Western (non-Roman) type scripts and mathematical symbols is not as developed.
- Scans at 300 dpi seem reasonably appropriate for the normal font size of 11 (this text is in 11 point font) or 12 points and higher. Smaller sizes call for a higher scanning rate and produce higher error rates.
- Typewritten copies often come with errors and corrections that humans can barely perceive, but emerge to wreak havoc with the conversion. You may be better off photocopying originals for the scanner.
- A single column of narrative is preferred. Tables and most document formatting are lost to most scanning programs. (Note: the software will occasionally see entries as text blocks. Unless that structure is turned off, it will strive to preserve the original integrity and make editing impossible).
- Take special steps to try to record handwritten notes and marginalia.
- Run post-production spell checking.
- This still requires manual proofreading—pay special attention to personal names, foreign language terms, mathematical symbols and any typical problem areas with the software—e.g., "n" rendered as "ri."

See also: Center of Excellence for Document Analysis and Recognition, SUNY, Buffalo (http://www.cedar.buffalo.edu/Publications/TechReps/OCR/overview.gif)

OCR Cautions.

Despite the advances and product hype, OCR is still an imperfect technology. As indicated in figure 6.7, errors will occur and may take a good deal of time to correct. In some instances, it is still better to rekey the text. It takes 5–7 times more effort for OCR than initial scanning.

MEDIA LAGNIAPPE

Lagniappe means "a little bit extra"—such as the following introduction to the conversion of audio and videotapes.

Print, Videotape, and Audiotape.

Media remains a secondary consideration for most repositories. They remain rooted in two-dimensional documents and images. Yet the future of the Web will be increasingly enlivened by audio and video presentations. Audiotapes and videotapes also appear as parts of many modern manuscript collections. And repositories are proactively engaging oral/video histories to flesh out their holdings.

SIMILARITIES. Media additions are, in fact, an extension of your experiences with print conversions:

- Project methodology continues to draw on the systems analysis and naming conventions that we have been using.

- HTML encoding uses a similar type of referential "imbedding" to retrieve the media; moreover, the equipment is getting ever easier to use.

- With a few exceptions, policy questions remain the same, but privacy rights may escalate—especially if the creator or per former is a recognized artist.

DIFFERENCES. But, print and non-print media are not identical. From an audio and video perspective, the differences include the following:

- Standards are more complex and not clearly established for multimedia presentations.

- Storage requirements dwarf those of text and images and also make extensive delivery through the Web problematic.

VoIP AND THE THIRD-GENERATION WEB

Voice recognition and Voice over IP (VoIP) are making significant advances for data entry and navigation on the Web. They promise to be the next major breakthrough for Web services—a third-generation Web. In early 2002, IBM announced a related eight-year Super Human Speech Recognition Initiative. The goal is for machines to interact seamlessly with people. The implementations would communicate and automatically take dictation and transcribe anything from customer service calls, telematics (wireless access for directions, news updates, e-mail), and voice mail, to multi-person oral history interviews and meetings. They would engage dynamic language translation that has been the stuff of science fiction. The technology draws on W3C's *XHTML+VoiceXML open system, artificial intelligence for content analysis, and the intriguing addition of visual assistance from lip-reading programs.

*SALT—Speech Application Language Tags—is the competing "open industry" initiative (http://www.saltforum.org).

The Colorado Digital Project *Digital Audio Guidelines* is an excellent introduction to audio projects (http://coloradodigital.coalliance.org/ digaudio.html.

TECHNICAL CONSIDERATINS.

Media digitization differs slightly from image conversion. Instead of converting visual content, devices convert mechanical waves interpreted by one type of machine into digital signals for another machine. There are additional technical factors to take into account:

- **SAMPLING RATE:** Kilohertz (kHz) reflect the number of times the amplitude of the wave is sampled per second. In-house preservation storage runs to 96 and 192 Khz. For Web purposes, use the CD base with a codecs at 44.1 Khz (i.e., 44,100 digital samples per second).

- **BIT DEPTH:** The breadth of the sampling rate is determined by the size of the storage byte: an 8-bit sample allows up to 255 measures, a 16-bit ranges to 65,535, and a 24-bit tops out at 16,777,215. For the spoken word on the Web, an 8-bit sample is sufficient, but many prefer to default to the CD's music-oriented 16-bit depth.

- **VIDEO IMAGES:** Video adds bit-depth considerations for black and white v. color and color depth; number of frames to refresh per second; and frame size/orientation.

- **STORAGE FORMATS:** Media formats are not as standardized for browser interpretation as those for print and images. You may need to consider offering a variety of formats—in particular:
  - **AUDIO:** Microsoft/IBM's Wave (*.wav* and *.wave*); Mp3 (MPEG-1, layer III, *.mp3*); Apple's Audio Interchange File Format (*.aif, .aiff*)
  - **VIDEO:** *.avi, .mov.*

- **WEB VIEWING:** Access through the Web has two options:
  - **DOWNLOADING,** in which the Web site acts as a transfer station for an entire file to the receiving computing and viewing is done offline—e.g., Mp3 for audio downloads
  - **STREAMING,** which decompresses packets for real-time viewing through specialized software—e.g., Real Media (http://www.real.com), Windows Media (http://www.

microsoft.com), and Apple QuickTime (http://www.apple.com), which is my recommendation and the basis for the MPEG-4 combined video/audio standard.

IMPLEMENTATION

The best advice for those considering media applications is to begin with digital recorders and avoid the analog step. You can easily record a minute of audio through the recording programs in Macintosh and Windows machines.

Working with media is truly an art form and will consume an immense amount of time to master—especially for competent editing. Yet the initial conversion of audio or videotapes is a relatively simple, albeit time-consuming process. Macintoshes and newer PCs come with the appropriate sound and video cards and input jacks.

In-House-Capture.

The first stage is the creation of the digital archival master. This involves importing an analog signal from a camcorder or videocassette recorder into the computer and digitizing it. You can use the programs built into Macintosh's OS X operating system or something like Adobe Premiere, which is described in the following steps.

1. Attach the cables from the input device to the computer and turn on both machines.
2. Launch Adobe Premiere or a similar program.
3. Load video—e.g., in *New Projects Settings* window, click *load/Regular Video/OK*.
4. Capture—e.g., *File/Capture.../Movie Capture....* A small "Movie Capture" window will appear.
5. Cue the input device. Start the play button. Starting images will be displayed, but you can also fast forward or rewind to select a smaller portion of the file.
6. Record—hit the *Record* button. Action takes place in the background in most PCs, or with flickering images in the Mac.
7. Name and *Save As*—be sure that you have a good deal of disk space available, or burn the results on a CD or DVD.

Web-Compression.

Few repositories can consider the online storage and delivery of complete audio and video files. Instead, the Web component is relegated to short "teasers" or clips, which demonstrate what is available for research and enhanced display. The second stage is thus shrinking the size for Web delivery or user copies. It involves a codec (compression/decompression algorithm) program, like those in Media Cleaner Pro or QuickTime, and conversion to Web-readable format.

1. Launch the program and open the digital video file.
2. Set Settings for either:
   a. Download—click CD-ROM in the dialogue box, use Continue to page through the screens and select the outputs: CD-ROM, High-End and Mid-Range, 8x or faster, QuickTime/Real Video/MS Media, Audio and Video Equally Important, Balanced Motion and Quality, Higher Quality, Normalize… Finish
   b. Web page—click WWW in the dialogue box and follow as above e.g., QuickTime/Real Video/MS Video, Progressive Download, High-Quality Image, Normalize Audio, Finish
3. Save (you have a renaming option—consider a "-user" designation to distinguish the user from the master copy;)—when finished, the program indicates "Compression completed"

MULTIMEDIA STANDARDS: MPEG AND SMIL

Two budding standards have surfaced for coordinating multimedia efforts. MPEG, the Moving Picture Experts Group (http://mpeg.telecomitalialab.com), works under ISO's umbrella. Its MPEG-21 is being proposed for overall interoperability among all types of media. The group is also responsible for the landmark MPEG-1, which produced CD standards and the Mp3 music download approach, along with the MPEG-4 controls for DVD encoding; MPEG-7 is being offered to standardize content description for media. SMIL (Synchronized Multimedia Integrated Language, pronounced "smile") is W3C's alternate open coding language for the coordination of multimedia presentations (www.w3c.org/TR/REC-smil). The first version appeared in 1998 with an HTML-like orientation. In August of 2001, SMIL 2.0 came forward as an XML DTD. Explorer 5.5+, QuickTime, and RealAudio multimedia browsers are already configured for it.

7 CREATING THE WEB SITE AND DISPLAY OPTIONS

Site Overview
• Web site guidance

Gateway
• Home page functions
• Digital access links
• Site search engine

Descriptive Strata
• Considering Finding Aids
• Pathfinders

Display Strata
• Online exhibits
• K-12 Document Packets
• Courseware

Resource Strata

Outsourcing
• RFI/RFP
• Contracts

This chapter begins to put together the pieces for the Web site. It offers general guidance and rules along with a multi-level image of Web digital archives. The text concentrates on a potpourri of emerging descriptive devices and displays for the medium—creations that hold the promise of redefining the roles of information professionals. It closes with a briefing on outsourcing alternatives.

SITE OVERVIEW

In the following top-down model, Web digital archives are cloudlike, open systems, designed to engage readily with external sites and search engines. Internal structures are expandable and permeable with access and navigation flowing down, up, and among the discrete parts:

- a formal gateway or entrance
- automated access through internal search engines
- descriptive strata of formal and informal tools
- display strata, including exhibits and educational packets
- resource strata holding the digital assets

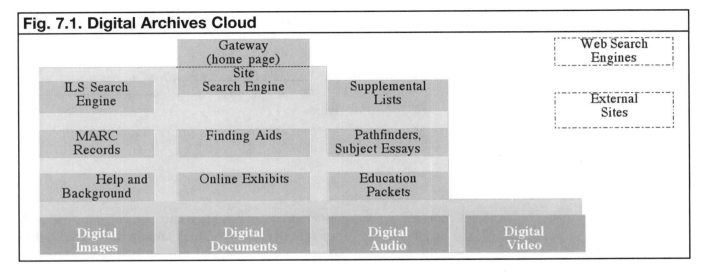

Fig. 7.1. Digital Archives Cloud

Gateway (home page)

Web Search Engines

ILS Search Engine

Site Search Engine

Supplemental Lists

External Sites

MARC Records

Finding Aids

Pathfinders, Subject Essays

Help and Background

Online Exhibits

Education Packets

Digital Images

Digital Documents

Digital Audio

Digital Video

WEB SITE GUIDANCE

Sophisticated institutional Web sites demand technical and aesthetic expertise beyond the approaches in this text. As mentioned in chapter 3, innumerable resources and experts are available to help with the task. The repository may outsource and/or develop its own staff expertise. It should not casually choose to utilize in-house staff, because it appears to save money; this course of action calls for Web editing software along with time, training, and perhaps extra staffing.

> **Note:** Trade-offs and scheduling requirements should be clear—part-time Web masters are too often overwhelmed by extra duties.

Whichever option it selects, management remains ultimately responsible for the look and utility of its site. Those in charge should understand that there are no perfect answers, since Web sites are always an evolving work in progress. The importance of simplicity and design for audiences will remain, as will concentration on effective navigation, naming conventions, and, above all, content. Any repository considering building a Web site must examine closely three elements in particular:

1. Universal Access Guidelines (UAG).

W3C recognizes that the Web should be a leveler for those with physical challenges. To Tim Berners-Lee, *"The power of the Web is in its universality. Access by everyone regardless of disability is an essential aspect."* Accessibility is one of W3C's three official goals, along with creating a semantic network and ensuring a "Web of trust.".

W3C's Web Accessibility Initiative responded with the *Web Content Accessibility Guidelines 1.0* (http://www.w3.org/TR/WAI-WEBCONTENT). It lists two unifying themes and, as seen in figure 7.2, fourteen rules:

The U.S. government adopted UAG in 2000.

> A. *ensuring the "graceful transformations" of displays on the Web for all people–regardless of physical abilities* (Rules 1–11)
> B. *making sure that the content is understandable and navigable* (Rules 12–14)

Easing Compliance.

Do not worry. Compliance does not have to be arduous or interfere with the beauty of the site. Some of the UAG rules anticipate future "transformational" technologies that are beyond our scope. Most sites can meet the demands or be easily retrofitted through such simple and appropriate steps as:

- having a linear site map available as one of the first links on the site;
- providing a no-frames option if you use frames;
- relying on clear textual descriptions; and
- using the "alt" attribute for image description.

UGA COMPLIANCE CHECKING

The WAI site includes a complete compliance checklist at (http://www.w3.org/WCAGID/full-checklist.html). You can get a quick check by running the site through the "Ask Bobby" analyzer (http://www.cast.org/bobby).

Fig. 7.2. UGA rules

1. Provide equivalent alternatives to auditory and visual content.
2. Don't rely on color alone.
3. Use markup and style sheets, and do so properly.
4. Clarify natural language usage.
5. Create tables that transform gracefully.
6. Ensure that pages featuring new technologies transform gracefully.
7. Ensure user control of time-sensitive content changes.
8. Ensure direct accessibility of embedded user interfaces.
9. Design for device-independence.
10. Use interim solutions (until user agent/assistive methods are ready).
11. Use W3C technologies and guidelines.
12. Provide context and orientation information.
13. Provide clear navigation mechanisms.
14. Ensure that documents are clear and simple.

---

2. Narrative Style.

Like any new technology, the Web changes the nature of writing. The limited viewing area and nature of the computer screen emphasize the importance of tight imagery. Reading is often in a staccato fashion and not the leisurely linear unfolding of a book or article. The reader expects to scan the page for key topics quickly and to wander in and out of a text through hyperlinks. Figure 7.3 contains practical suggestions for your Web compositions.

Fig. 7.3. Guidelines for Writing on the Web

1. Write in a visual style to facilitate scanning, but with UAG additions in mind
    a. Rely on frequent headings to make transitions and organize for the reader.
    b. Write in a terse style with short sentences and paragraphs.
    c. Use bulleted and numbered lists whenever possible.
    d. Consider enhancing content with images and perhaps media components.
    e. Ponder shading, color, and icons for aesthetics and to assist with scrolling and identifying locations (but ensure textual backup for UAG compliance).

2. Think about writing in hypertext
    a. Regularly build an interactive table of contents to the headings in the pages.
    b. Make logical connections for your readers with frequent links to related materials outside the page.
    c. Replace or augment end and footnotes with interactive references.

3. Differentiate between pages containing fixed narratives and those that are designed to be updated

4. Provide consistent identification for each page, including titles and dates

5. Consider delivery in PDF if you want to maintain print or typewriter style

---

3. Web Search Engines

Those looking to attract a public audience and naïve researchers (i.e., those who do not already know about your resources) must plan for Web search engines. Figure 7.4 provides hints to heighten the site's virtual visibility. For additional information, check Search Engines Showdown (http://www.searchengineshowdown.com/) and, especially, Danny Sullivan's Search Engine Watch (http://searchenginewatch.internet.com/).

Fig. 7.4. Tuning for Web Search Engines

• Enter a clear and concise official name for Title metadata.

• List your site with the Open Directory Project (dmoz.org). This volunteer-built guide to Web sites is actively referenced by the main Web-crawlers.

    • You are asked to select an appropriate categorization from the site's subject tree—the initial selection tool for many search engines. Most readers will begin with the main **Reference** category and add either the **Libraries** or **Museums** subcategory, plus a selection from the next level.

    • Complete the entry form:

Fig. 7.4. (cont.)

- Title of Site—your official title without promotional language; avoid the use of ALL CAPITAL letters
- Site Description—roughly twenty-five words in complete and clearly written sentences without HTML tags (See: Description metadata, below)
- E-mail address option
- Wait several weeks to see if you have been accepted. You can resubmit and also challenge rewording from the ODP editor.

- List your site with the individual search engines (group submission services may encounter problems). Most sites have "ADD URL" areas, which include methods for both free listings and paid entries. Have your Open Directory site description and categories in hand.

- Build relationships with other sites to ensure cross-listings.

- Add hyperlinks from the home page to relevant pages inside; repeat at the bottom of the page.

- Construct Keyword entries *<meta name="keyword" content= "list terms">*.
  - Remember that content for retrieval rests in the HTML tags, not image files or metadata.
  - Use "target phrases" of two or more words that reflect the main content and themes.
  - Place target phrases in the page title and internal headlines.
  - Check for frequency and placement of keywords. Engines often use a location/frequency method. They may analyze how often the keyword appears in relation to other words on the page

- Add Description metadata (a one sentence summary—180 character limit) *<meta name="description" contents="summary sentence">*.

- Add other metadata as you see fit.

GATEWAY

Digital archives require a formal entrance way. The goal is transparent navigation for first time users, but in a relatively fixed layout that becomes familiar to returning visitors. You also must consider the overall site's intended message, functions, language/terminology, and, especially, the audiences and type of information that they seek.

Some digital archives will have a dedicated interface, but many will be integrated with the repository's home page. As discussed below, this combination calls for careful analysis and will lead to individual solutions (see figure 7.5 for one example).

HOMEPAGE FUNCTIONS

The home page acts as a general-purpose introduction center. It serves several functions.

- **IDENTIFICATION AND BRANDING:** The first duty is to identify the site, its purposes, and your institutional "brand" as a trusted resource. The Web lacks quality controls and has many suspect authorities. Visitors should be assured that they are encountering an established cultural repository. They also expect to determine the "where" of your location and to encounter such information as the:
    - institution's name;
    - street address, phone number, and e-mail address;
    - hours of operation, visitor procedures, and policies; and
    - contact and directional information.
- **NAVIGATION:** The second role is to act as a virtual traffic cop—to route visitors efficiently to the information (the "who," "what," and "when") that they seek elsewhere on the site. Features may vary, but tend to include such links as:
    - calendar or events list (museums often add a focus area with extra detail on current exhibits);
    - staff listings/contacts along with the identification of board members and, perhaps, volunteers;
    - development/marketing to support the institution;
    - site map, especially for complex sites and UAG compliance; and
    - links to your digital resources and services links—the main object for most visitors and often clustered together.

- **POLICIES:** Current recommendations and legal considerations warrant posting policies for easy retrieval—e.g., on the opening page or through a navigation link off that page. Two statements are particularly crucial.

  - **COPYRIGHT:** You should prominently promulgate your adherence to copyright principles and access rights through Fair Use, and note the users' responsibilities:

    This site adheres to Copyright: Title 17 US Code. Materials are made available under its Fair Use Clause (Section 108). Their placement in no way transfers rights for reuse. Users must seek any releases on their own. The repository cannot guarantee the validity of information found through links off of this site.

  - **PRIVACY:** These statements are growing in importance:

    This site may collect information on use patterns, but does not retain personally identifi able data without the express permission of its users.

NARRATIVE INTRODUCTION

During the first years of the Web, many sites featured a written rationale and/or overview of the site and the institution's mission on the home page. This element remains, but often appears to be relegated to a separate page.

DIGITAL ACCESS LINKS

Although branding and promotion are important, do not lose sight of the users' desires. They want to be able to quickly mine the data or find entertainment on the site. Hence, be careful not to slow them down with overly detailed hierarchies and multiple steps for retrieval. The rule of thumb is to get to content within three or four clicks of entry into the site. For cultural repositories, such access starts with links to professional descriptions and exhibits, as listed below:

- library catalog
- collection or registrar's lists: e.g., Web Finding Aids and print copies
- pathfinders and subject essays
- online displays
- teaching packets

EXTERNAL PORTAL

Specialized collections have a general responsibility to their field of concentration. They should consider maintaining a portal to related resources—or providing a link to such information from a partner institution. Another option is joining or forming a Web ring—a Web software approach for voluntarily linking together a community of comparable sites (http://www.webring.com). **Note:** The exchange of links provides improved visibility for search engine ranking.

SITE SEARCH ENGINE

In theory, the well-structured site provides the best methods for systematically identifying and retrieving information. In reality, Web users want search engines for their explorations. Web digital archives necessitate a site search engine to accommodate user queries.

We can expect a growth of professional interest in search engines and related indexing/harvesting programs. Such instruments can provide valuable usage data to help fine tune operations. Repositories will need to be able to evaluate retrieval performance and to compare various software products for selection. At the moment, information remains sparse. We do not have clear metrics, and most products closely guard their methodologies.

HTML products are becoming more efficient knowledge managers—albeit with a minimal amount of metadata (title, keyword, and description tags). W3C and commercial interests are also pushing forward on the XML front with XML Query Engine (http://www.w3.org/XML/Query).

The Web team at the University of Pennsylvania offers an excellent project guide for search engine selection (http://www.upenn.edu/computing/web/webteam/rnd/search.html). SearchTools (http://www.searchtools.com) provides a solid resource to begin the data gathering. It lists some 240 search engines, which range in cost from free to hundreds of thousands of dollars. You should carefully investigate two types of services:

- **REMOTE SERVICES:** These are remarkably easy to install and may involve mere contact or cutting and pasting a few lines of java script. Once the program is in place, the service provider periodically comes through the site with its spiders to gather data and index. The drawback to many of the free products is that they require you to allow advertising.
- **LOCAL SERVER:** Those with their own servers or DBMS software can consider relying on their own internal engines.

SITE ENGINE RECOMMENDATION

At the moment, you may want to default to the ease and power of Google. At the high end, Google Search Appliance is a powerful and expensive option for large sites. At the low end, the company also provides a free service and download for smaller sites (http://services.google.com). The service's spiders will visit the site and gradually build up an index of your resources. If your institution owns and intends to digitize a large collection of images, you may find Google's other add-ons for searching PDF and image files worth installing.

Fig. 7.5. Sample Home Page/Digital Archives Gateway

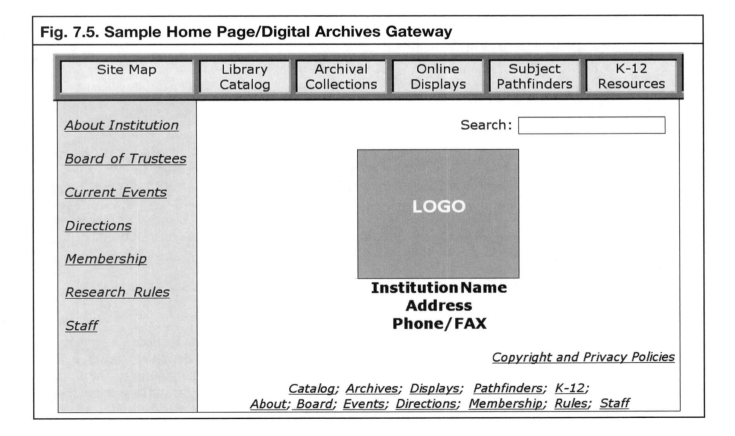

DESCRIPTION STRATA

The middle of the site provides a major activity zone for information professionals, a growth zone for the future. The Web forces Web designers to rethink content delivery mechanisms. On the one hand, the addition of thumbnail images and the interactivity offered by hyperlinks in the 856 field have enhanced MARC records. But on the other hand, the Dublin Core, or other methods, threatens to replace MARC. Other traditional descriptive devices are evolving in similar directions.

CONSIDERING FINDING AIDS

Findings Aids are following a logical path toward direct digital content. Online models increasingly feature sample photographs, and some include sound and video teasers. More importantly, inventories are being linked directly to their electronic assets. As pictured in figure 7.6, delivery may come with options. For instance, JPEG or PDF files can demonstrate the look of the original, but you may want HTML versions for manipulation and searching purposes.

Fig. 7.6. Direct Access Finding Aid, detail		
HTML	JPEG	**Box 2–Series II** 1. E. F. Doree depositions on behalf of amnesty for I.W.W. prisoners, Aug 1921
HTML	JPEG	2. E. F. Doree pardon; corresp., etc., Aug-Sep 19223. House Judiciary Committee hearing on amnesty for political prisoners; transcript, Mar 1922
HTML	JPEG	3. House Judiciary Committee hearing on amnesty for political prisoners; transcript, Mar 1922

HEFA and EAD models introduced navigational upgrades to Finding Aids. With the exception of links to external resources, neither model challenged the order or basic conceptualization of the Finding Aid format. The Web designer, however, may want to pursue several elements with a more critical eye:

- **AUDIENCE:** Trained researchers and archivists will remain as readers, but the Web opens the resources to the public. You may consider:
  - replacing archival terms with commonly understood terms;
  - tuning the reading level to college students, or perhaps an eighth-grade or newspaper reading level;
  - looking at the order established for the working archivist with the external user in mind; for example:
    - Start inventories with the description and not a box/folder number.
    - Add or substitute a thematic sort of folder heading versus displaying the original order.
- **NARRATIVE ELEMENTS:** As indicated in figure 7.3, writing for the computer screen requires "visual" and readily scanned information:
  - Use terse description, bullets, and numbered lists rather than long paragraphs.
  - Substitute chronologies, resumes, and organizational charts for narrative biographies and institutional profiles.
- **ONGOING DESCRIPTION:** You may need to rethink the fixed, print-era product in light of the mutable, dynamic description and ease with which Web pages can be updated. The Web Finding Aid could become a "living" document—one repeatedly embellished with new information and links to related collections or new publications.
- **MEDIA ADDITIONS:** As mentioned, the textual nature of the Finding Aid is changing. Photographs and graphics and even oral history interviews and video clips are being injected into Web versions.

Web Archival Resources Directories (WARDs).

The following Finding Aid variation arose at the Walter P. Reuther Library of Labor and Urban Affairs. The Reuther Library required a Web-based response to the records management needs of international unions, which had collections for multiple offices. Its projected audiences included union officials and records clerks at the headquarters, along with researchers, local unions, and the interested public.

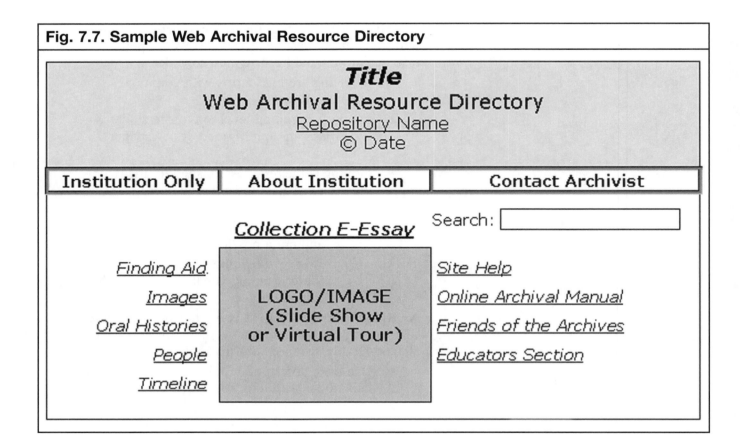

Fig. 7.7. Sample Web Archival Resource Directory

Figure 7.7 reveals a tripartite design. The top identifies the resources. The next level is for international communication, including a password-controlled interface for shipment management and provision of extra client services. The bottom level, divided into three sections, addresses other patrons and potential donors:

- THE **LEFT-HAND COLUMN** answers the "who, what, where, when, and why" for a research audience. But the focus goes beyond Finding Aid resources to highlight images and exhibits, oral histories, biographical entries, and a chronology.
- THE **MIDDLE COLUMN** is headed by an introductory archival e-essay on the overall holdings. Below that is either a fixed logo or a slide show of key images.
- THE **RIGHT-HAND COLUMN** is for potential partnerships and services, especially for the local

unions and their retirees. It ties to an e-book with records management and project tips for the locals (http://www.reuther.wayne.edu/services/making.htm). The area also provides links for financial development and teaching resources.

PATHFINDERS

The Web has had a profound effect on library pathfinders. These devices appeared in the 1960s as typewritten subject bibliographies. They were short and to the point—designed to help patrons get started with classroom assignments, deal with frequently requested topics, and/or orient users to the information resources in the facility. The format proved perfectly suited for the Web and quickly morphed into "electronic pathfinders."

As illustrated in figure 7.8, the results are suited to the left-hand navigation model. This layout also fits a stripped down, production mode with minimum design frills.

Fig. 7.8. Sample Pathfinder Title Box	
**Getting Started** _**Article Resources**_ _**Book Resources**_ _**Web Sites**_	**TITLE** Date Author Course Number: _____ _**©Repository**_
BACKGROUND	

OCLC'S CONNEXION

OCLC has converted the pathfinder into a regular feature of its CORC suite. Subscribers can use or modify a template to create their pathfinders, and find assistance with digital rights clearance. Also, you can enter information specific to your own repository, and Web links tailored to your patrons. Content is readily exchanged among the resources, including the ability to link to other pathfinders. The results are centrally managed as interactive bibliographic assets with Dublin Core tags.

Archival E-Essays

The pathfinder idea can be extended into larger, Resource Guides or intensive narrative analysis in the form of archival subject narratives or e-essays. The e-essays capture an archivist's intimate knowledge of the holdings and abilities to make linkages across disparate collections and to related external resources.

Unlike a print essay, when you write an e-essay, you assume it will receive frequent updates. These studies are enlivened by pictorial images and could include sound and video clips. Hyperlinks are imbedded throughout the document. They link to representative Finding Aids, pathfinders, documents, and even materials in other repositories. The treatment ends with a list of other resources and contacts.

You should expect synergies from a well-designed digital-archives package. With the capability to cut-and-paste from supplemental directories, the novice can master the process of inserting hypertext. . Other e-essays and pathfinders are available for nesting as reference resources. The archival e-essays can also work as qualitative reviews for collection development and other management purposes. The act of composition and review may even reveal hidden resources or point to items for digitizing.

AMATEUR ARCHIVES

Some of the best (and worst) archives exist only in cyberspace. Subject experts, aficionados, classes, and organizations put together dedicated subject sites without owning the digital resources. Instead of maintaining a vast number of resources and the responsibility for digitizing, they "cherry pick"—take the best available from any number of sites.

The presence of copyrighted images on another site can be annoying enough to lead some archives to defend their institution's interests. For most, such "borrowings" can be viewed as a mark of distinction and perhaps beyond your control. The best course is to ensure that your Web images contain a digital ownership mark. Secondly, if you receive a request to use an image, ask for a courtesy link back to your site. Finally, you can consider partnering with such sites and may even feel a professional responsibility to help preserve the more valuable endeavors.

DISPLAYS

The virtual sky is the limit for the display strata. We have only begun to explore alternative uses and methods for interpreting digital archives. The following section presents a few samples on the road to what may emerge as information professionals' main contributions in the Web era.

ONLINE EXHIBITS

Libraries and archives have jumped into the online exhibit business, but the clear leaders and experts are found in the museum and archive community. The Museum Computer Network provides a good portal to begin your data gathering on this subject (http://www.mcn.edu/resources/index.html).

This section can only touch briefly on the emerging art form of Web exhibit design. The online exhibit is the most formal element of digital archives. Implementation follows from the project planning for an internal exhibit installation. A storyboard is required to focus thematic development. You will want to create a timeline and to assemble a team with complimentary content, design, organizational, and technical skills.

Most importantly, since exhibits are a visual medium, images should dominate and text should play less of a role. Like a bricks-and-mortar exhibit, you have the option of providing supplemental "handouts," only on the Web you extend the research experience through hyperlinks.

Although they can and should supplement any of your physical displays, Web versions also clearly represent a different genre. In addition to normal HTML construction principles and metadata, you may need to consider these factors:

- It may be necessary to place limits on image size and standards to ensure reasonably fast downloading (See: chapter 6's GIF and JPEG discussions).
- The standard monitor size of 14" to 17" limits the viewing potential. Is the method of transiting from screen to screen to—scroll down, scroll across, or click?
- Internal design coherence among exhibits and with the site as a whole should be kept in mind.
- Many current exhibits unfold in a linear, step-by-step method, which is well suited to PDF or PowerPoint format, even with their limitations. The Web favors multiple points of entry—e.g., alphabetical, chronological, key figures, and thematic lines, or perhaps self-generated scenarios through role playing simulations.
- Similarly, current concentration is on images, but we should expect to add other media options.
- Other questions, especially for museums, concern the portion of the display to include on the Web, and how frequently you should update the site to attract return visitors.

QUIZZES AND GAMES

Online quizzes provide interesting diversions, especially for school-aged audiences. Yes/no and multiple guess questionnaires are easily composed with hyperlinks for the Web.

You can also turn creative juices to simulations and computer games. Clickteam (http://www.clickteam.com) is a good introductory site. Inexpensive, easy-to-use programming shells are available through sites like Stagecast (http://www.stagecast.com) and Adventure Maker (http://www.adventuremaker.com/). At the high end, you can take an online course through Games Institute (http://www.gamesinstitute.org) or look at Gaming World (http://www.gamingw.net).

Photo Galleries.

There is a simpler, but deceptively complex alternative to the formal online exhibit; namely, to allow patrons to browse through "Photo Galleries." These sites hold sample images with minimal organization (e.g., chronology or alphabetically by name) and limited tag-line descriptions. The genre employs the metaphor of photographic albums.

Photo galleries can be built easily by copying and pasting links from the scanning project log. Some sites may only need a single set of their key images. Most will link from the gateway to a supplementary list of photo albums.

PHOTO SITE OUTSOURCING

Instead of maintaining images and online albums, you may want to save disk space and consider commercial Web services. Policies and charges will vary widely, but you should check out the options at such locations as:

- Active Share from Adobe (http://www.activeshare.com)
- Albums OnLine, Triadigm Technologies (http://www.albumsonline.com)
- Cartographa from Hewlett-Packard (http://www.cartographa.com)
- Digital Fridge (http://www.digitalfridge.com)
- Gatherround, backed by Intel (www.gatherround.com)
- Homestead works with Shutterfly (http://www.homestead.com)
- Ofoto (http://www.ofoto.com)
- PhotoLoft (http://www.photoloft.com)
- PhotoPoint (http://www.photopoint.com)
- PhotoWorks (http://photoworks.com)
- Shutterfly (http://www.shutterfly.com)

K-12 DOCUMENT PACKETS

In what may prove to be its most significant contribution, the Web has dramatically opened the resources of cultural repositories to teachers and their students from the kindergarten to the high school level. Many repositories have begun to post key documents and subject guides for such clientele. Some have gone the extra step of producing formal lesson plans.

INSTRUCTIONAL RESOURCES

There are literally dozens of sites with lesson plans—e.g., the Educators Network (http://www.theeducatorsnetwork.com); LessonPlans with an online lesson plan generator (http://lessonplans.com); and Sites for Teachers (http://www.sitesforteachers.com). Many state archives have committed to document-based teaching models. On the Federal level, the U.S. Department of Education sponsors *The Gateway to Educational Materials* (http://www. thegateway.org). The Smithsonian has its Center for Education and Museum Studies with accompanying lesson plans (http://educate.si.edu/ut/about_fs.html). The National Park Service offers *Creative Teaching with Historic Places* (http://www.cr.nps.gov/nr/twhp/profdev.htm). The National Archives has an exemplary set of documents, plans, and instructions at its Digital Classroom (http://www.archives.gov/digital_classroom/index.html). Arguably the best resources for starting are found under The Learning Page of the Library of Congress's American Memory (memory.loc.gov/ammem/ndlpedu/index.html).

Lesson Plans.

Lesson plans must be well structured and should address education standards. They may include both teacher guides and student packages. Although the lure of didactic narrative is compelling, lesson plans should stress the visual, leaning toward Socratic, question-and-response discussions. Size is typically limited to one or two pages in outline form with such categories as:

- **HEADER**
  - **Title**
  - **Author**
  - **Subject Category** (e.g., Social Studies, Science)
  - **Grade Level**
- **GOALS AND OBJECTIVES**
  - **Educational Standards** (national and, especially, state requirements; See: Microsoft

Lesson Connection (http://www.k12.mcn
.com/) and its related StateStandards
(http://www.statestandards.com>)

- **LESSON/ACTIVITIES**

    Anticipatory set (preparations/context)

    Activities/document presentation

    Interpretive questions (see: Photo
    Analysis Worksheet—Figure 7.9)

    Sample activities

    Closure and/or homework

- **OTHER RESOURCES**

Networking.

The best advice for those contemplating lesson plans is to ally with
teachers and schools. In addition to the extra expertise, such networking provides pilot sites and helps ensure use of the material. You may
also gain unexpected insights and Web expertise from the students.
Consider, as well, submitting your packets to one or more of the lesson-
sharing sites.

WEBQUESTS

You may also investigate a WebQuest project. Developed by Bernie Dodge of San Diego State
University, these popular variants of the online treasure hunt spread out over the Web looking for collective answers and resources. They offer great promise for the studied interpretation of materials
across collections and repositories (http://webquest.sdsu.edu).

COURSEWARE

The Web offers new opportunities to work with professors and teachers
to work your electronic resources into their courses. You can go beyond
individual sessions to set up complete online curricula. In addition to
homegrown resources, packaged software programs are available to
help the development. These divide into two rough categories:

- **COURSE PACKETS**, like XanEdu (http://xane-
  du.com), are based on a distribution model with
  copyright clearance functions and often tie directly
  to ILS systems.

- **COURSEWARE**, like the proprietary Blackboard (http://www.blackboard.com) and WebCT (http://www.webct.com) or the open system of the Open Knowledge Institute (http://web.mit.edu/oki/), reflects administrative and grading-based approaches.

Note: The key to success is not necessarily technology. Interpersonal networking contributes significantly to users' knowledge about your holdings, and the cooperation of the IT staff is essential to publicize their availability. Secondly, you can make the appropriate pathfinders and hyperlinked resource lists readily available on the Web site.

Fig. 7.9. Photo Analysis Worksheet

(Based on NARA Digital Classroom Model)

Step1: Observation
  A. Study the image for two minutes (if this is a printed picture, turn it over to look at the back too).
  B. Consider the overall image.
  C. Concentrate on the items within the picture.
  D. Divide the photograph into quarters and study each section for more details.

Step 2: Inventory—List what you find in the chart below

People	Objects	Activities/Place

Notes:

Step 3—Analyze: Based on what you have seen, list three things that you believe you now know about this picture.

Step 4—Questions: What else would you need to know to interpret the image?

Step 5—Further Research: Where would you look for the answers?

RESOURCE STRATA

The inhabitants of the resource strata start out as raw born-digital and converted files. In a virtual environment, such resources are infinitely renewable and may be "located" in multiple positions. Creations from the display and descriptive strata can flow into this bottom layer to add their contents to the data mine.

In practice, the bottom layer acts as a virtual warehouse. The management model is an inventory control system. Materials are logged on entry, descriptions gathered, stored in identifiable locations, monitored, and retrieved on demand. The administrator faces two related operational questions:

- To what degree can we automate such activities—including the descriptive capacities of search engines?
- How much additional manual description/cataloging and metadata entries should be performed?

The nature of the electronic holdings establishes the type of digital archives. This can vary widely, from copies of institutional data files to scanned images of analog formats and new digital publications. Chapter 8 discusses these variations along with supporting maintenance and preservations methods.

OUTSOURCING

As repeatedly indicated, with enough funding, you can outsource most Web services. Web site design, for example, is often best left in the hands of professionals. Instead of an internal server, most institutions should also contract for the hosting of their sites. Those going the DBMS route also have the option of relying on remote access through an application services provider (ASP). The key is to be sure that staff can still easily update materials and that such outputs are part of their regular workflow.

RFI/RFP

Many institutions are required to put projects costing above a set dollar limit out for bid. In this scenario, you have two main options: Request for Information (RFI) or Request for Proposal (RFP). An RFP clearly spells out the scope of work and requests formal proposals. You issue an RFI to gain information and suggestions for treating the problem. It can come before an RFP or double as a request for bids. The elements in both are similar and typically include:

1. Title
2. Date of issue
3. Scope of work
4. Time frame for the scope of work
5. Relevant supporting information on the institution/services
6. Financial bid
7. References
8. Response date for the proposal
9. Contact person

Consider prominently posting the proposal request along with any supplemental information on your Web site. Depending on the type of product, you can consider advertising in the local paper and professional journals—for example, *Library Journal* maintains a section for such listings (http://www.libraryjournal.com). The best technique is likely networking to locate names of other institutions that have contracted for similar work, aside from visiting or collecting the names of vendors at conferences.

CONTRACTS

OCLC has a number of sample contracts to view on its site (http://www.oclc.org).

Formal contracts or letters of understanding are necessary. The contractor may have a standard form for your signature, though these are subject to change and negotiation. It is advisable to have your own default version at hand, especially for small endeavors, as well as volunteer situations. The model in figure 7.10 includes a crucial but easily overlooked clause to ensure copyright transfer to your institution.

Note: Without such a clause, you may find yourself limited in updating or making changes to the product.

Fig. 7.10. Sample Contract

Institution Name

1. **Scope of Work:** _Fill   in   name_ (Contractor) agrees to perform the following services for Institution (Client). _Complete description..._

2. **Independent Contractor:** Both Parties intend that this Agreement constitute a work for hire. Contractor shall control and determine the methods and working hours to perform the above Scope of Work.
   a. **Equipment and Supplies:**
      Contractor shall provide all equipment, tools, and supplies necessary to perform the Scope of Work.
      Client shall provide all equipment, tools, and supplies necessary to perform the Scope of Work.
      Contractor and Client will share costs. (Describe)
   b. **Subcontractors:** Contractor   shall or   shall not have the ability to sub-contract parts of the Scope of Work.

3. **Ownership:** All products generated through this Agreement remain the property of the Client.
   a. **Copyright warrant/transfer:** Contractor warrants ownership of the intellectual property rights to the products from the Agreement and transfers their ownership to the Client. (Option: Contractor agrees to share any intellectual property rights to the products from the Agreement.)

4. **Time for Performance:** The Agreement runs from _____ to _____, but may be extended by agreement of both parties. Contractor agrees to complete the Scope of Work by the date(s) specified. Contractor will provide reasonable follow-up to explain the products and implementation.

5. **Cancellation/Arbitration:** This contract can be cancelled by joint agreement with ___ days notice. In the case of an irreconcilable dispute over cancellation or satisfactory performance of the Scope of Work, the parties will submit the matter to an external arbitrator.

6. **Financial Consideration:**   Contractor donates the work to the Client.
      Client agrees to pay Contractor a sum not to exceed $_____ (Option: []that may be prorated at a rate of $_____ an hour).
      Client agrees to pay on completion within ___ days of Contractor's invoice.

Contractor: **Client: Institution Name/representative**

Signature: Date: Signature: Date:

8

MAINTAINING AND PRESERVING DIGITAL ARCHIVES

This final chapter considers the "nitty-gritty" of internal administration. It looks to methods for the maintenance, validity, and, especially, preservation of digital archives. The treatments are divided among three types of digital archives:

> **WEB MUSEUMS:** The basic model concentrates on the electronic display of traditional holdings.
>
> **INSTITUTIONAL ARCHIVES:** This advanced option addresses the management of born-digital information resources for organizations.
>
> **DIGITAL LIBRARIES:** The other advanced alternative stresses metadata and cooperative efforts to preserve digital publications and multimedia.

WEB MUSEUMS

Digital libraries can face an array of complex problems. For many cultural institutions, however, the issue is simple. They merely want to post electronic snapshots of their treasures on the Web. Suitable responses can range:

- At the low end, demand is met by posting samples or exhibits of representative materials. Reproduction quality is limited, based on the theoretical position that true value remains vested with the originals. "Real" research and viewing pleasure occurs on-site.

- At the high end, the Web site provides complete coverage of the holdings and the ability to make high-quality reproductions. The result is a virtual research environment that eliminates the need to travel to the repository.

MICHELANGELO EFFECT

Not everything can be digitized. Many analog materials include a complex range of information that is only evident in person: e.g., textures, scents, and inestimable associational values. Although unquantifiable, original materials can carry an undeniable effect. The scanned letters of Thomas Jefferson, paintings of Picasso, or sculptures of Michelangelo, will convey a satisfactory amount of information for most purposes, but they do not stimulate the emotional charge of touching or seeing the original object in person.

WEB RELIANCE

If the question of digital archives pertains only to the display of electronic facsimiles, they can get straightforward technical answers. Preservation per se continues through the original, while the Web offers relatively durable and reliable user copies.

As with the other scenarios, the medium's open codes and pervasiveness ensure a level of confidence beyond that of previous automation systems. Individuals around the world are committed to keeping their resources online on the original Web and commercial interests have converged on the medium. They have a vested interest in retaining format compatibility. While change and updating are inevitable, serviceable and sustainable digital archives can stem from:

- storage of the bulk of converted and born-digital documents in HTML (XHTML) for searching and/or PDF to maintain the look of the original;

- HTML to hold database displays through its tables function;

- images stored in such standard formats as *.jpeg* for color and *.gif* for grayscale;

- site discovery ensured through title/metadata controls, URL exchanges, listings with search engines, and other design features;

- clips of audio and video (given current bandwidth limitations these media are usually excluded or limited to short excerpts in standard formats).

Staffing.

Such enterprises can be assigned to an interested regular staff member acting as Web Manager and require a minimum of training. That person's duties divide into two phases:

1. initial editorial oversight to ensure the materials being submitted meet policy guidelines and site conventions
2. ongoing physical maintenance of the records, which also helps ensure preservation

TOOL SKILLS

As repeatedly emphasized, electronic records management relies upon naming principles: i.e., labeling the file clearly, saving in an open format, and storing in functional directories. Those steps are readily enhanced with several familiar measures:

- **METADATA:** Metadata heads the editorial side of the Web manager's duties. Such additions have limited, but significant presence for even "unstructured" HTML/word-processed situations. With the priority still on keeping the metadata as simple as possible, you have several options and a couple of demands to meet.

    - **ADMINISTRATIVE:** Many software packages automatically record background data and add that to the HTML header—e.g., the author's name and organization, along with date stamps and time on task information. Most of this can and should be met as a by-product of the set-up in the originating computers.

    - **DESCRIPTIVE:** The options are ensuring description, keyword, or professional metadata (e.g., Dublin Core) to assist with retrieval. The demand is maintaining compliance with Universal Access Guidelines—e.g., linear site maps and descriptive attributes for imbedded image and media files.

    - **STRUCTURAL:** The demand is an appropriate Web title for each page. New documents should be well structured, including meeting XHTML coding minimums—e.g., no upper case letters or empty elements. Such output can automatically arrive with new software. Older materials can be left alone or updated through HTML Tidy Online (http://infohound.net/tidy) and other validators.

- **UPDATING CONTENT:** Active administration involves updating content on a timely basis, which is crucial for integrating digital outputs into the regular workflow. The Web manager puts routine methods in place to refresh the information on the site. Typical approaches include:
  - **SNEAKER WARE:** The original and still effective technique involves physically carrying the data on disk or other media to load into the Web server. Staff submissions are left in a receiving tray.
  - **WEB TRANSFER DIRECTORY:** A directory is set aside in the LAN for staff to deposit their work.
  - **E-MAIL ATTACHMENTS:** Most We pages can ride the Internet's e-mail protocol as attachments.
  - **FTP:** The file transfer protocol is the Internet's other and the expert's most frequent recourse for transferring files, especially large files to a remote server.
- **BACKUPS:** Backups are one of the most significant measures to maintaining a digital library. Internal information systems and the Web site require duplication on a regular schedule—a weekly save and three-week rotation is typical. I also recommend a yearly archival copy, which could be burned onto CDs or DVDs. Ideally this involves storing the archival copy in an offsite facility, but a secure and reasonably fireproof location in-house can do the job, as well.

  Procedures should be seamless and recognized as part of the professional routine. To avoid interrupting regular work, many of the tasks can be scheduled by the computer for off-hours. The implications of such common sense practice and non-intrusive measures are immense for security, preservation, and migration purposes.

PRESERVING THE WEB SITE

Cultural repositories are often the "shoemaker's children" when it comes to preserving their own history. Few, for example, have taken the step of preserving the content and design of their ever-evolving Web sites. As suggested, proper backup procedures with an annual copy can adequately address this duty. The Web Wayback Machine may provide some respite by archiving selective sites since 1996 (http://web.archive.org/collections/web.html).

Fig. 8.1. Guidelines for Web Facsimile Archives

A. Editorial Responsibilities

1. **Metadata:** Entries must have clearly identifiable title tags and preferably a description element to help users orient themselves and search engines locate the page. Image and media files call for the added inclusion of descriptive attributes.
2. **File Naming:** Each record must have unique name or identifier(s) that the computer can recognize and staff can readily discern—e.g., the archival collection number.
3. **Open Format:** Files should be saved or readily convertible into open formats—e.g., ASCII, *.rtf, .htm, .html, .pdf* along with SQL for DBMSs and recognized XML/DTDs or schema.

B. Administrative Responsibilities

4. **Directory Controls:** Files are stored together within hierarchically arranged directories. These should be named and ordered to reflect functional activities. Those names and hierarchies are selectively mirrored on the Web site.
5. **Updating:** Methods must be in place to facilitate the entry of electronic products and to update content on the Web site.
6. **Backups:** Internal records and Web files must be duplicated on a regular schedule—preferably with off-site storage and an annual archival copy.

NINCH GUIDELINES

The National Institute for a Networked Cultural Heritage (NINCH) (http://www. ninch.org) has an excellent set of overall recommendations for Digital Asset Management—see the NINCH Guide to Good Practice (http://www.nyu.edu/ its/humanities/ninchguide/).

INSTITUTIONAL RECORDS

The electronic records management (ERM) of institutional files ratchets conversation into expert realms. The context is a governmental/business orientation—one that may be alien to cultural resources specialists. Rather than after-the-fact conversions, government and business implement the Institutional Records model. Activities begin before data is created. Instead of researchers, the primary goals are to serve the parent organization's information management system. Solutions require dedicated and trained digital specialists or outsourcing. Techniques such as the following are aimed at born-digital data:

- Initial design steps assist with the controlled entry of the information and automatic routing to the repository.

- Although long-term storage is on the table, the bulk of the information is understood as transitional with a limited lifespan.

- Administrative roles are vested in an electronic records manager, but with activities shared with technologists, across units, and ideally empower individual staff.

- Internal distribution is the primary intent. The open Web is viewed as an ancillary publication arm—one of several delivery mechanisms, but can be of special importance for government agencies or others with a mandate to present materials to the public.

ERM RESOURCES

A number of governmental archives and records services provide practical advice for the beginner. The Australian National Archives (http://www.naa.gov.au) and New York State Archives (http://www.archives.nysed.gov) are frequently cited for their informative and understandable introductions. Readers may also look to their state archives for assistance or check the excellent records management resources on the U.S. National Archives site (http://www.archives.gov).

THE RECORD

The ERM scenario reflects the centrality of the "record." The hard part is defining that concept within an electronic environment. For the New York State Archives, *"a 'record' is the complete set of documentation required to provide evidence of a business transaction."* Similarly, the Australian National Archives holds that a record is set within a context and requires content and structure; furthermore, it is transactional in nature:

Electronic records, in particular, are based on transfers which occur within and between computer systems. In many cases, these records may be updated, deleted, altered or manipulated without human intervention. In this process, the essential characteristics of the record—content, structure, context—may be altered or lost. In short, computer systems per se do not create or maintain records; specific intervention and planning is required to ensure that the essential characteristics of the record are built into electronic information systems and maintained.

ERM SKILL SET

The electronic records manager has expanded duties beyond being the Web manager in the previous scenario. The professional literature reveals an ever-expanding portfolio, including the following:

Access

Electronic records managers ensure that records are readily available for use and preferably used. Access first funnels through the internal LAN or Intranet. Staff and client use follows from functional design, naming practices, search engine capacities, and/or as a byproduct from turnkey software.

The Web site itself is secondary, but still needs to be clearly designed for navigation and preferably comes with a site search engine. Electronic records managers should ensure that each page is prepared with commercial search engines, browsers, and, increasingly, XML in mind. Depending on the type of institution, they may become involved with professional descriptions (e.g., EAD, MARC) and interpretive displays.

Authenticity

With Web Museums, authenticity was largely a byproduct of appraisal, whereby materials were judged for their validity before digitizing. With the Institutional Records scenario, the validity of most born-digital content is assured through the initial transfer process and a consistent chain of ownership. Yet certain situations call for extra measures—for example, institutions may have high-level security or financial concerns. Indeed, authentication procedures are rising to prominence for electronic records managers.

Technology complicates such matters. Unlike the fixed forms on paper, presentations are reborn on each view and only come together through an assembly of electrons. Data is discrete from its presentation software. Records may also be the multi-faceted union of several sources and composed of parts from several different files. The electronic records manager thus deals with several complex issues:

- **AUDIT TRAIL:** Governmental and business agencies are pushing for software systems that automatically document the chain of ownership and use for transactional records.

- **COMPLETENESS:** Given potential storage and delivery problems, issues arise over the construction of the record. As the Australians stress:

  A complete record is one which has the characteristics associated with time and place (dispatch and receipt), details of the sender and anticipated receiver (i.e., who it might be addressed to), an authority stamp (i.e., signature or code or PIN number), a title or subject and, of course, content expressing the will or requirement of the author. In electronic transactions which occur automatically the will is expressed in the system and process design, not at the individual transaction level.

- **LAYOUT VERSUS INFORMATION CONTENT:** A related question is the maintenance of the original look and feel of the item versus concentrating on its information content. Some purists demand retention of the originating software and hardware. The trend, however, is toward the primacy of the data—especially for born-digital records.

- **ORIGINAL AND SIGNATURE COPIES:** The idea of an original record is effectively lost in the computer world of digital conversions and the ability to make exact copies on demand. The digital alternatives are digital signatures and, in some instances, encryption.

> Major archival questions arise with media and the difficulties of capturing the full extent of an analog recording with digital measures.

Cost Analysis

> See also: Abby Smith, *Building and Sustaining Digital Collections*, CLIR, 8/2001, (http://www.clir.org/pubs/reports/pub100/contents.html)

In the rush to create digital archives some non-profits overlook the financial implications. The commercial side leaves no such room for ambiguities. Sun Microsystems' *The Digital Library Toolkit* (http://www.sun.com/edu or http://www.edulib.com) offers critical advice on launching an initiative. Author Peter Noerr stresses the importance of considering both start-up and ongoing maintenance over a period of time. Noerr also emphasizes that:

Introducing a digital library just because it is a technology that has caught someone's eye is wrong. It is important to consider the needs of the users, the resources in the library, the requirements of the organization, and the whole spectrum of available improvements. (p. 21)

Fig. 8.2. Expense Projections for Digital Archives	
(Average for 3–5 year period)	
A. Start-up Computer and Scanning Hardware—Capital • Software—Capital • Use licenses (per seat, simultaneous users) • Web site enhancements (or outsourcing costs) • Consultant fees and training expenses (in-house or offsite travel) • Storage (DVD, CD, tape) and backups • In-house development v. turnkey product (cost comparison) • Staff salaries/benefits (+ estimated work losses or replacement costs) **B. Ongoing (x number of years)** • Telecommunication and utility expenses • Upgrades • Licenses and Web costs • Help services _ Maintenance • Staff salaries/benefits (+ work losses or replacement costs)	**Amount**

Benefits.

Costs must be weighed against benefits and potential economic returns (what the business world calls ROI = return on investment). What are the demonstrable advantages for internal information management?

- Does the electronic strategy positively affect the services of the information bureau—e.g., reduce time spent on reference questions?
- Are the resources being sufficiently used by others in the institution?
- Does the material lend itself to promotional uses, financial development, or prospects for marketing derivative products?

> These formats have paper cognates, but there are genres that exist only in a virtual realm: e.g., Virtual reality or Geographic Information Systems.

Record types.

In most instances, records can be divided into one of two types of electronic documents:

- **FIXED:** Communications are most often exchanged as fixed entities that are not intended to be altered. The letter, e-mail, image, or media production is locked for documentation purposes. This follows in line with the analog conversions in the Web display scenario. HTML and PDF are readily adaptable for this type of publication.

- **MUTABLE:** Some information is living and intended to be in flux—e.g., the tabular arrays of spreadsheets and DBMSs. HTML can replicate such layouts through the tables command, but true functionality calls for XML or dynamic DBMS applications.

- Do you freeze living records for public display purposes, and if so, when? The normal resort for archival documentation is periodic capture dates—e.g., end of the fiscal year—which reflect a set of activity during a definable part of the institution's life cycle.

- Do you allow users to view the data only or engage the software functions?

- Do you only display completed reports or include working drafts to show the evolution of a project?

Scheduling.

Disposition schedules are essential components of a records management program. The ideal is a virtual conveyor belt to transit and bring order to the lifecycle of each type of institutional record. Every record series is premapped to respond to a pattern from creation and input to use, maintenance, and disposition. Consequently, the electronic records manager engages in multiple recurrent tasks:

- **RETENTION AND DISPOSITION:** The establishment of "Retention and Disposition" (R and D) schedules lies at the heart of records management. This skill ensures the presence of needed data and legal compliance, and guarantees that content of enduring value is not lost. Because computers can increase efficiencies and legal protections, they provide a particularly apt vehicle for automatically calculating, routing, and monitoring usage needs and demand.

- **VITAL RECORDS:** Some resources are "vital" for operations, particularly the records necessary to run the business in the event of a disaster—e.g., accounts receivable. The ERM job is to identify and offer them special protections.

- **AUTHENTICATED COPY PROCEDURES:** The electronic records manager may be called on to deliver authenticated copies, which can be approached in a number of ways. The simplest is maintaining a date-stamped "exemplar" or master copy in PDF format on a "write-once" CD or DVD. For extra verification, two copies should be generated at roughly the same time, but stored in separate and secured locations. The copies can be drawn together for verification purposes.

- **WEB TRANSFER:** The Information Highway adds responsibility for ensuring the regular Web publication of appropriate documents. For cultural institutions, on which the burden falls especially heavily, the shift to Web delivery of information is irreversible. Although Internet resources will likely build and accumulate over time, some materials become outmoded. They require monitoring to guarantee that they and their links are deleted on schedule—ideally as a part of site maintenance.

Security.

Security overlaps with disaster preparedness as an unfortunate fact of life accelerated with Internet access. While this responsibility must be addressed, there are no perfect protections. Working in concert with technicians or suppliers, electronic records managers must develop strategic responses to security and other risks of loss (e.g., fire):

1. warding off attacks;
2. discovering and recovering from an attack as quickly and with the least amount of damage as possible; and
3. tracking and prosecuting as another possibility for governmental and high security concerns.

SECURITY TIPS

Advanced technological measures are beyond our scope, but there are some simple and highly successful methods to consider:

- Use backing up as your primary tactic. Updating frequency determines your vulnerability—e.g., daily backups limit maximum exposure to twenty-four hours, weekly to seven days.

- Rely on the institution's technology department or include security as part of outsourcing.

- Ensure a fire wall and virus protection on workstations and servers.

- Display use policies and declare copyright for your Web publications.

- Consider watermarking, digital signatures, or other forms of identification (Note: these are not terribly effective today despite their cost).

- Use internal controls on the LAN to allow reading access, but set rights for writing, deleting, and posting to the Web.

- Maintain physical barriers between the LAN and the Web site, making the Web server a separate terminal. When materials for postings are routed to a staging area or receiving server, you can regularly upload them by disk or file transfer protocol over the Internet.

System Management.

Like security, the physical management and maintenance of the hardware and software system may fall to a separate technical staff. If so, electronic records managers are relegated to an advisory role, with three main areas of concern:

- ensuring the automation of backups, disposition, vital records protection, and disaster recovery;

- evaluating current services for problem areas and possible improvements—especially trying to make certain that the desired audiences are reaching and using the site; and

- monitoring the marketplace and professional standards to determine the appropriate moment for upgrading or launching new directions.

Evaluation Methods.

Currently, Web evaluation is an inexact science. We can measure the number of hits, but not the duration of use of HTML or XML records. A DBMS structure offers somewhat better tools, but still incomplete picture.

NISO discusses a Z39.7 standard in its *Report on the NISO Forum on Performance Measures and Statistics for Libraries* (http://www.niso.org/stats-rpt.html). In 1998, the International Coalition of Library Consortia offered *Guidelines for statistical measures of usage of web-based indexed, abstracted and full text resources* (http://www.library.yale.edu/consortia/webstats.html). ARL is seeking e-metrics for the use of commercial and local collections (http://www.arl.org/stats/newmeas/emetrics/index.html). ARL's Project Counter site issues its recommendations in 2003 (http://www .projectcounter.org).

WEB TUNE UPS AND LINK CHECKING

Sites like Web Site Garage (http://www.websitegarage.com) help to optimize services and ensure the links are working. Others resources check on search engine treatment—e.g., Marketleap Visibility Index (http://linkpop.marketleap .com), Link Popularity Check (http://www.linkpopularitycheck.com), and LinkPopularity (http://www.linkpopularity.com). For a fee, they also offer to improve performance. Most search engines provide their own mechanisms:

- AltaVista–finds a single URL using the "*url:http://url_name*" command string. To list the URLs included on the site, use "host:address" without the *http://* prefix. To check sites linking to yours–type "*link:url_name.*"

- Google uses "*allinurl:url_name*"; be sure to omit the *http://* prefix. To find all the URLs listed from the site use "*site:url_name*"; for sites linking to you, enter "*link:url_name.*"

- Inktomi employs "*originalurl:url_name*" for index information; "*domain: url_name*" for URLs included; and "*linkdomain:url_name.*"

- Yahoo allows for "*u:url_name*" to display its human-generated terms.

SOFTWARE REQUIREMENTS

The institutional records archive scenario closes with a brief overview of newly evolving requirements for ERM software applications. The United States' National Archives and Records Administration (NARA) and Department of Defense (DoD) are playing pivotal roles in this regard.

In the mid-1990s, DoD began working with NARA on the first official efforts to establish standard criteria for Records Management Application (RMA) software. Compliance testing would occur at the Joint Interoperability Test Command in Fort Huachuca, Arizona. DoD, the world's largest software consumer, determined that it would only purchase certified products.

ARCHIVAL SCHOOLS OF THOUGHTS

Two archival traditions and concomitant research projects directly influenced the development of the DoD's RMA standard:

- **AMERICAN PRAGMATIC SCHOOL:** The American tradition stresses functional analysis and variable treatments based on the assumed values of the materials. It is the direction of this text and best represented through the work of Richard Cox at the University of Pittsburgh. In 1993, Cox started a three-year study with funding from the National Historic Records and Publications Commission—*Functional Requirements for Evidence in Records Keeping* (http://www2.sis.pitt.edu/~rcox/FunReqs.htm).

- **EUROPEAN DIPLOMATICS SCHOOL:** Luciana Duranti from the University of British Columbia places the authentication skills of Diplomatics into the electronic arena. Her InterPARES project, an international cooperative effort, launched in 1994. The first InterPARES report *Long-term Preservation of Authentic Electronic Records* is available on the project Web site (http://www.interpares.org). Its success led to a multi-year investigation of extending the methodology to active records environments, which ends in December 2006.

DoD 5015.2-STD 2002.

The Department of Defense produced the official government guidelines for records management software in late 1997 as DoD 5015.2-STD. But, the Web had risen to prominence in the interim. NARA thus turned to DoD for an update and to guide portions of the nation's "E-Government" initiative. DOD issued its revision in June of 2002.

The new document had a global impact on software and information systems. The standard begins with an extensive glossary and then turns to a set of general requirements. The latter can inform the development of in-house software products—but is aimed at commercial-off-the-shelf (COTS) products.

File Plan.

The standard demands formal file plans. These can only come from and be changed by authorized individuals. Each plan must include a record category name, identifier, and description. It needs disposition instructions and authority. Records must come with indicators (e.g., form number codes) to signal if they are permanent or vital. As indicated in Figure 8.3, the standard demands a number of metadata elements. These will help coordinate all governmental records and likely form the baseline for administrative and structural metadata in the world political arena.

Fig. 8.3. DoD 5015.2 Required Record Metadata Components	
Required Record Metadata Components	
• unique record identifier–computer generated • supplemental marking list • subject or title _ media type • format _ record dates • date filed • publication date • date received	• author or originator • addressee • other addressees • originating organization • additional metadata • location • vital record indicator • vital record review • user-defined fields

RMA Software Elements.

DoD 5015–2 provides a detailed outline of requirements and options for an ERM environment. These are broken down among as many as twenty functional categories and subcategories—for instance:

- **SCHEDULING RECORDS,** including lifecycle, retention, disposition, interim transfer, and rescheduling
- **DECLARING AND FILING RECORDS** with mandates for metadata and demands for synchronizing multiple databases and repositories
- **E-MAILS** declared as the equivalent of any other record and needing to hold:
  - an intelligent name of the sender
  - an intelligent name of primary addresses
  - all other addresses
  - incoming data and time of receipt
  - the subject of the message
  - the presence or absence of an attachment

- **STORING RECORDS** to prevent unauthorized access and preservation to ensure correct information duplication
- **RETENTION AND VITAL RECORDS** to screen records and allow vital records cycling
- **FREEZING AND UNFREEZING** of schedules
- **TRANSFERRING AND DESTROYING** routines with an audit trail and authorizations
- **SEARCHING AND RETRIEVING** through any combination of the record and its metadata with wild cards, Boolean operators, and null values
- **ACCESS CONTROLS** with authorization levels for who can see, use, or alter along with encryption, password, biometrics and other filters
- **SYSTEM AUDITS** to automate the logging of date, time, users, user actions and protection against mishandling
- **SYSTEMS MANAGEMENT** requirements for the operating system or database and to ensure automatic backups with recovery/rollback and rebuilding facilities
- **NON-MANDATORY OPTIONS** are site specific with features for documentation, system performance, transmission protocols, training...
- **ANOTHER USEFUL CATEGORY** lists desirables from global changes, bulk loading, and interface with other systems to document imaging, fax tools, bar codes, forms management, GILS (Government Information Locator System) registration, and Web capacity.
- **MANAGEMENT OF CLASSIFIED RECORDS** adds an extra layer of security. It calls for a variety of access controls from passwords to biometrics along with encryption options. Classified records need an automated audit history of the uses and users of the record. The section demands an indication of the record's initial and current classification level, as well as whether the classification is derived from a related type of record. It requests a formal guide to the reasons for the classification, any exemptions, and periodic reviews of the classification. The guidelines require defined triggers for

declassification. As with regular disposition approaches these are set by:

- a time period (e.g., ten years);
- an event (case file closed); or
- a time/event combination.

DIGITAL LIBRARIES

The final scenario is an overview of developments in the library field. Early in the new millennium, leading libraries are moving to transform their practices. Like the copying mission of monastery libraries in the Dark Ages, libraries are asserting a new preservation mission, which assumes the digitization of analog treasures and creation of Web Museums. But major libraries are also seeking to assert their stewardship over new born-digital genre (e-books, electronic journals, and Web sites) and multimedia.

The amount of activity and new initiatives is dizzying, but the basic pieces of the digitization puzzle and policy elements are coming into place. As seen in the following overview, these initiatives feature cooperative ventures within and among the major universities, the online bibliographic utilities, and the government.

The nature of library staffs is changing with a cadre of digital librarians and non-librarian information technologists all striving to be at the cutting edge of the Web. In this effort, the importance of catalogers who come preequipped with metadata skills, is only now being realized.

- Descriptions and processing draw heavily on metadata approaches.
- While many continue with the original Web, the technological locus is rapidly moving toward the second-generation Web and XML hierarchical database schema.
- Internal files will likely be managed by DBMS engines and involve massive electronic storage arrays.
- The rub is with establishing methods for Digital Rights Management and the contracting libraries' responsibilities to limit access to their constituents.

PRESERVATION STRATEGIES

Digital preservation is a hallmark, but the definition of that phrase is evolving away from the conservation of original documents. As one dealing with the remnants of five- and even eight-inch floppies can attest, electronic storage is fraught with peril. At one time, preservation remedies attempted to maintain "Smithsonians" of obsolete equipment—or reliance on paper and microfilm copies. Fortunately, the open source movement helped revolutionize the picture.

PRESERVATION RESOURCES

The amount of information and available resources for digital preservation is expanding rapidly. In addition to the NDIPP (http://www.digitalpreservation.gov), the Council on Library and Information Resources (CLIR) (http://www.clir.org) picked up part of the gauntlet through its Commission on Preservation and Access. The related Digital Library Federation provides a major resource (http://www.diglib.org/preserve.htm). The Northeast Document Conservation Center (NEDCC) offers advice with *A Handbook for Digital Projects* (http://www.nedcc.org). ARL has a number of solid "Spec Kits" available in print and on the preservation section of its Web site (http://www.arl.org/preserv). Other online resources include Australia's PADI (Preserving Access to Digital Information) (http://www.nla.gov.au/padi) and COOL conservator's resource site (http://palimpsest.stanford.edu). Finally, Gregory Hunter's *Preserving Digital Information* in the same series as this book provides an excellent overview.

Pragmatic Turn.

Once again, in a less-than-perfect world, there are no perfect solutions. Recent literature reflects that reality and a maturing move away from print-era orientations. Absolutist demands for exact replication of the "original" encoding and "permanence" are giving way. The unity and indivisibility of ink on paper is simply not applicable to the digital realm. Instead, market forces and the practical limits of the technology come to the fore. Preservation and permanence are recognized as misnomers—"long-term" maintenance is in vogue.

In CLIR's *The State of Digital Preservation* (http://www.clir.org/pubs/abstract/pub107abst.html) for the NDIIPP, Kenneth Thibodeau of NARA and project leader for DoD 5015.2 lists four "obvious" principles:

- **FEASIBILITY:** *requires hardware and software capable of implementing the method.*
- **SUSTAINABILITY**: *means either that the method can be applied indefinitely into the future or that*

there are credible grounds for asserting that another path will offer a logical sequel to the method, should it cease being sustainable. The sustainability of any given method has internal and external components: internally, the method must be immune or isolated from the effects of technological obsolescence; externally, it must be capable of interfacing with other methods, such as for discovery and delivery, which will continue to change.

- **PRACTICALITY:** *requires that implementation be within reasonable limits of difficulty and expense.*
- **APPROPRIATENESS:** *depends on the types of objects to be preserved and on the specific objectives of preservation.*

Preservation Strategies.

Basic preservation strategies are evolving, based on the open source codes and standards. Reliance on backups and "Digital Masters" of media seems established for unique materials. The maintenance of electronic publications appears destined to be a cooperative venture with redundant copies among multiple licensees. We also note a rough consensus on two main "refreshing" strategies to handle long-term storage:

- **MIGRATION:** Information is periodically recopied onto newer, standardized formats and media. This is the dominant trend and recommendation from the Web Museum scenario. Migration occurs across:
    - **EXTERNAL STORAGE MEDIA**—e.g., among various types of diskette, to CD, to DVD, to DAT… (Note: DAT is out of favor)
    - **INTERNAL COMPUTER STORAGE** from hard disk to hard disk as new machines come online
    - **SOFTWARE PRODUCTS** as the product lines upgrade or a new leader emerges—e.g., Word Star, to WordPerfect, to MS Word
    - **STORAGE FORMATS** as standards evolve or are replaced—e.g., HTML 1.0 to 4.0 to XHTML, SGML to XML, ASCII to RDF)

- **EMULATION:** Future computers are to be configured with retro-capacities. They will be fitted with special software to mimic as closely as possible the original program and recreate its original look, feel, and functions.

Scientist Jeff Rothenburg led the drive for emulation in his oft-cited 1999 article "Avoiding Technological Quicksand" (http://www.clir.org/pubs/abstract/pub77.html). As he noted, standards are never fixed—they alter significantly over time and with new generations. Something as seemingly stable as TIFF comes in at least two flavors. Equally important, the rules are at the whim of commercial powers, which understandably feel free to "play" for their own purposes. This is especially the case with digital multimedia and competing business standards.

Media Techniques.

Interesting debates have transpired over the importance of saving the original analog signals versus the digital master. Analog files can produce extremely "dense" signals. Digitization can make exorbitant storage demands, demand possibly distorting compression programs, or be technically beyond the power of some equipment. Moreover, can we stem the tide of technological obsolescence?

- The use of analog media is inherently destructive. Each play produces wear and tear. Every copy or new generation results in a loss of signal.
- The copying of digital records occurs without generational loss. Every version can be an exact duplicate of its parents or offspring
- The commercial marketplace is replacing previous media equipment with digital versions and making it difficult—if not impossible—to maintain viewing of older materials.

Methods.

Techniques for digital media follow the same path as other types of digital collections, but with one variation. Given the amount of data involved, storage and retrieval is typically removed from the active file system. Instead, one produces "Digital Masters" in a compact storage format—e.g., CDs or DVDs, which are commonplace and quite affordable. Practical suggestions include:

- If authentication is an issue, use "write-once" disks versus rewritable.

- Make a back-up copy, which is preferably stored in another location.
- At this time, rely on MPEG-4 and DVDs as the preferred vehicles.

Fig. 8.4. Digital Video Storage Delivery Formats				
	DVD=DivX (MPEG-4)	CD=VCD (MPEG-1)	CD=SVCD (MPEG-2)	MiniDVD (DVD-on-CD)
Video Resolution	560x240 (Widescreen— variable)	352x240 (*NTSC)	480x480 (NTSC)	720x480 (NTSC)
Video Quality	Low-High (SVHS)	Low (VHS)	Medium-High (SVHS)	Best (SVHS)
Audio Resolution	Stereo,16bit, 48kHz (MP3— variable)	Stereo, 16bit, 44.1kHz	Stereo, 16bit, 44.1kHz	Dolby Digital (AC3)
Audio Quality	Low-Best	Medium	Medium	Best
File Size (1 hour)	150– 500+ MB	500+ MB	400+ MB	1500+ MB
*NTSC is the US's television transmission standard—PAL the European.				

Digital Rights Management.

Libraries are not necessarily the copyright holders of the new digital genre that they hope to preserve. Since licensing agreements have superceded right of sale privilege, libraries are forced to seek arrangements with data aggregators or the copyright holders of e-books, electronic journals, and newscasts.

Distribution details, royalties, audit trail, and role-definition for this type of operation are not clearly defined at the moment, but suggest intense negotiations with publishers for cooperative efforts for long-term or permanent archival rights. Library leadership will rest with the Library of Congress's Copyright Division and the National Digital

Information Infrastructure Preservation Program. The Copyright Clearance Center (http://www.copyright.com) will also likely take a prominent role in future developments.

RESEARCH LIBRARIES

Research libraries are pushing toward a digital library scenario on an individual basis and through collaborative ventures with ARL, the Council on Library and Information Resources, the Digital Library Federation, RLG and ad hoc linkages. The overriding theme is improved research and educational supports for their parent institution. The drive also responds to historical responsibilities to preserve information along with escalating costs for materials and their storage.

DLXS AND FEDORA SOFTWARE

The academic community has produced at least two software programs to help implement the vision of digital libraries on the second-generation Web. The University of Michigan has a working suite with its DLXS (Digital Library eXtension Service) product. DLXS is for a Unix environment and is not cheap. But it does come with software tools for mounting sites and the powerful XPAT search engine, which is tuned to use all our metadata and XML tags.

The University of Virginia, a pioneer on the digital library scene, is leading a consortium in developing Cornell University's FEDORA (Flexible Extensible Digital Object and Repository Architecture). Currently, FEDORA remains in a pilot mode, but when ready, it will be released as an open source program, which works by modularizing of data, interface, and program segments.

Foreign Materials.

Economic pressure emerged for foreign language resources. In the early 1990s, the Mellon Foundation became aware of a decline in the purchase of non-English language materials. With Mellon Foundation funding, the Association of American Universities and ARL started a Global Resources Program. Their North American Digital Library initiative involves several Web-based pilots. The University of Texas took one lead with an outstanding LARRP site on Latin American Resources (http://www.lanis.texas.edu). Other pilots are aimed at Germany, Japan, and Southeast Asia.

Digital Collection Development.

The digital library scenario involves other areas of collection development. New collection development specialists increasingly factor digital archives as a given and deal with:

- **ARCHIVES:** The manuscript, image, and media files that the institution holds the copyright to, which may include faculty production.

- **FREE WEB:** Many resources are now available without charge, but often without any guarantee of future availability. Such a threat may lead to formal arrangements to mirror and even archive content.

- **LICENSING:** Those periodicals, databases, and other information services that are under contract. Questions include the ability to deliver offsite, participation in cost-cutting group arrangements, and the ability to license for long-term/archival access.

A COUNTER RIGHTS WAVE AND DEPOSITORY FUNCTION

The university library or archives often acts as the official depository for theses and dissertations. Only now, electronic submission is replacing the traditional requirements for print versions. In such a scenario, logging, preservation, and most policy matters would remain the same. But the option for Web publication would demand consideration.

Similarly, universities are objecting more often to paying twice for their professors' work—once for the salary and the second to license back the use of their articles. The result is a drive for at least shared copyright of their intellectual productions. In addition to enhanced depository function for digital archives, this movement could substantially alter the nature of a publishers market, which dates to the print revolution. One also notes collective efforts by professional history associations to provide electronic access to their journals to subscribers—including their institutional members.

LIBRARY OF CONGRESS

Given the immense scope of these challenges and interests, it is not surprising that the government has taken a growing interest. The Library of Congress retains a singular leadership role for the library field in all these matters. The world's largest library holds a pivotal legal position as a U.S. government's agency and its copyright depository. In addition to cooperation with research libraries and other federal agencies, LC maintains many of the key standards and authors or sponsors research initiatives. LC's emerging goal appears no less than a cooperative, multi-institutional National or Global Digital Library.

National Digital Information Infrastructure (NDIIPP).

In December of 2000, Congress appropriated $100,000,000 for the Library of Congress to head a National Digital Information Infrastructure Preservation Program (PL106–554). The *Preserving Our*

Digital Heritage plan of 2002 and a number of "environmental scans" of the current state-of-the-art in digital preservation are available on its Web site (http://www.digitalpreservation.gov).

NDIIPP is a cooperative venture with a twenty-seven-member board of federal and major library stakeholders along with business interests. The program includes:

1. a focus on building from LC's position as the nation's copyright depository to address digital rights management;

2. a general focus on collaborative digital preservation with ongoing research, a functional business model, and evolving "best practices";

3. the technical focus on born-digital publications—a baseline study, *Building a National Digital Stratagem* (http://www.clir.org/pubs/abstract/pub106abst .html), for example, appeared in early 2002 with discussions on six major areas of interest:
   - electronic books
   - electronic journals
   - large Web sites
   - digitally recorded sound
   - digital film
   - digital television.

IMLS FRAMEWORK

The Institute of Museum and Library Services (IMLS) plays a related federal role through grants that set the directions for the both the library and museum fields. Its *Framework of Guidance for Building Good Digital Collections* sustains the subtle new tone for digital archives (http://www.imls.gov/pubs/forumframework.htm). The document turns from electronic facsimiles toward born-digital publications. It defines the attributes of "good" digital archives:

1. *A good digital collection is created according to an explicit collection development policy that has been agreed upon and documented before digitization begins.*

2. *Collections should be described so that a user can discover important characteristics of the collection,*

including scope, format, restrictions on access, ownership, and any information significant for determining the collection's authenticity, integrity and interpretation.

3. *A collection should be sustainable over time. In particular, digital collections built with special funding should have a plan for their continued usability beyond the funded period.*

4. *A good collection is broadly available and avoids unnecessary impediments to use. Collections should be accessible to persons with disabilities, and usable effectively in conjunction with adaptive technologies.*

5. *A good collection respects intellectual property rights. Collection managers should maintain a consistent record of rights holders and permissions granted for all applicable materials.*

6. *A good collection provides some measurement of use. Counts should be aggregated by period and maintained over time so that comparison can be made.*

7. *A good collection fits into the larger context of significant related national and international digital library initiatives. For example, collections of content useful for education in science, math and/or engineering should be usable in the NSDL.*

Object Definitions.

The IMLS Framework also defines the attributes for "a good digital object":

- *It will be produced in a way that ensures it supports collection priorities.*

- *It is persistent. That is, it will be the intention of some known individual or institution that the good object will persist; that it will remain accessible over time despite changing technologies.*

- *It is digitized in a format that supports intended current and likely future use or that support the development of access copies that support those uses. Consequently, a good object is exchangeable across platforms, broadly accessible, and will either be digitized according to a recognized standard or best practice or deviate from standards and practices only for well documented reasons.*

- *It will be named with a persistent, unique identifier that conforms to a well-documented scheme. It will not be named with reference to its absolute filename or address (e.g. as with URLs and other Internet addresses) as filenames and addresses have a tendency to change. Rather, the filename's location will be resolvable with reference to its identifier.*

- *It will either have a known preservation strategy (e.g. as with SGML-encoded ASCII texts where migration through changing regimes is both known and deemed viable and cost effective) or a good chance of evolving such a strategy (e.g. where widespread commercial investment in the format—PDF—makes development of an effective preservation strategy highly likely).*

- *It can be authenticated in at least two senses. First, a user should be able to determine the object's origins, structure, and developmental history (version, etc.). Second, a user should be able to determine that the object is what it purports to be.*

- *It will have and be associated with metadata. All good objects will have descriptive and administrative metadata. Some will have metadata that supplies information about their external relationships to other objects (e.g. the structural metadata that determines how page images from a digitally reformatted book relate to one another in some sequence).*

OAIS REFERENCE MODEL

Arguably, the most important direction for digital archives and enhanced preservation emanates from outside the repository world. American space agencies have long engaged data mines. They seek methods to capture, access, and store mind-boggling amounts of data that stream from satellites.

NASA's Consultative Committee for Space Data Systems put forth a call for an Open Archival Information System—OAIS (ISO 14721:2002) in 1999. The goal was the "long-term" preservation of digital assets through a confederation of trusted archives. In this model, archives were defined as:

Consisting of an organization of people and systems, that has accepted the responsibility to presser information and make it available for a Designated Community...

Ontology.

OAIS provides a shared set of definitions—an ontology that reduces confusion among the contributing disciplines. As illustrated in figure 8.5, the standard emerges as a "black box" to define all aspects of the digital archives Instead of concentrating on material as received by the repository, the reference model represents the interactions of the real world. It reflects three sets of players: producers, archives, and information requesters. OAIS takes into account market forces, evolving trends, and sets the base for future standards. Operations are arrayed among six functions, which are captured in three types of application or "information packages."

1. **SUBMISSION INFORMATION PACKAGE (SIP)** is issued by the producer of the digital content as an ingest function to initiate an Archival Information Package.

2. **ARCHIVAL INFORMATION PACKAGE (AIP)** of descriptive information for the Archives has four subcomponents: Content Information (CI), Preservation Description Information (PDI), Packaging Information (PI), and Descriptive Information (DI). AIP involves four interrelated functional engines:
   - Archival Storage for long-term preservation
   - Data Management for database administration, queries, and system updates
   - Administrative Services as the motor to handle operations
   - Preservation Planning for monitoring the technology and migrations or other strategies that are implemented by Administrative Services

3. **DISSEMINATION INFORMATION PACKAGE (DIP)** emerges from Consumer queries or delivery orders through the Access Function.

Fig. 8.5. OAIS Conceptual Framework

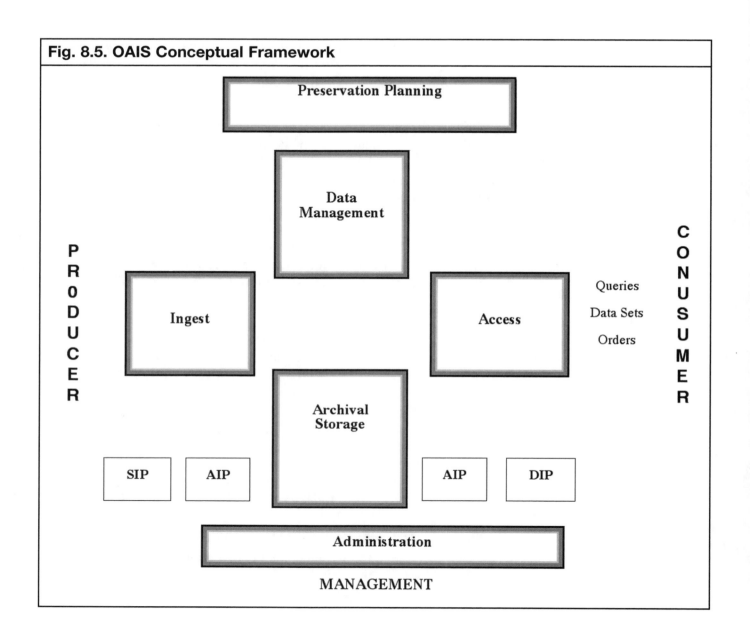

METS AND METADATA

We have encountered a number of metadata schemas with potential for digital archives—such as MPEG-7 for media. METS is among the most intriguing, because it offers a broad and unifying framework for controlling "libraries" of digital objects (http://www.loc.gov/mets/). Maintained at the Library of Congress, METS is also the centerpiece of the Digital Library Federation's long-range commitment to the Web.

METS AND MOA

METS derived from the landmark Making of America (MOA) project at Cornell and Michigan and MOA2 from Berkeley. Those efforts provided searchable, full-text access to thousands of monographs and journal articles (See: http://www.hti.umich.edu/m/moagrp/). They also developed a shared metadata strategy to coordinate their efforts: sunsite.berkeley.edu/MOA2. The scheme, like other library projects, divided tags among administrative, descriptive, and structural elements.

METS is especially applicable to large-scale applications and the digital libraries of the future. It embraces the new opportunities offered by XML and OAIS. METS goes beyond the exchange of individual digital objects to handle related families—e.g., complete collections, displays that range from thumbnails and JPEG on the Web to in-house TIFF masters. The standard itself is built through five metadata categories:

1. **DESCRIPTIVE METADATA** points to an external descriptive record, like a MARC or EAD entry, and/or contains its own descriptive elements. The descriptive metadata section is composed of Descriptive Metadata Sections <dmdSec>. These wrappers can indicate either:

   - **EXTERNAL DESCRIPTIVE METADATA (MDREF):** elaborates on the address with attributes for the type of location (URN, URI, PURL), encoding type, and type of metadata; the last has specified values for: DC, DDI (Data Documentation Initiative), EAD, FGDC (Federal Geographic Data Committee), LC-AV, MARC, NISOIMG (NISO for digital still images), TEIHDR (TEI and header)

   - **INTERNAL DESCRIPTIVE METADATA (MDWRAP):** either XML-encodes metadata outside the METS namespace—e.g., EAD and DC—or uses other binary or textual formatting

2. **ADMINISTRATIVE METADATA** indicates background on the origins of the object, including provenance, copyright, and migration or transformation information. <amdSec> holds administrative metadata about the digital asset, but can also refer to the original. There are four subsets available:

   - **TECHNICAL METADATA** on the creation, format, and use nature of the file

- **INTELLECTUAL PROPERTY RIGHTS METADATA** on copyright and licensing
- **SOURCE METADATA** about the original
- **DIGITAL PROVENANCE METADATA** with background about origins, migrations, transformations of the digital object and its relations to the original

3. **FILE GROUPS** list all the electronic files that collectively make up the object. *<fileGrp>* elements group the related files around a digital library object—e.g., preservation master, pdf version, thumbnail image, downloadable media and streaming media versions.

4. **STRUCTURAL MAP** provides the *<structMap>* at the heart of a METS document. *<structMap>* outlines the hierarchical order for digital library objects. It links the elements of that structure to content files and metadata that pertain to each element. The area is split into nested series of division *<div>* elements. These are defined through attributes to declare the type of *<div>*, e.g., oral history, photograph collection, article. The wrapper can hold METS pointers *<mptr>* to other METS documents and file pointers *<ftpr>* to those inside the structural map. The following example of *"an extremely simple structural map"* is taken from the METS tutorial on the LC site (See: Figure 8.6).

5. **EXECUTABLE BEHAVIORS** or "verbs" for the contents can come with METS. This is especially appropriate to OAIS operations. For instance, imbedded METS tags could automate review and migration actions similar to that of book conservation programs.

OAI—HARVESTING METADATA

The Open Archives Initiative came from the same MOA roots as METS. OAI provides METS with an XML action component to "harvest" the metadata. According to the *Open Archives Initiative Protocol for Metadata Harvesting Protocol Version 1.1*, the goal is for *"an application-independent interoperability framework that can be used by a variety of communities who are engaged in publishing content on the Web"* (http://www.openarchives.org/OAI/openarchivesprotocol.htm). OAI harvest requests are sent out to the XML data sets of individual or service group providers to gather metadata for comparison and subsequent retrieval of pertinent records.

Fig. 8.6. Mets Structural Map

```
<structMap TYPE="logical">
  <div ID="div1" LABEL="Oral History: Mayor Abraham Beame" TYPE="oral history">
    <div ID="div1.1" LABEL="Interviewer Introduction" ORDER="1">
      <fptr FILEID="FILE001">
        <area FILEID="FILE001" BEGIN="INTVWBG" END="INTVWND" BETYPE="IDREF" />
      </fptr>
      <fptr FILEID="FILE002">
        <area FILEID="FILE002" BEGIN="00:00:00" END="00:01:47" BETYPE="TIME" />
      </fptr>
      <fptr FILEID="FILE003">
        <area FILEID="FILE003" BEGIN="00:00:00" END="00:01:47" BETYPE="TIME" />
      </fptr>
    </div>
    <div ID="div1.2" LABEL="Family History" ORDER="2">
      <fptr FILEID="FILE001">
        <area FILEID="FILE001" BEGIN="FHBG" END="FHND" BETYPE="IDREF" />
      </fptr>
      <fptr FILEID="FILE002">
        <area FILEID="FILE002" BEGIN="00:01:48" END="00:06:17" BETYPE="TIME" />
      </fptr>
      <fptr FILEID="FILE003">
        <area FILEID="FILE003" BEGIN="00:01:48" END="00:06:17" BETYPE="TIME" />
      </fptr>
    </div>
    <div ID="div1.3" LABEL="Introduction to Teachers' Union" ORDER="3">
      <fptr FILEID="FILE001">
        <area FILEID="FILE001" BEGIN="TUBG" END="TUND" BETYPE="IDREF" />
      </fptr>
      <fptr FILEID="FILE002">
        <area FILEID="FILE002" BEGIN="00:06:18" END="00:10:03" BETYPE="TIME" />
      </fptr>
      <fptr FILEID="FILE003">
        <area FILEID="FILE003" BEGIN="00:06:18" END="00:10:03" BETYPE="TIME" />
      </fptr>
    </div>
  </div>
</structMap>
```

This structural map shows that we have an oral history (with Mayor Abraham Beame of New York City) that includes three subsections: an opening introduction by the interviewer, some family history from Mayor Beame, and a discussion of how he came to be involved with the teachers' union in New York. Each of these subsections/divisions is linked to three files (taken from our earlier example of file groups): an XML transcription and a master and derivative audio file. A subsidiary <area> element is used in each <fptr> to indicate that this division corresponds with only a portion of the linked file, and to identify the exact portion of each linked file. For example, the first division (the interviewer introduction) is linked to a portion of the XML transcription file (FILE001) which is found between the two tags in the transcription file with ID attribute values of "INTVWBG" and "INTVWND." It is also linked to the two different audio files; in these cases, rather than specifying ID attribute values within the linked files, the begin and end points of the linked material within the files is indicated by a simple time code value of the form HH:MM:SS. So the interviewer introduction can be found in both audio files in the segment beginning at time 00:00:00 in the file and extending through time 00:01:47.

TRUSTED REPOSITORIES

Finally, we can point to initiatives to add a layer of professional credentials for digital archives. In 1996, a joint committee with RLG's Task Force on Archiving of Digital Information and the Commission on Preservation and Access issued a forward-looking report (http://www.rlg.org/ArchTF/ tfadi.index.htm). The committee noted the need for national and internal systems of digital libraries. Concerted efforts were in order to guarantee the world's "long-term" access to the cultural, economic, intellectual, scientific, and social information in electronic formats.

OCLC and RLG pursued this vision with renewed vigor in the aftermath of the OAIS's call for trusted repositories. The utilities commissioned a joint effort in March of 2001. The RLG-OCLC *Attributes of a Trusted Digital Repository* (http://www.rlg.org/longterm/attributes01 .pdf) appeared with remarkable speed in August of 2001. The report suggested that a "trusted repository" must demonstrate five attributes:

- administrative responsibility
- organizational viability
- technological abilities
- security
- accountability

The Committee continued its work with *Trusted Digital Repositories: Attributes and Responsibilities* in January of 2002. This report calls for more research and new tools, and advocates relationships of trust between the repository, content creators, and holders of the information rights—as well as present and future users. It proffers a series of defining characteristics for a trusted digital repository:

- *Accept responsibility for long-term maintenance of digital resources on behalf of its depositors and for the benefit of current and future users.*

- *Have an organizational system that supports not only long-term viability of the repository, but also the digital information for which it has responsibility.*

- *Demonstrate fiscal responsibility and sustainability.*

- *Design its systems in accordance with commonly accepted conventions and standards to ensure the* ongoing management, access, and security of material deposited within it.

- Establish methodologies for system evaluation that meet community expectations of trustworthiness.

- Be dependent upon to carry out its long-term responsibility to depositors and users openly and explicitly.

- Have policies, practices and performance that can be audited and measured.

Ultimately, the report acknowledges that most established archives, libraries, and museums are trusted, but goes further to recommend a formal certification process. The likely criteria are found in Appendix C, which is reproduced below.

Fig. 8.7. Operational Responsibilities Checklist for Trusted Repositories

Negotiating for and Accepting Information from Content Providers

☐ Well-documented and agreed-on policies about what is selected for deposit, including, where appropriate, specific required formats.

☐ Effective procedures and workflow for obtaining copyright clearance for both short-term and immediate access, as necessary, and preservation.

☐ A comprehensive metadata specification and agreed-on standards for its implementation.

☐ Procedures and systems for ensuring the authenticity of submitted materials.

☐ Initial assessment of the completeness of the submission.

☐ Effective record keeping of all transactions, including ongoing relationships, with content providers.

Obtaining Sufficient Control of the Information

☐ Detailed analysis of an object or class of objects to assess its significant properties. Analysis should be automated as much as possible and informed by the collections management policy, rights clearances, the designated community's knowledge base, and policy restrictions on specific file formats.

☐ Verification and creation of bibliographic and technical metadata and documentation to support the long-term preservation of the digital object according to its significant properties and underlying technology or abstract form, with monitoring and updating of metadata as necessary to reflect changes in technology or access arrangements. This involves understanding how strategies for continuing access, such as migration and emulation, influence the creation of preservation metadata.

☐ A robust system of unique identification.

☐ A reliable method for encapsulating the digital object with its metadata in the archive.

☐ A reliable archival storage facility, including an ongoing program of media refreshment; a program of monitoring media; geographically distributed backup systems; routine authenticity and integrity checking of the stored object; disaster preparedness; response and recovery policies and procedures; and security.

Fig. 8.7. (cont.)

Determining the Repositories Designated Community
☐ *Analysis and documentation of the repository's current designated community as well as the possible needs and modes of access of future users.*
☐ *For federated or cooperating repositories, a shared understanding of the designated communities that are to be served.*
☐ *Ensuring the Information to Be Preserved Is Independently Understandable.*
☐ *A "technology watch" to manage the risk as technology evolves and to provide continuing access and updated methods of access as necessary, such as new migrations or emulators.*

Following Documented Policies and Procedures
☐ *Policies for collections development (e.g., selection and retention) that link to technical procedures about how and at what level materials are preserved and how access is provided both short and long term.*
☐ *Policies for access control to ensure all parties are protected, including authentication of users and disseminated materials.*
☐ *Policies for storage of materials, including service-level agreements with external suppliers.*
☐ *Policies that define the repository's designated community and describe its knowledge base.*
☐ *A rigorous system for updating policies and procedure in accordance with changes in technology and in the repository's designated community.*
☐ *Explicit links between these policies and procedures, allowing for easy application across heterogeneous collections.*

Making the Preserved Information Available to the Designated Community
☐ *A system for discovery of resources.*
☐ *Appropriate mechanisms for authentication of the digital materials.*
☐ *Access control mechanisms in accordance with licenses and laws, and an "access rights watch."*
☐ *Mechanisms for managing electronic commerce.*
☐ *User support programs.*

Advocating Good Practices in the Creation of Digital Resources
☐ *Effective mechanisms for advocating good practice for content providers.*

AFTERWORD: SETTING THE HISTORICAL CONTEXT

Si fieri potest, ornentur codices pulchro decore, ut etiam aspectu sui ad lectionem provocent intuentes. Hoc enim veteres magno studio procurasse cognovimus, ut venustas exterior interiorem codicum pulchritudinem commendaret.... Covendum tamen est, ne ipse ornatus sit curiosus, ne pulchritudinem rectitudini preponamus, quia ubi honestas admittitur...

> *As far as possible, manuscripts should be decorated so that their appearance alone will produce study. We understand that the ancient writers took great care in matching exterior beauty with internal contents.... However, we should also be aware that such ornamentation must not prevail over truth—that only honesty rules...*

> Johannes Trithemius, *De Laude Scriptorium (In Praise of Scribes),* Published in Mainz, Germany, 1494 from the manuscript of 1492.

Johannes Trithemius provided a prophetic vision for those in the current communication's revolution. As he suggested, information should be attractively presented—but truthful content must rule. Trithemius shared present concerns about the loss of quality and preservation problems with a new medium. In his case, newfangled paper would only last 200 years. Despite his fears, the abbot had taken a crucial step. He had embraced the new technology and turned it into a tool for his institution.

HISTORICAL MUSINGS

Cultural repositories have repeatedly reordered themselves in response to technological change. Indeed, we can gain valuable lessons from our past. The mechanization of printing provides the most significant examples and metaphors for understanding the current revolution. Print even supplies the starting spot for the terminology and reading methods that we use on the Web today.

GUTENBERG AND TIME

For an online review of the print thesis see: H-Net, H-Ideas... Series, http://www .hnet.msu.edu/^ideas.

Gutenberg's fifteenth-century innovations were the dividing line for modern society. They radically altered the nature of information and redefined its supporting institutions. Copying traditions that dated to Ancient Sumer and Egypt were destroyed. The scribal-librarian disappeared, and archives divided from libraries.

Other interested parties appeared on the scene. State-sponsored copyright appeared and individual authorship blossomed. Moreover, a new group of players wrested control of production from the repositories. Arguably the world's first capitalists, publishers took command of the book and pushed into unknown territory. Their experiences provide illustrations and ongoing precedents for today's communication revolution.

A major lesson then and now was the importance of the time. Time was needed for innovation and the evolution of the media. It took a fifty-year break-in period, the Incunabulum, before what we would recognize as a modern book emerged. Publisher/printers had to develop the trappings of paragraphing, tables of contents, and indexes. Contributions included a revolutionary new form of publicity. Instead of a closing colophon, the title page emerged as the main method for identifying a book. It would become the key tool for the newly recast field of librarianship.

Publishers made the crucial advance beyond massive volumes and dense gothic lettering for readings at lecterns. The Venetian printer Aldus Manutius sculpted a light humanistic type font as part of his invention of the pocketbook—the birth of portable and personalized reading.

Even more time was needed for the formats and reading conventions that we now take for granted. During the sixteenth century, the world gained vernacular literature, religious tracts, and rudimentary schoolbooks. In the process, Cartesian logic and the scientific method took hold. The scholastic concentration on uncovering the truths from the Bible and a few authoritative volumes gave way to multiple texts and a very different approach to the organization of knowledge.

With the centuries came a panoply of previously unknown types of publication and concomitant responsibilities for the redefined librarian. The coming years yielded broadsides and early forms of the newspaper, the novel, hornbooks, and encyclopedias. Each new genre demanded subtly different reading and navigational skills. And much more was in the offing from still another communications revolution.

MASS CULTURE FERMENT

Despite the advances, printing did not approach its potential for three more centuries. It only matured within the ferment of the nineteenth century, when early industrialization enhanced methods for printing, bindings, and inexpensive wood pulp paper. Such capacities set one side of the stage for the rise of mass culture. Technology needed a market, which it found in the burgeoning offspring of compulsory education laws. Literacy had become the norm for the first time in history. A large audience developed with newly standardized methods for reading and shared grammar lessons.

To the chagrin of arbiters of good taste, literacy enabled a new consumerism. People were eager for entertainment. The modern press and propaganda were born along with illustrated magazines and dime novels. Print did not stop. It continued to evolve into new formats. People began to intuit such diverse formats as phone books, comic books and, recently, computer manuals.

Today's cultural information professionals are in many ways the proper products of mass culture, but also a byproduct of the overlapping forces of Nationalism. Emerging nation-states and entrepreneurs sought institutions to chronicle and celebrate their advancements. Something was needed to assist the educational messages, manage the explosion of information, and define or perhaps defend cultural spheres.

Led by the French Bibliothèque Nationale and the British Museum, Western archives, libraries, and museums were reinvented as nationalistic expressions. Such drives reached down to the municipal level. The American invention of the public library quickly evolved into a requisite symbol to distinguish a progressive and civilized community.

Nationalism and technology also melded with the "New University" movement. Rather than the classical liberal arts, higher education turned to creating and supporting "professions." Newly created land-grant colleges and older institutions also reflected the era's penchant for scientific taxonomies and classification. Librarianship, which had been largely a scholarly or antiquarian retreat, became a distinct field with training in its own right.

By the early twentieth century, the Dewey Decimal and Library of Congress Classification System entered the public consciousness. The first generation of university-educated specialists stepped forward on their own. Librarians and curators created tools to further classify and handle expanding resources.

The fields also continued to share in, and evolve in response to, technological advances. Edison would conquer the night and open new hours with the electric light bulb. Air conditioning entered the scene. It enhanced the patrons' experience and incidentally contributed significantly to preservation. Professional practices developed in response to an ever-unfolding range of technologies, which would coalesce with automation:

- **DESCRIPTION:** Printed catalog cards appeared in the early twentieth century and helped stimulate national and international cooperation. By mid-century, such efforts devolved into the Anglo-American Cataloguing Rules and, in the 1960s, MARC for the computer age.
- **MEDIA:** The output of the presses would be joined by phonograph recordings, films, audiotapes, videos and a move forward to CDs and DVDs.
- **REPRODUCTION:** The mini-press of the typewriter appeared. With assistance from carbon paper and mimeographs, it allowed for local directories and archival Finding Aids. The photocopiers and cassette recorders of the 1960s added reprographic potential. In the 1980s, computer printers entered the scene. Today, digital scanners have risen to the fore.
- **STORAGE:** New filing cabinets from the late nineteenth century morphed into card catalogs. Princeton files and plastic enclosures were supplemented by the massive potential of hard disks, CDs, and DVDs.
- **TELECOMMUNICATION:** Alexander Graham Bell's telephone also rang in changes and new services. By the close of the twentieth century, the device would be supplemented by facsimile transmissions, overlap with computers through wide and local area computer networks (WANs and LANs), and spread globally through the World Wide Web.

POLITICAL AND COMMERCIAL CONTEXT

Technology and good intentions do not fully explain the nature and direction of the Web—politics and entrepreneurship are also factors. At a macro-level, the nationalism of print is being replaced by the globalism of the Web. The Information Highway was born of multinational cooperation and rests on international standards. The medium is transforming business practices and turning information into a world commodity–one that knows no boundaries. Such power has spawned an empire of complimentary and competitive forces across the virtual landscape:

- **W3C** became the titular seat of the empire. The organization has declared itself vitally concerned with:
  - maintaining open systems;
  - insuring the Web is useable for all people—regardless of their physical limitations; and
  - enabling content for computer understanding.
- **TECHNICAL STANDARDS ORGANIZATIONS** have involved themselves in a collective drive for open, non-proprietary systems (e.g., ISO-International Standards Organization, NISO-National Information Standards Organization, etcetera). W3C looks to the Internet Engineering Taskforce for communications structures.
- **GOVERNMENTS** play an increasingly important role. They are involved with telecommunications infrastructure and the onset of coordinated "e-government." Officials are integrally involved on the regulatory and legal side with copyright, content questions, privacy rights, and taxes. The European Union, in particular, seems interested in vying for leadership with the United States.
- **ACADEMIC RESEARCH COMPLEXES,** including universities and governmental research interests, have joined in a push for some of the most powerful applications.
- **COMMERCIAL INTERESTS** include the for-profit kings of IBM and Microsoft. They extend to such lesser royalty as Sun Microsystems and Xerox, along with the knights-errant of the software clans. These have their research interests and may control the final destiny of the medium.

CULTURAL PROSPECTS

> Note: We would still face another fifty years if we wished the Web to reach the maturity that print reached in the nineteenth century.

We sit within a "Cyber-Incunabulum" with the need to work with technology and political factors. Time remains the crucial variable. Web creator Berners-Lee projects development in Web years of 2.6 months. If so, the end of 2002 marked a rite of passage. Like the fifty years of the print Incunabulum, the Web should have incubated to a stable level. The Information Highway will have the basic conventions that future generations will take for granted.

2002 did mark the coalescence of a number of major directions on the Web. Yet new Web options continue to appear almost daily. The interplay between HTML and XML has hardly begun. Will structured RDF and metatags triumph, or will the fuzzy knowledge management offered by search engines and other software? Moreover, sound, color, and video facilities have barely been scratched. What new genres will appear to capture the full range of the Web's potential? How will reading or viewing habits be redefined in a multimedia era?

At a parochial level, what will be the role of our cultural institutions in this new age? Will fields long separated by subtly different objects of study and subtly divergent descriptive devices be reunited by digital products? Will the archival, library, and museum communities have a definitive say with the Web or be relegated, as with print, to the backwaters behind commercial interests? I believe that the future potential of cultural repositories for the Web depends on a coming together and a remixing of the skills of our three major fields.

- **ARCHIVISTS** are needed for insights into the nature of unique collective resources of unique materials and integration within active information systems.
- **LIBRARIANS** are vital for uniting diverse types of original and supporting materials within a descriptive framework for public access.
- **MUSEUM CURATORS** are crucial for display, interpretation, and outreach to make the documentary heritage a living legacy.

Ultimately, the present time seems too precipitous a date for closure. The future likely awaits the insights of those without the built-in biases of our print culture. The world will experience the creations of the first generations raised with an inherent knowledge of hypertext— those for whom the Web and hypertext navigation are assumed facts of life. My best bet is that the Cyber-Incunabulum has time to run, and perhaps 2010 is a better benchmark for stability.

Long-range predictions about the Web are obviously fraught with uncertainty. The closing advice is thus a return to KISS. Like Trithemius, engage the new technology, but strive to set a solid truthful base of digital content. You may approach this as part of the second generation with interactive databases, multimedia, and internal information management. Or you may still make invaluable contributions through the original Web with word-processing and displays. Whatever the case, you can rest assured that we have only begun to scratch the surface of digital archives.

WEBLIOGRAPHY

The following "webliography" lists the links mentioned or referenced during the creation of the text. They were valid at the time the book was published.

A

Active Share (Adobe), <http://www.http://http://www.activeshare.com>
Adobe, <http://www.http://http://www.adobe.com>
Adventure Maker, <http://www.http://http://www.adventuremaker.com>
Albums OnLine, <http://www.albumsonline.com>
AltaMyra Press (PastPresent Software), <http://www.altamyra.com>
AASLH (American Association for State and Local History), <http://www.http://http://www.aaslh.org>
American Heritage Virtual Library Project, <http://sunsite.berkeley.edu/FindingAids/EAD/ameriher.html>
ALA (American Library Association), <http:///www.ala.org/oif>
AMICO, <http://www.http://http://www.amico.org>
ANSI, <http://www.http://http://www.ansi.org>
ArchivesUSA, <http://www.http://http://www.chadwyck.com>
ARL, <http://www.http://http://www.arl.org>
Ask Bobby (Center for Applied Special Technology), <http://www.cast.org/bobby/>
Attributes of a Trusted Digital Repository, <http://www.rlg.org/longterm/attributes01.pdf>
Australian National Archives, <http://www.naa.gov.au>

B

Bath Profile (Z39.50), <http://www.nlc-bnc.ca/bath/bp-current.htm>
Bentley Historical Library of the University of Michigan, <http://www.umich.edu>
Berkley (University of California) Finding Aid Project, <http://sunsite.Berkeley.edu/FindingAids>
Blackboard, <http://www.blackboard.com>
Building and Sustaining Digital Collections, <http://www.clir.org/pubs/reports/pub100/contents.html>
Building a National Digital Stratagem, <http://www.clir.org/pubs/pub106abs.html>

C

Canadian National Archives, <http://www.archives.ca>
Cartographa, <http://www.cartographa.com>
Center for Education and Museum Studies (Smithsonian), <http://educate.si.edu/ ut/about_fs.html>.

C-Net Central, <http://www.cnet.com>
CIMI (Consortium for Computer Exchange of Museum Information), <http://www.cimi.org
Clickteam <http://www.clickteam.com>
Colorado Digital Audio Guidelines, <http://coloradodigital .coalliance.org/digaudio.html>
Conservation OnLine (COOL), <http://palimpsest.stanford.edu>
Copyright Act: Title 17 US Code, <http://www.loc.gov/copyright>
Copyright Clearance Center, <http://www.copyright.com>
Copyright Management Center, <http://www.copyright.iupui.edu>
Copyright Management Center, <http://www.copyright.iupui.edu .about.htm>
Copyright Web Site, <http://www.copyrightwebsite.com/info/notice.asp>
CORC, <http://www.oclc.org/connexion>
Corel Software, <http://www.corel.com>
Council on Library and Information Resources (CLIR), <http://www.clir.org>
Creative Teaching with Historic Places (National Park Service), <http://www.cr.nps.gov /nr/twhp/profdev.htm>
CPB/WGBH National Center for Accessible Media, <ncam.wgbh.org>
CUSTARD (Canadian United States Task Force on Archival Description), <http://www.archivists.org/newscustardproject.asp>
Cyberspace Law Institute, <http://www.cli.org>

D

Designing More Usable Web sites, <http://trace.wisc.edu/world/web/>
Digital Classroom (National Archives), <http://www.archives.gov/ digital_classroom/index.html>
Digital Fridge, <http://www.digitalfridge.com>
Digital Imaging Tutorial, <http://www.library.cornell.edu/preservation/ tutorial/index.html>
Digital Library Federation, <http://www.diglib.org/dlfhomepage.htm>
Digital Millennium Copyright Act (DMCA), <http://www.loc.gov/ copyright/legislation/dmca.pdf>
DFLNewsletter, <http://www.diglib.org/pubs/newsletter.htm>
DLib Magazine, <http://www.dlib.org>

DLXS, <http://www.dlxs.org>
Digital Library Toolkit, <http://www.sun.com/edu or http://www.edulib.com
Dmitry's Design Lab, <http://www.webreference.com>
Dublin Core, <http://www.dublincore.org>
Dublin Core to MARC Converter, <http://www.bibsys.no/meta/dzm/>

E

EAD standards site, <http://lcweb.loc.gov/ead/>
EAD exchange site, <http://jefferson.village.virginia.edu/ead>
EBSCO, <http://www.epnet.com>
Educators Network, <http://www.theeducatorsnetwork.com>
European Archival Net, <http://www.european-archival.net/>
European Copyright User Platform <http://www.eblida.org/ecup>
Ex Libris' SFX Open URL, <http://www.sfxit.com>

F

FEDORA, <http://www.fedora.info/>
Framework of Guidance for Building Good Digital Collections (IMLS), <http://www.imls.gov/pubs/forumframework.htm>
Functional Requirements for Evidence in Records Keeping, <http://www2.lis.pitt.edu ^nhprc>
Funnel Web Analyzer, <http://www.quest.com>

G

Gatherround, <http://www.gatherround.com>
Gale, <http://www.galegroup.com>
GamesInstitute, <http://www.gamesinstitute.org>
Gaming World, <http://www. gamingw.net>
The Gateway to Educational Materials, <http://www.thegateway.org>
Getty Provenance Index, <http://www.getty.edu/research/tools/provenance/>
Getty Thesaurus of Geographic Names (TGN), <http://www.getty.edu/research/tools/vocabulary/tgn/index.html>
Google's search engine download, <http://services.google.com>
Guidelines for Selecting Materials for Digitization (RLG), <http://www.rlg.org/preserv/joint/ayris.html>
Guidelines for Statistical Measures of Usage of Web-based... Resources, <http://www.library.yale.edu/ consortia/webstats.html>
Guidelines for Web Document Style and Design, <http://sunsite.berkeley.edu/Web/guidelines.html>

H

A Handbook for Digital Projects, <http://www.nedcc.org>
Harvard University Digital Selection Guide, <http://preserveharvard .edu/resource/digitization/selection.html>
H-Net, <http://www.h-net.msu.edu/~ideas>
Homestead, <http://www.homestead.com>
HTML Help, <http://www.htmlhelp.com>
HTML Tidy, <http://tidy.sourceforge.net>
HTML Tidy Online, <http://infohound.net/tidy>

I

IMLS, <http://www.imls.gov/>
Informedia Terabyte Project (Carnegie-Mellon), <http://www.informedia .cs.cmu.edu>.
International Center for Disability Resources on the Internet, <http://www.icdri.org/>
ISAD(g) (General International Standard of Archival Description), <http://www.ica.org/eng/mb/com/cds/descriptivestandards.html>
ISAAR (International Standard Archival Authority Records), <http://www.ica.org/ isaar_e.html>
Institute of Museum and Library Services (IMLS), <http://www.imls.gov>
Internet Archive, <http://www.alexa.com>
Internet 2, <http://www.internet2.org>
Internet Engineering Task Force, <http://www.ietf.cnri.reston.va.us/home.html> and Internic <http://www.Internic.net> Internet 2, <http://www.internet2.org>
InterPARES <http://www.interpares.org>
Introduction to Metadata, <http://www.getty.edu/gri/standard/>
ISO, <http://www.iso.ch>

J

Java Homepage, < http://java.sun.com>
Journal of Online Law, <http://www.wm.edu/law/publications/jol/ index.shtml>

L

LARRP (Latin American Resources), <http://www.lanis.texas.edu>
Learning Page (LC's American Memory), <http://memory.loc.gov/ ammem/ndlpedu/index.html>

LessonPlans, < http://lessonplans.com>
Library Journal, <http://www.libraryjournal.com>
Library of Congress, <http://www.loc.gov>
LinkBot (now WebQA), <http://www.watchfire.com/products/webqa.asp>
Link Popularity Check, <http://www.linkpopularitycheck.com>
LinkPopularity, <http://www.linkpopularity.com/>

M

Making of America (MOA), <http://www.hti. umich.edu/m/moagrp>
Making of America Metadata, <http://sunsite.berkeley.edu/MOA2>
Making Local Union History, <http://www.reuther.wayne.edu/services/making.htm>
MARC, <http://lcweb.loc.gov/marc/>
MARC SGML/XML Converters, <http://www.loc.gov/marc/marcxml.html>
Marketleap Visibility Index, <http://linkpop.marketleap.com>
METS, <http://www.loc.gov/mets/>
Microsoft Lesson Connection, <http://www.k12.mcn.com/>
MPEG (Moving Picture Experts Group), <http://mpeg.telecomitalialab.com>
Museum Computer Network, <http://www.mcn.edu>
MyStuff, <http://www.collectify.com>

N

National Archives, U.S., <http://www.archives.gov>
National Digital Information Infrastructure Preservation Program (LC), <http://www.digitalpreservation.gov>.
National Initiative for a Networked Cultural Heritage, <http://www.ninch.org/>
National Endowment for the Arts, <http://www.nea.gov/>
National Endowment for the Humanities, <http://www.neh.fed.us/>
NCSA Beginner's guide to HTML, <http://www.ncsa.uiuc.edu/General/Internet/WWW/HTMLPrimer.html>
NHPRC, <http://www.nara.gov/nhprc/sites>
NetMechanic, <http://www.netmechanic.com>
New York State Archives <http://www.archives. nysed.gov>
NISO, <http://www.niso.org/>
NISO Committee AX (OpenURL), <http://library.caltech.edu/openurl/>
NISO, *Forum on Performance Measures and Statistics for Libraries*, <http://www.niso.org/stats-rpt.html>

Q

QuickTime (APPLE), <http://www.apple.com>

R

RAD (Rules for Archival Description), <http://lib74123.usask.ca/scaa/rad>

RDF (Resource Description Framework, <http://www.w3.org/TR/REC-rdf-ssyntax>

Real Media, <http://www. real.com>

Records Management Resources, <http://home.flash.net/~survivor/sitefram.htm>

RLG (Research Library Group), <http://www.rlg.org>

RGL *EAD Applications Guidelines,* <http://www.rlg.org/rlgead/>

Reuther Library's HEFA Help, <http://www.reuther.wayne.edu/services/hefa_resources.htm>.

RLG, <http://www.rlg.org>

RLG DigiNews, <http://www.rlg.org/preserv/diginews/>

S

SALT (Speech Application Language Tags), <http://www.saltforum.org>

Scientific American, <http://www.sciam.com>

Search Engine Watch, <http://searchenginewatch.internet.com/>

Search Engine Selection (University of Pennsylvannia), <http://www.upenn.edu/computing/web/webteam/rnd/search.html>

Search Engines Showdown, <http://www.searchengineshowdown.com/>

SGML/XML International Users group, <www/isgmlug.org>

Shutterfly, <http://www.shutterfly.com>

Sites for Teachers, <http://www.sitesforteachers.com>

SMIL (W3C's Synchronized Multimedia Integrated Language), <http://www.w3c.org/TR/REC-smil>

Social Welfare History Archives of the University of Minnesota, < http://special.lib.umn.edu/swha/manuscripts.html>

Society of American Archivists, <http://www.archivists.org>

Stagecast, <http://www.stagecast.com>

Standards for Archival Description, <http://www.archivists.org/catalog/stds99/index.html>

State of Digital Preservation, <http://www.clir.org/pubs/issue28.html>

StateStandards, <http://www.statestandards.com>

Sun Microsystem, <http://www.sun.com>

T

TCP/IP primer, <http://info.acm.org/crossroads/xrds1-1/tcpjmy.html>
Technical Metadata for Digital Still Images (NISO Z39.87-2002), <http://www.niso.org/committees/ committee_au.html>.
TEI (Text Encoded Initiative), <http://www.tei-c.org>
TEI "Lite" (University of Virginia), <http://etext.lib.virginia.edu/ TEI.html>
Tibco XML Software, <http://www.tibco.com/products/>
Tools for Building the Digital Library, <http://sunsite.berkeley.edu/ Tools/>

U

UNESCO Archival Portal, <http://www.unesco.org/webworld/ portal_archives/>
URN (Uniform Resource Names), <http://www.ietf.org/html. charters/urncharter.html>

W

W3C, <http://www.w3.org>
Web Content Accessibility Guidelines, <http://www.w3.org/TR/WAI-WEBCONTENT>
Web Content Accessibility Guidelines 1.0, <http://www.w3.org/ TR/WAI-WEBCONTENT/>
WebCT, <http://www.webct.com>
Web Pages That Suck, <http://www.webpagesthatsuck.com/>
WebQuest, <http://webquest.sdsu.edu>.
Web Ring, <http://www.webring.com>
Web Site Garage, <http://www.websitegarage.com>
Windows Media, <http://www.microsoft.com>

X

XanEdu, <http://xanedu.com>
XDirectory, <http://www.esprit-is.com/xdir.htm>
Xenu's Link Sleuth < http://home.snafu.de/tilman/xenulink.html >
XMetal, <http://www.softquad.com><http://www.corel.com/xmetal>
XHTML, <http://www.w3.org/XHTML>
XML, <http://www.w3.org/XML/>
XML Query Engine, <http://www.w3. org/XML/Query>
XSL FAQs, <http://www.dpawson.co.uk/xsl/xslfaq.html>

Y

Yale Archives and Manuscripts Tutorial, <http://www.library.yale.edu/
mssa/tutorial/tutorial.htm>
Yale Web Manual, < http://info.med.yale.edu/caim/manual/>

Z

Z39.50, <lcweb.loc.gov/z3950/agency/>

INDEX

Be sure to refer to the chapter outlines at the start of the book for additional concepts.

M

N

O

P

ABOUT THE AUTHOR

Frederick Stielow is librarian and archivist with long-standing ties to the National Park Service and museum community. Fred is also the author or editor of ten books, including 1999's *Creating a Virtual Library* for this Neal-Schuman *How To* series. Trained in the US Army for computer operations, he went on to earn an M.L.S. from the University of Rhode Island and a Ph.D. in History from Indiana University. Dr. Stielow headed the Amistad Research Center, Mid-Hudson Library System, and Walter P. Reuther Library of Labor and Urban Affairs. He also served as a faculty member in the library schools at Catholic University and the University of Maryland, as well as adjunct faculty at the University of Illinois, University of Puerto Rico, and Wayne State University.

Stielow participated in the development of the HyperTIES hypertext program and Sirs-Mandarin's M-3 ILS projects. In addition to contributing to over sixty Web sites, he was named chair for ALA's Web Advisory Committee, 2001-2002. A Fulbright Fellow in Italy and Jameson Scholar at the Library of Congress, Stielow was also selected as a 1998 "Cybrarian of the Year" by MCI. He now consults and writes under FSR Associates in Annapolis, Maryland (Stielow@netscape.net), is an adjunct professor at Catholic University, and Project Manager for the Special Collections of the National Agriculture Library.